Additional prais
The Privatization of L   j......g

"From water systems to private prisons, charter schools to exclusive patents on life-saving drugs, Cohen and Mikaelian describe an astonishing array of privatization scams and schemes and, helpfully, where some communities are successfully resisting."
—Annie Leonard, executive director, Greenpeace USA,
and author of *The Story of Stuff*

"Connects the dots between privatization and our current political crisis, showing how it has been enabled by and fed racism and the deterioration of our democratic culture. A must-read for policymakers and activists who want to rebuild government and democracy."
—Deepak Bhargava, distinguished lecturer, CUNY School of
Labor and Urban Studies, and former director,
Center for Community Change

"A well-researched call to action that reveals with crystal clarity the stakes of the stealth project to destroy the commons."
—Heather McGhee, author of *The Sum of Us: What Racism Costs
Everyone and How We Can Prosper Together*

"A compelling and poignant case for why our public goods deserve to be in the hands of the public and how privatization exploits our most vulnerable while exacerbating social, political, health, and economic barriers to equality."
—Rosa DeLauro, congresswoman and
author of *The Least Among Us*

"Brings us up to speed on one of the most important shifts in our political economy in a generation. And somehow makes it a fun read!"
—George Goehl, director, People's Action

"Exposes with incredible detail and acuity the market-driven, anti-government ideology that now pervades every corner of our society, and offers a rousing defense of public goods as essential to our collective well-being."
—Astra Taylor, author of *Democracy May Not Exist,*
but We'll Miss It When It's Gone

"The issue of privatization is one of the subtlest, most insidious bait-and-switch schemes of the last century. It happened gradually but relentlessly, and so it is the hardest kind of problem to address. *The Privatization of Everything* tells us how. Every American should read this book."
—Abigail Disney, activist and filmmaker

"A dozen years ago, after years of organizing against and research about privatization as it spread across all sectors, we concluded that 'Damn! They really do want it all.' *The Privatization of Everything* skillfully documents the extent to which this is even more true today, and how we can fight to take back what's rightfully ours."
—Si Kahn and Elizabeth Minnich, authors of *The Fox in the*
Henhouse: How Privatization Threatens Democracy

"A passionate defense of the idea of public goods and a detailed account of the myriad problems that are caused by turning them over to private corporations. Exploring the gritty, compromised way that privatization actually works cuts through ideological celebrations of the market's glories and offers a political language with which to defend the public sector."

—Kim Phillips-Fein, author of *Invisible Hands: The Businessmen's Crusade Against the New Deal*

"Pulls the lid off one of the longest cons in American history—the wholesale privatization of public goods, which enriches the wealthy and corporations while immiserating everyone else. For the last four decades we've been scammed into selling our infrastructure, our public health, and even our drinking water to for-profit businesses. This book cogently explains how we can stop the scammers and retake the public sector, creating a more prosperous future for everyone."

—Nick Hanauer, entrepreneur and author of *It's Never Our Fault (And Other Shameless Excuses)*

"*The Privatization of Everything* reveals how the private sector has taken over public functions—from providing clean water to forecasting the weather—long performed better and less expensively by government agencies, and how taking back public control will make us a better, healthier country."

—David Michaels, former administrator of OSHA and author of *The Triumph of Doubt: Dark Money and the Science of Deception*

"Pulls back the curtain on the multi-decade effort by profiteers to privatize and monetize America's public goods at the expense of the American people. This book is a must-read for anyone who values the importance of our public schools, libraries, transit and health systems, and a clean and healthy environment in creating vibrant communities and a strong democracy. Public goods are indeed for the common good and it's vital we turn the tide on the privatization agenda that has only succeeded in draining our communities and making the rich richer. Donald Cohen and Allen Mikaelian give us the road map to do just that."

—Randi Weingarten, president, American Federation of Teachers

"In the face of pandemic and catastrophic climate change, our atomized, privatized society does not and cannot provide for our well-being. *The Privatization of Everything* explains how we arrived at this critical juncture and where we must go from here. This fascinating, lively book reveals how, over decades, the American public's power over essential goods, including everything from water and roads to education and health care, has been transferred into the hands of corporate entities that, by definition, seek private profit over the public interest. It is a clarion call to reclaim our citizenship and rebuild the public sphere."

—Vanessa Williamson, senior fellow, Brookings Institution, and author of *Read My Lips: Why Americans Are Proud to Pay Taxes*

"*The Privatization of Everything* warns of the dangers of leaving our collective future and well-being in the hands of private market interest alone. We lose sight of our interdependence and create barriers to the care and support we all need. The book's clarion call for a movement for the public good is just what we need to build a caring economy and society, rooted in the complexities of humanity."

—Ai-jen Poo, executive director, National Domestic Workers Alliance

"An important and groundbreaking book, detailing the decades-long campaign/grift to turn public goods and services into private profit-centers. Instead of saving the taxpayer's money, the scheme enriched private business at the expense of both our pocketbooks and civic life. We've been had and Donald Cohen and Allen Mikaelian show us exactly how the scheme worked—and what we as Americans can do to fight back."

—Helaine Olen, author of *Pound Foolish*

"In *The Privatization of Everything*, Donald Cohen and Allen Mikaelian expose how right-wing ideology and class profit-seeking masquerading as social science undermined our national interests and values over many decades. Cohen and Mikaelian reframe the concepts of democracy, freedom, competition, and efficiency in this timely and essential book."

—Thea Mei Lee, deputy undersecretary for International Labor Affairs and former president of the Economic Policy Institute

"Nearly fifty years ago, large corporations and their Wall Street backers adopted a two-pronged strategy to seize power: they would use monopolization to concentrate control over our markets and privatization to assume the authority of government itself. This smart and engaging book moves far beyond the conventional debates about privatization. Filled with shocking stories of the cooptation of democracy by corporate interests, it shows that what's at stake is nothing short of our liberty as a free and self-governing people."

Stacy Mitchell, co-director, Institute for Local Self-Reliance

"Not just an invaluable critique of corporate America's fifty-year campaign to turn public goods into private profit centers—it also includes reproducible examples of successful anti-privatization fights."

—*Labor Notes*

"The book demonstrates why racial justice is a foundational principle for our democracy and how the racialized dismantling of the public is an attack on our core values as a nation. Racial justice and democracy are inextricably intertwined, and we cannot have one without the other. Both require robust public institutions driven by our values. The authors provide compelling, detailed and unassailable history and case studies on how privatization impoverishes our government and divides our people from each other. It is a powerful call to end these practices and build our public institutions through an equitable vision. We would be wise to heed that call."

—Glenn Harris, president, Race Forward

"Essential reading for understanding big business's movement to privatize public goods and how we can fight back and create an economy that works for all."

—Dorian Warren, president, Community Change

THE PRIVATIZATION OF
EVERYTHING

HOW THE PLUNDER OF PUBLIC GOODS TRANSFORMED AMERICA
AND HOW WE CAN FIGHT BACK

DONALD COHEN
ALLEN MIKAELIAN

NEW YORK
LONDON

Requests for permission to reproduce selections from this book should be made through our website: https://thenewpress.com/contact.

Published in the United States by The New Press, New York, 2021
Paperback edition published by The New Press, 2023
Distributed by Two Rivers Distribution

ISBN 978-1-62097-653-1 (hc)
ISBN 978-1-62097-797-2 (pb)
ISBN 978-1-62097-662-3 (ebook)
CIP data is available

The New Press publishes books that promote and enrich public discussion and understanding of the issues vital to our democracy and to a more equitable world. These books are made possible by the enthusiasm of our readers; the support of a committed group of donors, large and small; the collaboration of our many partners in the independent media and the not-for-profit sector; booksellers, who often hand-sell New Press books; librarians; and above all by our authors.

www.thenewpress.com

Book design and composition by Bookbright Media
This book was set in Times New Roman and Oswald

Printed in the United States of America

HC: 10 9 8 7 6 5 4 3 2 1
PB: 10 9 8 7 6 5 4 3 2 1

Contents

THE PRIVATIZATION OF EVERYTHING

Part I
UNDERSTANDING PRIVATIZATION

1

Public Goods for the Common Good

ON MARCH 13, 2020, THE DAY THAT PRESIDENT DONALD TRUMP FINALLY declared the COVID-19 pandemic a national emergency, the stage was set for bold, sweeping action. The crisis demanded it. Vice President Mike Pence, newly appointed as head of the White House Coronavirus Task Force, spoke of a "whole-of-government approach" backed by "an all-of-America approach." But when he got down to details, the government and the public were conspicuously absent. Instead, he offered one "historic public-private partnership" after another. Private companies would produce tests and sell them on the open market, Google would provide online triage, and "incredible companies" like CVS, Target, Walgreens, and Walmart would "give a little bit of their parking lot" for drive-through testing, he crowed.[1]

Within hours it was evident that these "historic" partnerships were largely aspirational—no private company was ready to produce massive numbers of tests, Google wasn't actually working on a nationwide triage website, and the gift of a few parking spots from the "incredible" retailers made little sense without the first two pieces in place. Within a few weeks, the administration quietly threw up its hands and pulled funding for testing sites. Walmart's online market, meanwhile, was taking a cut of some incredible price gouging on products like hand sanitizer and face masks—to the point where thirty-three state attorneys general demanded it stop.[2]

Within days it was evident that private enterprise and the free market alone would not meet the nation's need for medical equipment; Trump came under pressure to use the Defense Production Act, which would allow him to order manufacturers to do what the invisible hand was failing to do. Trump refused, saying he would seek only voluntary commitments from producers and falsely claiming that any use of the DPA would amount to a government takeover: "We're a country not based on nationalizing our business. Call a person over in Venezuela, ask them how did nationalization of their businesses work out. Not too well." The DPA does not allow the government to nationalize a business, but Trump was apparently heeding the guidance of his top economic adviser, Larry Kudlow, who was insisting, even as the economy sank in the last weeks of February, that the pandemic would never "sink" the economy. Only "the socialism coming from our friends on the other side of the aisle" could do that.[3]

So, rather than focusing on public health through public solutions, the administration's pandemic response was, in the words of Dr. Deborah Birx, the task force's response coordinator, "centered fully on unleashing the power of the private sector." The administration's priorities were plain. When a private laboratory developed a COVID-19 test that could provide results in as little as five minutes, Trump called it "a whole new ball game," particularly since states were facing deep backlogs—California was behind by nearly 60,000 samples, and 115,000 patients from around the nation were in a queue at Quest Diagnostics' labs. The federal government, however, made almost no effort to get the test to the states, trusting instead in the free market. The Department of Health and Human Services ordered a mere 5,500 tests; its spokesperson explained why: "We wanted to leave market share for hospitals and other healthcare providers to purchase through the commercial sector." Preserving market share, letting the market decide who would get the tests, took priority.[4]

Public health is a public good, but the Trump administration handed it over to corporations. Shocking as this was, the Trump administration's stance was simply an extension of what it had been doing since it came into office, and what politicians of all stripes have been doing for some fifty years.

Many define privatization as simply the outsourcing of a good or a service to a private company, but it is much more than that. Privatization has broad effects and needs a broad definition. Privatization is the transfer of control over public goods to private hands. Sometimes this happens during procurement—the outsourcing of public services to a private contractor. In other cases it's due to austerity—reducing public funding of a vital public good and letting private options take over. Or it can happen through deregulation—when we eliminate or fail to enforce public control through important regulatory safeguards for consumers, workers, or the environment. In all these ways, privatization is a transfer of power over our own destiny, as individuals and as a nation, to unelected, unaccountable, and inscrutable corporations and their executives.

Public Power over Public Goods

If privatization is the transfer of control over public goods, what do we mean by *public goods*? Economics textbooks have a pretty strict definition, but ironically it's one that effectively excludes the public. If we want to have any say in what counts as a public good, we need to let our definition expand. Most economics textbooks, and many economists, define public goods in pretty strict terms: they are things that are *nonexcludable* (meaning that it's either impossible or impractical to prevent people from using them) and *nonrivalrous* (meaning that one person using them does not take away from another person's use). In theory, at least, things that fit this definition are hard to make money from because profit comes from exclusion and rivalry. Therefore, if the market can't exploit it, it's a public good, and it's okay for the government to get involved. So those who want to limit government often use this theory of public goods to draw a bright line between what private businesses and the market does and what the government should be *allowed* to do.

This theory of public goods sidelines the public almost completely. It assumes that the market can and will provide just about everything. According to conservative economists, the government should step in only when markets fail. In those rare instances where someone can't make money from a particular good or service, it becomes *permissible* for the government to take it on. In this framing, the market decides what is public and what is private, and the public must follow the market's dictates. Privatization is often a logical outcome. When a good or service is privatized, it means that someone has figured out how to make money from it or that they want to exclude segments of the public. And when that happens, according to free-market adherents, the public needs to get out of the way.

This classic and narrow definition of public goods is fundamentally opposed to democracy and leaves decision-making about vital issues to the whims of the market. We therefore propose flipping the definition on its head. In a democratic society public goods should not be defined by the market. They should be defined by the public and its values. Just because some people *can* be excluded from having a public good does not mean we should allow that to happen. In fact, after we the people define something as a public good, we must use our democratic power to make certain that exclusions do not happen. And even if it's possible for there to be rivalries for a particular public good, we will make sure that, in these narrow arenas, winning and losing don't carry devastating consequences.

Clearly, it is *possible* to exclude some people from schools. Clearly, there can be intense rivalry over who gets a seat. But we decided long ago that this would not happen at K–12 public schools. We *could* make all our roads exclusive, but we decided that it would be better for both the economy and each of us individually if the public controlled most roads, paid for them, and permitted access.

During the coronavirus pandemic, the tools of public health fell into private hands, as did the ability to make public health policy. The president's son-in-law and senior adviser Jared Kushner was blunt about this after hearing complaints that the competition for protective equipment—masks, gowns, and other essentials—was driving prices beyond reason. "Free markets will solve this," he reportedly replied. "That is not the role of government." But the free market failed spectacularly, and Trump heard about it firsthand from the nation's governors. "I'm bidding up other states on the prices," explained New York's Andrew Cuomo. Masks that once cost $0.85 each soon were $7. Louisiana found that ventilators were 23 percent more expensive than they'd been before the outbreak, but the same company was selling them to Washington State for just slightly more than the pre-COVID price. No one could say why.[5]

Free-market solutions are often touted as a way to hold government spending down and prevent waste, but in this market Louisiana had to order far more ventilators than it needed because it was uncertain that any of its orders would be met. None of this helped ensure that ventilators would get to the places of greatest need in time—instead of public servants making these policy decisions, private companies made the decision that maximized their private profit, regardless of the public good. Dr. Joseph Kanter of the Louisiana Department of Health was at a loss: "The private sector can be a dizzying place. When it's life and death, there needs to be some measure of additional coordination."[6]

Massachusetts governor Charlie Baker, on a conference call with the president, pointed out that on three separate orders of desperately needed medical equipment, the state "lost to the feds." An apparently unconcerned and possibly proud Trump actually chuckled over that fact, according to news reports, and went on to explain the obvious: "Price is always a component of that also. And maybe that's why you lost to the feds, okay, I'll tell you, that's probably why." To Trump, the market was working exactly the way it was supposed to.[7]

The market is allegedly the most efficient way to bring the right amount of a good or a service to the right customer at the right time at the best price. Such assumptions fed Trump's assertion that states could get supplies "faster if they can get them directly" from suppliers. When the product is a public good, however, the market can put lives at risk. The free-market chaos that the states had to face did not serve public health or the public good. It benefited only those able to exploit the chaos by driving up prices.[8]

In a democracy, it is the public's job—not the market's—to decide what to cede to the private sphere. In some cases, even if something is not a public good in the economists' sense, the public has the ability to decide that *we will treat it as such*. In a democracy, *we* get to decide that there should be no exclusions—no winners or losers—when it comes to education (or clean water, or a fair trial, or a vaccine), even if it's possible to do so. We decide there are things we should do together. We give special treatment to these goods because we realize that they benefit everyone in the course of benefiting each one—and conversely, that excluding some hurts us all.

That starts with asserting public control over our fundamental public goods. We lift these goods out of the market or restrict what the market can do, taking concrete steps to make sure that no one is excluded and that there is enough to go around (and, we should note, that doesn't mean that there can't be private schools or bottled water or privately produced COVID testing kits). Public control is exercised in different ways; the public tool kit includes establishing public-goods standards for public money spent on procurement, providing public services, and creating regulations and safeguards for public goods created privately. What's important is that public goods exist only insofar as we, the voters and the people, create them. That's how democracy should and often does work.[9]

But it really works only if we can hold on to an idea of the common good. Is it good for individuals *and* the whole? Public goods can be slippery things if we don't keep our ideas about the common good in view. A democracy could conceivably be convinced that everyone should have 72-inch OLED televisions. A lobbyist from the gigantic TV manufacturers' association could spin out an argument that universal access to such items should be a public good. But it's harder to do so if we start with public values and use those as a ruler. Does universal access to big TVs serve our common vision of what's necessary, even to the point of justifying the cost of providing them? Does access to ginormous, high-definition TV screens meet a moral need? Most of us would say no. It does not greatly benefit me if my neighbor has a huge TV. But it benefits me tremendously if she has an education, if his children are fed, and if they are vaccinated. And making sure all those things are provided is also just the right thing to do.

Public Goods in Private Hands

Privatization is the transfer of control over public goods into private hands. In all of our thinking about how public goods are created and distributed, our concern should be focused on control: Who has ownership, rights, and the power to make decisions? As public agencies go about their business of serving the people, they will use all manner of arrangements, including contracting, outsourcing, and public-private partnerships, to get things done. All of these arrangements should be judged by how much control the public retains. We should not object to government contracting or outsourcing per se, but we should resist giving control of a public good over to a private concern.

It usually makes sense for a city or state to hire contractors to build a road. These contractors can be held accountable by public managers who ensure that the work is done, meets public standards, and doesn't waste public resources, and the public will still own and control the finished product. But when the public cedes control over all aspects of construction, planning, financing, operations, and maintenance (as often happens in so-called public-private partnerships), it loses control over a public good. Politicians in Colorado, instead of budgeting for the cost of operating the Northwest Parkway in Denver, gave the Portugal-based corporation Brisa Auto-Estradas a contract to tend to the road and profit from its tolls for a term of ninety-nine years. When residents wanted to improve a local road nearby, one that was still in public hands, the multinational company objected, pointing to contract language that barred localities from competing with the toll road, and it demanded compensation. A public road became unwelcome competition; the public could be charged for their attempts to lessen congestion and emissions.[10]

In 2008 Chicago's mayor and city council provided a case study in how badly things can go wrong when the public gives up control over public goods. It was a terrifying time financially. The 2008 recession meant plummeting revenues for the city, with no bottom in sight. The group of private investors led by Morgan Stanley rode in like white knights with $1.16 billion, and all Chicago had to do was give up control of its 36,000 parking meters, which were in need of modernization anyway, for seventy-five years. The sudden decision was made without public involvement or much scrutiny of the contract.

The city got fleeced: Chicago's parking meters raked in $138.7 million in 2019. All told, private investors have earned $1.6 billion so far. That's nearly $500 million more than their initial, $1.16 billion investment— with sixty-four years' worth of parking-meter revenues to go. Chicago's inspector general later found that the city stood to *lose* nearly a billion dollars over the course of the contract by taking a billion up front. But that massive revenue shortfall was only part of what Chicago lost. When investors got control over the meters, they also gained control over public space and even future development. When the investors penned the contract, they insisted that the city "true up" any loss caused by the city's changing with the times, which is what cities do and what the public expects. If a bus lane, bike lane, housing development, street fair, tree planting, or any other initiative is perceived to reduce parking revenue, the city must pay. Those payments could add up to $20 million a year. That has the effect of limiting choices made through the democratic process. Chicago invited a powerful, unaccountable, and unelected player to the table. The parking-meter conglomerate is not a citizen; it has no vote, but it holds the power to resist the city's efforts to serve the public good until the contract expires in 2083.[11]

A discussion about the parking-meter deal based on the idea that public space is a public good and deserves public control would have ended in a very different place. A decision that prioritized public control would have accepted the need to increase revenue for the common good, through either taxes or a bond, and would have recognized that giving up control over public space is a profoundly shortsighted way to bring in cash. Instead, Chicago's city leaders lost a billion dollars after being hypnotized by the promises of Wall Street wizardry and the myth of private-sector efficiency.

The Market Mythology of "Run It Like a Business"

We've been taught for so long that bureaucracies can't beat the private sector when it comes to quality and efficiency, so privatization proposals like the Chicago parking-meter deal get barely a second thought. The idea that the private sector will always perform better is so ingrained that we even accept the idea that prisons can be run for profit.

Back in 1983, the private prison industry emerged from the idea that when it came to incarceration, "you just sell it like you were selling cars, or real estate, or hamburgers," or so one of the co-founders of the Corrections Corporation of America (CCA) told a reporter. The founders had a good hustle, but their venture clearly didn't deliver a superior product. On their first contracts, because their facilities weren't ready, they housed prisoners in motel rooms, and several of them made easy escapes after removing their A/C window units. So it wasn't quality that carried the day. CCA (now known as CoreCivic) did not get its start as a scrappy entrepreneurial venture innovating its way into the market with a better mousetrap; it succeeded because of its founders' political connections and their ability to exploit state financial crises.[12]

The founders of CCA—T. Don Hutto, Thomas Beasley, Doctor R. Crants—knew how to work the system. It's unlikely they would have succeeded if they didn't. Hutto was a director of corrections for Virginia and a president of the American Correctional Association. He also had experience running Arkansas's corrections department and had previously attempted to monetize prisoners under his control (the U.S. Supreme Court chided him and his colleagues in Virginia for attempting "to operate their prisons at a profit," and painted a picture of prison labor not unlike the Jim Crow era's convict-lease system). Beasley was chairman of the Tennessee Republican Party and had served on a committee investigating prison conditions in the state, which led him to the conclusion that a private prison company would be a winning business. Crants was a Nashville-based lawyer and Harvard MBA grad. Investors in CCA included a venture capitalist who'd funded Kentucky Fried Chicken and Leslee "Honey" Buhler, the wife of Tennessee governor Lamar Alexander.[13]

CCA succeeded because, as Beasley noticed during his time on the investigating committee, prisons were overcrowded due to the war on drugs and tough-on-crime measures, but states were operating on shoestring budgets due to Reagan-era tax cuts and promises to reduce the size of government. This left governments in a bind and gave CCA its opening.[14]

Prisons are labor-intensive operations. Some 65 to 70 percent of the costs associated with publicly run prisons are related to the workforce. So when a politician gives a management contract to a private prison company, they can claim to have dramatically reduced the number of government employees. They are really just relabeling a large part of their workforce, but the move looks good on paper. This is of course *nothing* like selling hamburgers or cars or real estate. In most cases, the privatizer offers no new innovation or improvement to the public good, but they don't need to. In reality, the product is not what is being sold; it's the disingenuous promise of "no new taxes." In the end, what they are really selling is a way for politicians to both externalize a cost and backstop an antigovernment, antipublic ideology.[15]

The rise of for-profit prisons gives us a window into what privatization is really all about. These prisons have never been better than the public alternative—in many cases they are demonstrably worse. They don't beat competitors with better products. Instead, they work the system, play to politicians' weaknesses, make money by cutting wages and payrolls, and obtain contracts that help them eliminate risk (many private prisons, for example, get paid based on capacity, not on actual prison population). Like many privatization schemes, private prisons also profit on the backs of the disempowered, the poor, and minorities.

And yet private prisons and many other privatization schemes thrive under the unproven assumption that they will automatically be more efficient than the government ever possibly could be; that the profit motive will always be more effective than the desire to serve the public. In part, these companies and their political allies have convinced us that we should evaluate each public policy decision more as consumers than as citizens.

Citizens and Consumers in the Public Square

Privatization advocates depend on transforming us from citizens into consumers. They tell us that education policy should be guided by school choice, as if we were choosing between appliances. That water is simply a product like other "foodstuffs." That libraries are unnecessary when we have Amazon and Starbucks. These advocates relentlessly argue that government creates a monopoly whenever it takes on a service, and that monopolies stifle innovation, quality, and freedom. They offer instead the free market's panoply of choice, and a promise that any low-quality offerings will wither away as consumers learn to avoid them.*

Their sunny view of the free market obscures the rivalries and exclusions that markets create. In fact, we enable this process by competing with and excluding fellow citizens from the best of what the market has to offer. There are limited spaces at the best private and charter schools. You have to be willing to spend to sit at a Starbucks. And how would the free market distribute limited supplies of a lifesaving vaccine? It certainly wouldn't follow public health experts' recommendations on how to reduce the spread of the disease. It wouldn't target the low-wage or minority communities hit hardest by the disease, for example. "Being a consumer is a matter of trying to get what I happen to want," Michael S. Sandel, professor of government at Harvard University, notes. "Being a citizen involves deliberating with my fellow citizens, about what should be the fate of our collective destiny, of the political community as a whole." What we have instead, argues Sherrilyn Ifill, president and director-counsel of the NAACP Legal Defense Fund, is a fully privatized citizenship:

> What we're seeing in our country today: the rhetoric, the hate, the ignorance, the coarseness, the vulgarity, the cruelty, the greed, the fear is the result of decades of poor citizenship development. It is a reflection of the fully privatized notion of citizenship, a feral conflict for the scraps left by oligarchs.

When she was growing up in the late 1960s, Ifill was fully aware of the importance of public things—libraries, transportation, parks, schools: "My entire early life was supported by public goods and policy decisions designed to promote the public good." She then lived through a seismic shift in American life. As the nation took steps toward desegregation,

---

* Sadly, even the word *citizen* has in some contexts come to be used as something exclusionary. We are using the word in its original sense—it was derived from *city*—of a member of a community who has rights and accepts responsibilities. In our use, it is a mindset rather than a legal definition and it is meant to include, not divide.

white people had to start visibly sharing public things with black people. It became easy for those opposed to big government to use racism in "a deliberate effort to denigrate public life and goods by associating them with race. . . . And once it's associated with black people, it becomes denigrated. It becomes something that you don't want. The private becomes better: private education and your private car and your own big Mc-Mansion."[16]

We are both citizens and consumers, but privatization encourages us to approach public goods merely as a shopper while convincing us to forget that fellow citizens need that public good too. We come to believe that our own satisfaction is paramount, even if gaining that satisfaction leaves others behind. We have long been told that the customer is always right, and reject the idea that we should work with others so we can all achieve a common goal. As consumers, our only responsibility is to ourselves.

As consumers, we promote exclusions, but at the same time we are excluded. We do not have power over what is given to us; we have no right to expect a voice in what choices we have. Private corporations decide for us. Sometimes they might be responding to broad consumer demand, other times they might be driving it. In either case, they are not accountable to us. As consumers, we take what others have made, and have no connection to the process of creation.

There are plenty of times when there's nothing wrong with being a consumer, so long as we can get the best for ourselves while balancing our desires against the consequences of our choices. But for things that we value both for ourselves and for the common good—clean water, education, public health, safe roads and bridges—let's approach these as citizens of a democracy, as co-creators of public goods and not merely consumers of others' work, as part of something larger and not merely as isolated individuals, and as a people defined by our responsibilities rather than merely by our desires.

The difference between citizen and consumer, between private desires and public needs, came into focus as never before during 2020's pandemic, and it revealed a dark thread running through several seemingly unrelated topics. Suddenly, individual consumer choices threatened the lives of fellow citizens. Fulfilling our desires to eat in a restaurant, dance in a bar, or cheer at a sports game meant participating in the spread of a deadly virus. Public health experts asked us to sacrifice and to think of the common good, but much of the nation had been primed to treat these recommendations as it treated every other science-based policy: first, as utterly political, and second, as purely a matter of personal choice.

"We are being destroyed by the idea that we are not interdependent," warned Ifill. And in the same vein but in comments focused on the pandemic, former secretary of labor Robert Reich lamented, "In America, the word 'public'—as in public health, public education or public welfare—means a sum total of individual needs, not the common good." It was March 2020, and the country was at an inflection point. Many politicians, mostly Republicans, were following Trump in his morbid calculus that pitted the economy against American lives and concluding that the economy, driven by free and unfettered consumer choice, should take priority. The following month saw small but well-organized protests against public health recommendations nationwide. The same month saw media talking heads and lobbyists from the right-leaning American Legislative Exchange Council (ALEC) "value-pushing" against lockdowns and closures. ALEC's position was: "It is possible and preferable for employers to implement best practices to protect the health of their customers and employees—without micromanagement from the government." Here again, the public needed to stand aside for individual choice; in this case it was the individual choices of the employers, while in the case of the right-wing protesters it was their choice to refuse to wear a mask, to ignore lockdown orders, and go to bars and restaurants. They claimed that public decisions—those that take into account the health of all citizens—were nothing more than limits on freedom. The results were predictable and terrible.[17]

Some recalled their responsibilities as citizens, but those who continued to embrace individual consumer choice at the expense of public health found themselves walking with extremists, showing once again how unbending individualism and hardened racism often travel hand-in-hand. The Michigan Freedom Fund, which relied heavily on donations from Education Secretary Betsy DeVos's family, helped organize protests against the state's sensible public health restrictions. The fund's

Operation Gridlock in Lansing succeeded in blocking ambulances from getting to the hospital; a doctor had to beg with protesters to let them through. The public transportation agency announced it was "unable to accommodate life-sustaining and medically necessary trips" to sections of the city because of the intentional gridlock. Firearms and Confederate flags were in abundance. The Proud Boys, classified as a hate group by the Southern Poverty Law Center and prone to violence, made their presence felt.[18]

Abandon our obligations to each other, and racism and bigotry are not far behind. Secretary DeVos had no compunction about supporting these protests, just as she has no qualms about tax dollars going to schools that discriminate against LGBTQ+ employees, parents, and students. Following the reasoning of DeVos and others like her, excluding certain people is after all an individual choice, a consumer choice, that in her worldview must be protected from government intervention.

In the minds of many of those who refuse to acknowledge public health or entrenched societal racism, there are no systemic problems—no problems that can be addressed by a public working together. This antipublic attitude was on display in the pandemic's conservative protest movement and especially in counterprotests against those decrying police violence. "There is no racism, there is no oppression," one woman screamed while painting over a public display of the words *Black lives matter*. There are, in this mindset, only individual choices, and those individual choices never add up to something that demands we take collective responsibility and action.

Privatization often relies on such attitudes, and it often works to advance them. It is a huge help to privatizing corporations if we think of water as a mere consumer good or think selling incarceration is just like selling hamburgers. It helps them if we believe we just need to take care of ourselves, and that our consumer choices have no impact on public welfare. It's a huge help if those with power and privilege deny any responsibility for or kinship with the minority communities that privatization often targets. But it is much worse than that. Privatization also operates to further racism's animating principle—the denial of systemic racism—by convincing us that our consumer freedoms mean we can safely ignore our responsibilities as citizens.

A Fight We Can Win: Why There's Hope

In spite of the vast amounts of power and money focused on privatizing public goods, there remain several reasons to be hopeful, and there is much that we can do. In the end, as paradoxical as it seems, privatization is not just about money or about who provides what service; privatization is about values, about whether we are committed to promoting the general welfare as enshrined in the preamble to the Constitution, and about what we the public deem to be public goods.

Public values are powerful things, and when they are clearly articulated in a democracy, they, not the privileged few, can guide the discussion and the politics. This is why we are hopeful. In California, the small city of Felton took back its water infrastructure from the privately owned California American Water after finding that a public co-op would be better and cheaper. In Pomona, California, voters turned out in overwhelming numbers to block the privatization of city libraries—even those who never used the library saw its value as a public good. In Atlanta, a coalition of public transit users, employees, and teachers stopped a plan to transfer control over city buses to private enterprises. In Florida, a Republican lawmaker waged war against private prisons, documenting waste, fraud, and abuse and making the case that the power to punish should belong to the public. Voters in Massachusetts resisted multimillion-dollar campaigns funded by out-of-state billionaires that attempted to expand school privatization. These are small victories but represent something much larger. We are hopeful because these victories, although seemingly isolated and local, were an expression of public values and involved citizens defining public goods.

Our national malaise, which feeds division and isolation, is partly due to a sense that our problems are too large for citizens to remedy. Economic inequality, power imbalance, the dissolution of communities, and segregation seem like issues that average people can do little to address, much less repair. But this is not the case. Privatization is a driver of all of these issues: it facilitates the upward transfer of wealth, exacerbates inequality, creates powerful interests, separates us from each other, and segregates us by race and class. And privatization is *not* too big for the average citizen to take on. It happens at very local levels and involves corporations and politicians who are acutely susceptible to public pressure.

Reclaiming public goods addresses the big problems in very specific, concrete ways. Citizen activism can be directed at *this* road, *these* schools, *that* library—local institutions that have an impact on our daily lives and a broader impact on the health of our communities. At the same time, this road, these schools, and that library are more than individual institutions; they are embodiments of a set of public values. When we act to protect these public goods, or create new ones, we have an opportunity to communicate what it is we value and how we want to see those values reflected in our lives. Reclaiming public goods is about more than who picks up our trash or bills us for our water; it is about who we are and what we believe. When we point to those values while fighting for this school or that library, we can win.

Why This Book

The work of a pro-public movement will happen on two parallel tracks. One track will reintroduce public values into the conversation. We will reclaim the idea of the public; we will honor and celebrate our connections to each other and make decisions based on awareness of those connections. We will reclaim our governments as tools of the public—not as distant power centers or as tribute-taking idols, but as useful instruments for making public values manifest. We will use public conversation and debate to define public goods, and we will act to ensure that those goods remain under public control.

On the other track, we will confront privatization whenever it threatens a public good. The values chosen and public goods defined in our national and local conversations will help determine what we can cede to the market and what must remain with the public. We will learn what we need to know about these public goods to help determine what can be allowed to be sold on the market. We will insist that the democratic practices of transparency, accountability, equal treatment, and equal access be preserved, whether a particular service is delivered by a public servant or a private contractor.

This book travels on both tracks. Each part looks at a key public good, makes a case for the public values that support it, and indicates where we have ceded too much to private interests. We look at what the public has historically accomplished in each area, why public control is essential, and the impact of privatization. Our approach is both idealistic and practical. We want readers to see the lofty values and big ideas behind the creation of public goods, and we want readers to feel empowered to question those values and introduce new ones. We want to help change the conversation, so we can stop talking about "government monopolies" and return to talking about public control over public goods.

The next chapter argues that privatization is primarily a political strategy—one designed to separate us from public goods, our government, and each other. Part II discusses the privatization of water and food inspection, but it's more broadly about public health. Part III goes into the privatization of transportation and communication infrastructure, but it's really about building an equitable economy. Part IV covers examples that seem very disparate—environmental policy, private prisons, and forced arbitration—but all show how privatization is undermining democracy and liberty. Part V is about the social safety net, student loans, and wages under privatization, but it's more broadly about inequality. Part VI shows how privatization erodes community, drawing examples from charter schools, public parks, presidential libraries, and Social Security. Part VII covers education in the competitive marketplace, and part VIII looks at what happens when public knowledge becomes private. Finally, part IX wraps up the book with concrete suggestions about how to become pro-public, reinvigorate American democracy, and take public control of public goods.

We also want to provide a clear path toward seeing public values and the promises inherent in public goods delivered. We want to change the conversation, but not for cosmetic reasons—a stronger and more honest language will help us better analyze the changes privatization is proposing. The stories in this book of failed privatization schemes are shocking, but they aren't just for rhetorical effect; they are intended as vivid illustrations of what happens when we lose sight of the common good. And the stories of successful struggles against privatization aren't meant only to inspire, but also to help serve as a road map.

Whenever we feel powerless to stop the steady transfer of public goods into private hands, we can be sure that the advocates of privatization did their jobs well. The vision that they are selling is of consumers stripped of all connections to each other and utterly impotent in the face of market forces. Freedom is reduced to consumer choice, which amounts merely to a choice between a limited number of products that someone else chose to produce. Citizens' freedoms are more than that. Citizens have freedom not only to consume but also to create, and to create great things together. Citizens created safe public water and the very idea of public health. Citizens created transportation and communications systems that create diverse economies. Citizens created democracy, expanded voting rights, and have held the powerful to account. The chapters that follow are about privatization, but they are also about reclaiming real freedom, redefining our public values, and putting them to work for our common good.

2

The Roots and Reasons of Privatization

A Very Brief History

UNDERSTANDING PRIVATIZATION MEANS UNDERSTANDING THAT IT IS FIRST and foremost a political strategy. It was born this way, and so it remains, but it has also become a grab for billions of dollars in contracts and fees. In the years since it sprang from the mind of Milton Friedman as a way to undercut government "monopoly," it has also become a way for profiteers to tap into the $7 trillion of public revenue (which swelled to $9 trillion during the COVID crisis) spent by local, state, and federal government agencies each year and carve out a piece (sometimes a very big piece) for themselves. Privatization has also in recent history become remarkably bipartisan—Democratic president Bill Clinton arguably did more for the privatization project than did his Republican predecessor Ronald Reagan. And it has become surprisingly pervasive, to the point where there are now 2.6 times as many federal government contractors as there are government employees, and there is literally no public good that is not at risk of being privatized. But it started very humbly, with ideas from the conservative intelligentsia that became a way to achieve political ends without incurring public disfavor.[1]

School Choice and the "Iron Fist" of the Bureaucrats

In the 1950s, conservative economist Milton Friedman felt increasingly out of step with what he saw as "the general trend in our times toward increasing intervention by the state" and "the trend toward collectivism." He strongly preferred a government that provided only enforcement and avoided providing any services. Yet he also believed that democratic governments tend to naturally grow larger due to self-interested groups and the self-preservation instincts of politicians and bureaucrats (in Friedman's imagination, people often seem incapable of acting for the common good). Privatization was an effective, though imperfect, counterweight to these tendencies. In his landmark 1955 essay on school choice, Friedman admitted that few citizens would want to do away with universal public education, and suggested providing parents with "a specified sum to be used solely in paying for [their child's] general education" and allowing them "to spend this sum at a school of their own choice." This would satisfy a public desire while preventing the growth of bureaucracy. Sixty-two years later, President Donald Trump chose a secretary of education whose *only* experience in education was her advocacy for Friedman's ideas, now packaged in the consumer-friendly term *school choice*.[2]

Friedman's vision for market-managed public services was remarkably clear-eyed; he was under no illusion that any profit-generating enterprise would act for the common good. He lambasted the very idea that a business could have social responsibilities, and insisted that executives have responsibilities only to the business owners. To even suggest a responsibility to something larger was to invite "the iron fist of Government bureaucrats." So Friedman's voucher-supported private schools, despite taking public money, would have zero responsibility to the public.[3]

The implications were clear by the time Friedman's essay was published. *Brown v. Board of Education* had already spurred a "school choice" movement in segregated states. Private schools, bereft of social responsibility, offered something their white customers wanted—segregation— and politicians hoped to support this deplorable choice with public money in the form of vouchers. The racial implications of privatization should have been perfectly obvious to a man of Friedman's intelligence, but they apparently did not enter his thinking until someone pointed them out to him, after his landmark essay was largely complete. The issue of how the free market encourages racial segregation gets no more than an awkward footnote.[4]

Outside of Friedman's self-generated bubble, school choice was a raw expression of white supremacy. The white parents of Prince Edward County, Virginia, were happy with their public schools until the court forced those schools to accept black children. Vouchers came into play as part of a segregationist strategy that started with the county's pulling funding for all public schools. Next came a "tuition grant program" that gave parents vouchers up to $150 for private school. White parents rallied together to create a "segregation academy" that could legally bar black students. Prince Edward County ultimately closed its public schools completely and chained their doors. This example inspired racists everywhere; in 1969 over two hundred segregation academies were thriving in the South, and seven states had instituted voucher programs.[5]

The Prince Edward County school story offers a clear example of the ways in which privatization helps the powerful and well connected circumvent civil rights and the law. Putting public goods in private hands helps them evade accountability and protections. It prioritizes individual choice, even if that choice is one of racial oppression. While Friedman first devised privatization as a way to avoid the iron fist of government, his vouchers merely forged another fist, one specifically designed to curtail the rights of African Americans and other racial minorities.

The Reagan Revolution and Privatization's "Golden Opportunity"

Privatization's next big moment would not come until the 1970s, when it emerged as a response to the country's urban fiscal crises. Cities were going bankrupt, and conservative thinkers had a ready scapegoat and a ready solution. They blamed overspending on government pensions and social programs for the drain on funds; in fact, these deficits were largely the result of a diminishing tax base as white residents fled desegregating urban neighborhoods and schools. The conservatives' solution was to slash services, but when it came to services that voters wanted they offered privatization. It was clear that what they really wanted was for the public to have no role whatsoever in providing services, but they settled for limiting government to being something that merely manages contracts and writes checks to private companies. Ultimately, privatization would be a way station on the road to the smallest government possible.

In the early 1970s Emanuel Savas, a professor of public affairs who served as assistant secretary of the U.S. Department of Housing and Urban Development under Reagan, embedded privatization in the conservative movement by changing the way it was framed. In an essay co-authored with Friedman, he claimed that cities could lift themselves out of crisis by opening up "competition to reduce the monopolistic control many governments have over their customers." Savas's enticing but thoroughly dishonest language turned governments into "monopolies," while citizens became "customers" and "competition" emerged as the panacea. Savas also perfected the art of the attack on public servants—even teachers and firefighters—whom he saw as utterly self-interested to the point of, in the case of his hometown, "victimizing the entire city, and holding all eight million New Yorkers hostage." The budget crisis, he wrote, was "a golden opportunity" for privatization.[6]

Savas's influence cannot be overstated. Though hardly a household name, he has been one of the foremost advocates of privatization for over four decades. Prior to his post in the Reagan administration, he was the manager of urban systems at IBM Corporation and was a deputy city administrator from 1967 to 1972 under New York mayor John Lindsay. Today's advocates of privatization consistently employ Savas's language and lines of attack, including images of lazy, unionized bureaucrats; looming bureaucracies that are remarkably both inefficient and nefarious; and the utopian promise of competition. And Savas was more than a theorist; he helped found the Reason Foundation, a leader of antipublic thought that paved and lit the way for conservative free-market groups such as ALEC, the Heritage Foundation, and the Cato Institute, all of which played major roles during the Reagan revolution.

But the key to the ideological push for privatization was how it complemented an antigovernment political strategy. Robert Poole, a co-founder of the Reason Foundation with Savas, saw privatization as a way of "dismantling the state step by step." He revealed in an interview how he believed that "socialism" in America would be undone "by privatizing one function after the other, selling each move as justified for its own sake rather than waiting until the majority of the population is convinced of the case for a libertarian utopia."[7]

Shrinking government through privatization is a fundamentally dishonest strategy. It has to be. Small-government conservatives' biggest problem has always been how voters tend to actually *like* government services (and somehow fail to see the totalitarian Bolshevism lurking behind the smile of their kindly kindergarten teacher). Privatization became a way to reconcile a small-government philosophy with voters' embrace of public services. "Cities have been discovering that public services do not necessarily have to be reduced by government or paid for by taxes," claimed the Privatization Council's David Seader in 1986. Through the magic of privatization, we could have it all.[8]

At about the same time, Stuart Butler of the Heritage Foundation referred to privatization as a way to eliminate inconvenient pro-public interest groups. His goal was, as political scientist Jeffrey Henig put it, to "reshape the interest group environment." By changing how services are delivered, the idea went, loyalties would shift away from public entities. The interest groups to which he referred included the standard bugbears of unions and organizations like the AARP that fight for the health of public programs, but more broadly he was referring to all of us. This framework can't avoid casting aspersions on the people served by those organizations as well. The Reagan revolution helped crystalize a strategy to characterize any group of citizens that benefits from a public program as a "special interest group"; privatization would help divide them internally and from each other. The presumption here, and in some cases it has been proven right, is that it's not hard to turn a citizen, one who thinks broadly about the ownership of public goods, into a consumer who cares only about whether certain goods are available to him.[9]

The attack on public services was also an attack on the idea of the public, and it continued through the Reagan era with the Reason Foundation's evolving prescriptions. Continuing Savas's line of thinking, Poole inventoried in 1983 the services that citizens receive. He saw no reason to consider them public goods: "Most local services have few attributes of true public goods. Most of them—garbage collection, park and recreation services, libraries, airports, transit, and aspects of police and fire protection—have specific, identifiable users, who are the services' beneficiaries."[10]

This brings us to another salient fact about privatization: it is easier to justify if you deny the public a role in deciding what is a public good. Poole was arguing that since not everyone uses a library, it is not a public good and should not be treated as such by city budgets. Rather, only those who use them should pay for them. And once you accept that, it's very easy to argue that private entities should be allowed to take over and should be allowed to profit from them. In the end, Poole's argument rests on the idea that the public has no role in defining what counts as a public good. As we will maintain throughout this book, that's undemocratic and antipublic.

The stark divide between citizen and consumer is evident from this line of thought. A consumer should never pay for a service he does not use. Citizens, on the other hand, agree to pay for services that they don't directly use because they can see how they benefit all of us, and they see the indirect benefit to themselves. As citizens, we realize that even if we never set foot on a city bus the fact that others do alleviates congestion, reduces air pollution, benefits the economy by getting people to work, and benefits all of us by getting the people we rely on—bank workers, the dry cleaner, the barista, or our mother's caregiver—to their jobs. So it is something that *all* citizens benefit from by subsidizing. A consumer may not see that, but it is obvious to citizens.

The Reagan-era privatizers succeeded in obscuring citizenship and aggravating consumer-style grievances. The president himself perfected the art of alienating the public from the government; citizens became mere taxpayers (a term that can be used to exclude the poorest among us), public servants became mere bureaucrats, and public services became handouts. Privatization became a universal solution, as evidenced by the staggeringly long list of services targeted for transfer to private control by the President's Commission on Privatization—public housing, federal loan programs, air traffic control, education vouchers, the Postal Service, prisons, Amtrak, and Medicare, just to name a few. The vision was enormous and comprehensive. It really was the privatization of everything. Reagan's proposals amounted to "the greatest effort to return the provision of goods and services to the private sector that we've seen in this century," boasted Richard Fink, president of Citizens for a Sound

Economy, an organization created and funded by businessman and philanthropist David Koch.[11]

It's worth pausing to parse one important part of Fink's statement: many of the items targeted for privatization, like weather satellites, had originally been created, owned, and operated by the public and thus could not be "returned" to private control. But privatization advocates typically try to create a mythical golden age of free enterprise, dishonestly dismissing how much private enterprise owes to public investment. And it also helps make their plunder of public goods seem more like a reclaiming of the private sector's due. Ronald Reagan reflected this thinking when he announced the President's Commission on Privatization and claimed that privatization was in the "great tradition of free enterprise and private ownership of property" and was a descendant of the Northwest Ordinance and "homestead program."[12]

Reagan was likening public things that the public had voted and campaigned to make public—water, Social Security, trash collection—to "private property" that should rightfully be in private hands (and he further likened these public creations to land that had been taken from Native Americans). His sunny comment blithely ignored dark moments in American history while revealing an expansive view of what should be considered private property. It foretold of a privatization takeover.

A Democrat Runs with It: Privatization in the Clinton Era

Democrats in Congress repeatedly thwarted Reagan's vision, but the road map remained, and the political strategy turned out to be infinitely adaptable. Bill Clinton, looking to prove his centrist, "third way" bona fides, found privatization useful for precisely the same reasons the Reagan Republicans had—it gave the appearance that government could be cut without cutting services. Clinton, the New Democrat, had Vice President Al Gore lead an initiative to "reinvent government." The resulting proposals were radical, but hardly inventive: Ron Utt, who had served as Reagan's "privatization czar," pointed out that the Clinton reform agenda was "virtually all drawn from recommendations made in 1988 by President Reagan's Commission on Privatization" and amounted to "the boldest privatization agenda put forth by any American president to date." Looking back some years after Clinton had left office, Robert Poole approvingly noted that "the Clinton administration's privatization successes exceeded those of Reagan."[13]

Clinton-era privatization was as broad as any Reagan-era conservative could have wished for, but two efforts stand out in their scope and audacity: the acceleration of prison privatization and the creation of a new private industry that profited from the dismantling of the Great Society safety net. Both of these industries were symbiotic with a new breed of Republican politician that came to power with the help of the American Legislative Exchange Council.

ALEC is a behind-the-scenes organization made up of business interests and right-leaning politicians that creates model legislation—for example, bills to protect businesses from class-action suits and an array of laws targeting unions—largely for state lawmakers. In the 1990s ALEC helped shape the early careers of Republican governors like Wisconsin's Scott Walker and Florida's Charlie Crist. Both championed ALEC model legislation in their respective statehouses and scored victories that made them heroes of big business and big campaign donors. And it was in the mid-1990s that ALEC sparked the era of mass incarceration with its three-strikes and truth-in-sentencing model legislation, proposals that became laws in twenty-seven states.[14]

Why would an organization primarily concerned with creating business-friendly policies suddenly take up issues of incarceration? To understand, one need only look to ALEC's criminal justice task force, which authored at least eighty-five tough-on-crime measures. Representatives of the Corrections Corporation of America weren't just in the room; they co-chaired the committee. CCA's public relations people, who have a gift for generating incredulity, insist to this day that CCA did not help shape or vote on the three-strikes or truth-in-sentencing legislation that emerged from this committee. Apparently we are supposed to believe that CCA's representatives sat silently in the co-chair's seat while their disinterested colleagues drafted proposals that would add billions to CCA's bottom line.[15]

ALEC's deft political maneuvering brought profits to its members and

solidified a bond between social and economic conservatives. Privatization held it all together. ALEC and corporations like CCA helped nur-
ture politicians who used privatization to advance a socially conservative
agenda and strategically undermine sources of political power on the left.

In the 1990s, for example, Scott Walker was a Wisconsin state legislator who made his mark advancing ALEC-inspired tough-on-crime legislation. Walker has spoken openly about ALEC's influence, and while
serving in the Wisconsin state assembly two of his top fifteen donors
were with CCA. Both were based in Tennessee but seemed highly interested in the outcome of Walker's Wisconsin state assembly race. Within
weeks of the victorious vote for ALEC's truth-in-sentencing law, Walker
sounded the alarm on prison overpopulation, a natural outcome of harsh-
er sentencing. Since Wisconsin state law prohibited prison privatization,
Walker pushed for shipping prisoners to private prisons out of state, and
CCA was ready to receive them. As an elected official in Milwaukee, he
also pushed for the privatization of the transportation of these prisoners, which CCA was more than willing to handle. Of course, he then
argued to abolish a law banning private prisons, claiming that shipping
prisoners out of state (something he'd helped bring about) amounted to a
bleeding of jobs and tax revenue. Walker went on to national prominence
as a governor willing to wage war against public-sector unions, public
universities, and public assistance; in each of these efforts, privatization
was his weapon of choice.[16]

While the privatization of prisons largely flew under the public's radar,
the transfer of the public safety net into private hands was trumpeted
as a major reform of a long-standing entitlement. Aid to Families with
Dependent Children, popularly known as welfare, dated back to the New
Deal but was a strikingly small part of the federal budget. When Bill
Clinton signed the Personal Responsibility and Work Opportunity Act of
1996, he eliminated AFDC and replaced it with Temporary Aid to Needy
Families (TANF), a system of block grants to states that came with a
significant mandate—get people off the program—and little guidance
on how to accomplish it. States were free to experiment, and many ultimately did so by giving control to private entities.[17]

Several things happened in this effort that were astounding and new.

Private, for-profit enterprises—including companies traded on Wall Street—sprung up around welfare reform, guaranteeing that a significant portion of the few remaining public dollars sent to the social safety net would wind up in the wallets of the wealthy. In addition, in the name of "innovation," many states utterly gave up on public control of the safety net. The private companies did not just carry out the will of the public like contractors, but also set policy and made decisions about whom they would serve and how.[18]

In New York City, the perennial problems associated with the loss of public control emerged even before the bidding started. Mayor Rudy Giuliani's administration, according to the city comptroller, tipped its hand to a preferred candidate—Wall Street darling Maximus Inc.— months before it opened bidding for the $500 million in contracts. Despite the possibility that NYC had violated fair bidding rules, the city awarded Maximus the contract.[19]

The overarching goal of Clinton's reform was to get people off public assistance. How this was accomplished was secondary, and the states and cities that received the block grants got the message. According to a Giuliani-era NYC commissioner, the intent of the changes was to provoke "a crisis in welfare recipients' lives, precipitating such dire prospects as hunger and homelessness." Through this paternalistic program, the poor were assumed to be too comfortable on welfare to want to improve their lives and would start work only if the clock started ticking on their benefits. Maximus's job was to guide these newly threatened citizens into jobs or job training and to enforce the new rules regarding who could and could not continue to receive benefits.[20]

Maximus agreed to a goal of placing 46 percent of participants in jobs, and the city gave them tremendous leeway in how to accomplish their objectives. Maximus failed miserably. A 2004–2005 review found only 8 percent of participants had been placed in jobs; 3 percent still held those jobs after six months. Most of the jobs obtained paid $8.00 per hour or less, and many were part-time or temporary. Despite the legal requirement to offer job training, and a strong preference among clients for further education, only 18 percent of Maximus's clients received any training or education.[21]

Outside audits were clear about the reasons: there was no incentive in the contract to obtain training or good jobs for clients. All the rewards were tied to getting people off public assistance; finding low-wage, unstable jobs was much easier than offering people a viable path out of poverty.

The other way to slash the welfare rolls was, of course, to kick people off for rules violations. Here Maximus proved to be a master of efficiency, expelling 76 percent of its clients from the program for failure to adhere to labyrinthine rules that seemed designed to be misunderstood. But in the new world of welfare reform, this counted as a success. Maximus's contract was renewed in 2006.[22]

During the 1990s privatization allowed politicians to take a big step back from their responsibilities. The tough-on-crime politicians, often the same politicians who promised to slash the size of government, knew that their policies would mean a larger government. Incarceration is labor intensive and requires a large bureaucracy. They owed the public an explanation, but instead hid the growth of government behind private prisons. Politicians who promised welfare-to-work programs immediately backed away from the "work" and settled for simply stopping public assistance payments. Privatization allowed them to punt the hard policy decisions to a private entity while claiming that the private sector would develop new solutions to endemic poverty. Adding insult to injury, it was public money that supported this shell game and allowed Wall Street investors to enthusiastically trade stock in companies that profited from widespread misery—hunger, homelessness, and incarceration.

The 1990s saw the use of privatization as a political strategy and as a way for government to dodge responsibility. The major shift, however— the real innovation—was toward private control over what had once been public decisions. The wide latitude given companies like Maximus allowed private interests to redefine public goals. Given enough leeway, these companies were able to put the profits of their shareholders over the will of the people, even as they continued to receive the people's money.

Each Crisis an Opportunity: Privatization After 2000

The push for privatization accelerated under the administration of George W. Bush, even though he was unsuccessful when it came to the privatization of Social Security. Aside from that one exception, however, the floodgates were open. Privatization even seeped into how we fight our wars, with the military expanding its use of contractors, including the notoriously unaccountable private security firm Blackwater. What was new here wasn't just the increasing reliance on private employees; the nature of their work changed as well. The Pentagon had a long history of using contractors to fill support roles and civilian jobs, but in Iraq and Afghanistan contractors were increasingly placed on the front lines and ran as a parallel military force, often without the discipline and account-ability of regular uniformed personnel.

Worse still, uniformed service members found themselves doing the exact same job as contractors for a fraction of the pay. When it came time to reenlist, many made the obvious choice: leave the military, take a job with a contractor, and return to the field with a six-figure salary. In this way, privatization—intended to help alleviate person-nel shortages—actually made them worse and drove up the cost of the post-9/11 wars. These twin outcomes—the creation of an environment of unaccountability and a cycle of dependency as talent leaves for the private sector—are common in all manner of privatization schemes; in the national security arena they have expanded consequences. In far too many cases, contractors operated in sensitive areas like security and intelligence, where they were given power without clear accountability. Neither military nor local laws strictly applied to them, and in the legal gray area they inhabited, abuses became endemic. Meanwhile, profits for these companies, derived almost entirely from public money, soared.[23]

While Bush furthered the outsourcing of national security and made his play for the privatization of Social Security, the transfer of public goods to private hands was encountering little resistance at the state and local levels. Deep Republican tax cuts forced increasingly anemic bud-gets on statehouses and city councils, which propelled this quiet take-over. As a wave of public servants retired, the bills for their pensions came due. Promises made at a time when the stock market was soaring and taxation was more equitable now became scapegoats for state and local deficits. Again, the answer from the antitax, antigovernment side of the aisle was to avoid responsibility by eliminating government jobs and replacing them with private contractors, who hired nonunion workers without pensions and in many cases without any benefits. If they were underpaid and unable to cover their own retirements, that was not the public's problem (even though they were doing the public's work).

The trends only accelerated after the 2008 market crash devastated pension funds and further shrank state and local budgets. Stretched beyond the breaking point and stubbornly refusing to raise revenues via more reasonable and equitable tax rates, governments took previously unthinkable steps to quickly raise revenue and cover budget shortfalls. For example, water systems, the very lifeblood of cities and towns, came to be viewed as both a burden and a source of quick cash. Cities that had long neglected their water systems were faced with massive repair and upgrade bills at the very moment when they could least afford it. Multinational corporations with Wall Street backing started turning up at small-town council meetings with an enticing offer: sell the entire system to us. We'll take care of repairs, you don't have to be responsible for water any longer, and your city gets a big, one-time payday that will help paper over the fact that you've failed to raise enough revenue to provide for public goods. By 2014, one mayor who had seen this play out in his state several times over declared, "Water is the new oil." The reason for this and other lootings of public goods was simple, according to the chairman of a major privatization financing company who saw huge opportunities in the immediate aftermath of the 2008 crash: "Desperate government is our best customer. There will be a lot of desperate governments out there."[24]

By 2008 privatization had become such a fixture on the political landscape that even Barack Obama, who spoke more eloquently about the role of government and the power of the public than any president since FDR, could not avoid it. Nor would resistance on Obama's part have been terribly effective; many of the most important decisions about public goods had devolved to the states and cities, where it is easier for private entities to exert influence and where the conversion of public goods to profiteering hands can be more complete. The short, eventful history of privatization is the history of a political and ideological strategy expanding quietly over time and seeping into every corner of American life, from the water we drink to the wars we fight. The political and ideological phase of this transfer of power is all but complete. Now we are living through the reaping as corporations sit upon their harvest of the $7 trillion or more that governments spend each year in the name of the common good. They could not have asked for a better friend than Donald J. Trump.

Donald J. Trump, the Antipublic Epitome

At some point in the last few years, public schools became "government schools." Few noticed it in 2016 when presidential candidate Donald Trump repeatedly referred to government schools during his rare forays into education policy, but during his 2020 State of the Union address the phrase became much more pointed. And they weren't just government schools; they were invariably "failing government schools." Trump was channeling the language of small and devoted Tea Party groups and conservative politicians who made the conscious decision to stop talking about public schools and speak only of government schools. It's a snarl, but it caught on. And it makes clear how much we need to change the conversation. Somewhere along the way, we mentally separated the government from the public, reflexively assuming that it is something distant from us and something incompatible with free markets.[25]

A Republican Kansas state senator recently embraced the term in a screed against providing free lunches to poverty-stricken children, claiming, "Our local grade school is now the government school. Our children have become government children. Think about it—it's true." According to this lawmaker, schools transformed children into "government children" by offering the poorest among them free lunches; soon, he claimed without evidence, even those who brought lunches from home were clamoring for hot government meals, and before you knew what was happening, "the good parents began to be bad parents. Government was at the heart of this, of course."[26]

There's a lot to chew on here, including the utter lack of evidence, the automatic assumption that only "bad parents" are unable to afford healthy meals, and so on. But there is more than antigovernment animus behind the pernicious twisting of language that has given us the phrase "government school." This effort is not just antigovernment; it is antipublic. It is an attempt to dissolve the entire idea of the public working together on a problem, like feeding hungry children. It is an attempt to separate us from each other. It's a declaration that the government serves underserving others. It is an attempt to deny that there is an "us."

When we lose the public, when we speak of schools as run by a distant government and not by empowered citizens working together in a democratic process (which in fact they are), we lose the idea of a common good. It is *we* who decided that children should not be hungry, and we did so not just for emotional reasons like guilt or empathy. We decided that providing for hungry children uplifts all children, that it is a drag on communities as a whole to allow some of us to attend school unable to focus because of malnutrition. It was not a program devised simply to serve those children, or their parents, or "the government"—it was created to serve all of us.

Trump's counterpoint to "failing government schools" is school choice, and during his 2020 State of the Union he put on a little show to illustrate. In the audience was a supposed victim of a failing government school, Janiyah Davis, a fourth-grader from Philadelphia. Trump claimed that she was one of tens of thousands of students waiting for government scholarships and then, with much flourish, announced that she was now officially a scholarship holder and could attend a private school. As it turned out, this was not due to some new policy or big administrative achievement. Quite simply, his education secretary, Betsy DeVos, had reached into her vast family fortune and donated some of it to this young girl. The message seems to be that we fail when we work together. Instead, we need to rely on the billionaire class to provide us with choice and opportunity and ultimately to save us from our own government.[27]

We knew even before he took office that Trump would out-privatize his predecessors. At least thirty-two Trump transition team members had either worked for privatizers or had touted the philosophy. Betsy DeVos was likely the most visible example, but the list also included Tom Price, tapped to head Health and Human Services, who was well known as an advocate of privatizing Medicare. The person Trump wanted in charge of the Centers for Medicare and Medicaid services, Seema Verna, who took over as HHS secretary after Price resigned following a series of embarrassing abuses of office, had been a consultant on Iowa's troubled Medicaid privatization experiment, a wide-ranging disaster detailed later in this book. On transportation and infrastructure, Trump brought in a director of "public-private ventures" at the American Road and Transportation Association and a former official who'd authored Virginia's Public-Private Transportation Act. The administration took office fully committed to the privatization project.[28]

Yet he went further still. On education, for example, Republicans had gotten used to supporting both charter schools and school vouchers under the umbrella of "school choice." Trump and DeVos proposed to zero out federal funding for charters and throw everything behind vouchers with a $5 billion tax credit. He further supported the privatization of public education by making private K–12 tuition payable from tax-free 529 college savings plans. Those who could afford it now had a chance to essentially launder their income through a 529 before paying private school tuition, getting a big tax break and imposing a significant burden on their states, which were forced to help pay for Trump's privatization policy.[29]

Trump went further still on student loans. Republicans had long yearned for a return to a student loan market run by banks, despite the public savings of $68.4 billion Obama had won by bringing the loans back into the federal government. Trump and DeVos made every attempt to undermine the federal program and undo the minor relief Obama had instituted. Then they went further. In 2019 the Trump Department of Education proposed replacing student loans with income-share agreements, whereby investors would back a student's college education in exchange for a percentage of their future salary. It was just different enough from a loan to get around caps on student loans and maybe just flexible enough to avoid laws on indentured servitude. And since these loans were creations of Wall Street investors, they could do things the government couldn't do—like undermining students' choices by giving subprime rates to humanities majors and plum rates to majors with supposedly more profitable career paths. It was in effect the sale of our children to hedge funds and private equity.[30]

Trump went further still on prisons. Obama had taken steps to pull the federal government back from the private prison industry, and candidate Hillary Clinton had promised to stop using them altogether. Trump, by contrast, packed his administration with prison advocates, and then he went further. Private prisons flourished under Trump as he filled their expensive beds with unnecessarily detained immigrants.[31]

George W. Bush had taken significant and ultimately dangerous steps to privatize American wars and intelligence analysis, but Trump wanted to go further. In 2018 a top Trump fundraiser helped package a proposal that would outsource clandestine field work—intelligence collection and covert operations—in order to get around the "deep state" (which is really just a synonym for oversight and rule of law). While it's unclear how far this proposal went, its cousin appeared in Scott Pruitt's Environmental Protection Agency, which hired an opposition research firm that monitored EPA employees suspected of being insufficiently loyal.[32]

In these cases, Trump proved willing to aggressively undermine law, regulation, and existing policies by shifting into private mode. It was no different during the pandemic crisis, when it was most clear that lives were at stake. In the midst of a destructive PR war with his own Centers for Disease Control, Trump abruptly moved data gathering from hospitals away from the CDC and handed it to a private company with a no-bid contract, upending a system that had worked well for the better part of a decade. No one had asked for this. The hospitals that the administration said would benefit from the change howled in protest. A valuable hospital-capacity map run by the CDC suddenly went dark. The contractor refused to answer senators' questions, claiming it had a nondisclosure agreement with the Department of Health and Human Services. And the COVID-19 data that had long helped drive criticism of Trump's abhorrent handling of the crisis were out of public hands.[33]

From segregationist school vouchers to Trump's privatized COVID memory hole, privatization has been a way to get around the law, civil rights, and accountability. From the early proposals to outsource all municipal services to the more recent attempts to outsource America's wars, privatization has been a strategy for separating the public from the government, and from each other. Along the way, privatizing corporations have grown exceedingly rich and powerful.

This decades-long concentration of power and profit means that Democrats are not immune from its sway. While it's heartening to see a platform statement from the Democrats that includes the line, "Private profit should not motivate the provision of vital public services, including in the criminal justice system," other Democrats have proposed making water privatization easier. And the lure of the public-private partnership for infrastructure, and even for school construction, remains strong. Democrats have a history of helping to advance the privatization of everything, and won't reverse course without public awareness and pressure.

We need that public pressure because of what privatization really means. All of the political, social, and fiscal costs of privatization have come at the expense of our public goods. In other words, they have had a distinct, measurable, and sustained human cost. Those human stories, of what happens to us when we are separated from public goods, constitute the real history of privatization and will be the focus of the following chapters.

Part II

PUBLIC GOODS FOR LIFE

The Dangers of Privatizing Public Health,
Water, and Food Safety

THE ARCHITECTS OF PRIVATIZATION ENCOURAGED A LANGUAGE AND A MINDset in which public goods are transformed into consumer goods. If we follow their lead, we can easily forget that these goods are broader than ourselves and that wide use benefits all of us. We might lose sight of why these things were ever under public control.

If our response to a pandemic is to treat each individual patient as a health care consumer, if our tests and treatments are targeted at meeting only individual needs, we lose sight of public health. If we treat water just the way we treat sports drinks, and give control over pricing, conservation, and policy to private corporations, we lose sight of how publicly controlled water is essential for preserving public health and maintaining policies that benefit the public. Such decisions will inevitably come back to haunt us. We can't do much for individual health in a perpetually sick society.

Advocates of privatization fight to maintain a consumer-based approach with broad and aggressive swipes. During the pandemic, the free-market absolutists attacked public health workers and even denied the very notion of public health as a public good. In their missives, they claimed public health was indistinguishable from partisan politics, a threat to freedom, and a pseudoscience that could be safely ignored. When it comes to water, the privatizers insist that it's merely a "foodstuff," denying its connection to our health, our well-being, and our very lives.

Such attacks are reckless, dangerous, and out of step with what the public wants. Throughout our history, we have advocated for public health through publicly controlled water and publicly run food inspection. Although privatization has made significant inroads toward the privatization of the water supply, in many places citizens have pulled it back. And in 2020 a majority of the public recognized the failures of Trump's free-market response to the pandemic and endorsed a public health approach as the only one that had a chance of working. Those majority preferences didn't always translate into policy, but we all learned, in our isolation, how interconnected we are and how our individual choices ripple through society.

Yet it remains very easy for public health to slide into private control.

Often all it takes is a tight local or federal budget, a denial of public needs, or a noisy minority insisting that consumer freedoms trump individual responsibility. The reason this public control is so fragile lies in our nation's refusal to fully embrace public health generally and health care for individuals as public goods. We make exceptions for those struggling with poverty through Medicaid, for the elderly through Medicare, and for veterans through Tricare or the Veterans Health Administration, but despite our public successes in those areas we insist that, for all others, access to health care should be a consumer product, not a public good. As long as we accept this framework for individuals, effective public health policy for the country as a whole will be largely out of our hands.

3

Privatizing Public Health Makes Us Sick
An Epidemic of Market Failures

THE TRUMP ADMINISTRATION'S RESPONSE TO THE 2020 PANDEMIC WAS "centered fully on unleashing the power of the private sector," according to Deborah Birx. And when it came to getting medical supplies to the right place at the right time, Jared Kushner insisted that "free markets will sort it out" and "this is not the role of government." While these positions were unwavering, it was a difficult time to reflexively deny an active role for government. The political right could see how price gouging and chronic undersupply might cause public attitudes toward the free market to turn ugly, but their response wasn't to temper expectations about what markets can do. Instead they tried to stake out even more extreme positions.[1]

A senior writer at the *National Review* blamed government for getting in the way of testing production and demanded utter deregulation of both tests and drugs—"an absolute free-for-all"—to the point where "the normal FDA regulations could be waived to allow for more radical treatment, even experimentation on humans." Other commentators embarrassingly misrepresented what had happened in South Korea, where infections and deaths were markedly lower per capita compared to the United States; one claimed that the South Korean testing achievement was an exemplar of free-market solutions. In fact, it was plainly due to the government, which has a single-payer health plan and a robust public health apparatus and which told companies to drop everything and make millions of tests, stat. And despite daily reminders of how irrational markets can be during a pandemic, James C. Capretta, the Milton Friedman Chair at the American Enterprise Institute, insisted that "market incentives may be instrumental in getting the country, and the world, out of its current mess."[2]

The market cannot and will not save us because market incentives are directly opposed to public health. Despite conservative commentators' complaints about government interference, the testing market *was* largely driven by market incentives during most of 2020. The results were not surprising. For example, if you were a professional athlete, you were likely tested for COVID on a shockingly routine basis. During one week in November the National Football League tested 7,856 players and employees 43,148 times. That averages out to more than five tests per person per week. Meanwhile, a survey of nurses reported that two-thirds of them had *never* been tested. By and large their hospitals could not afford it, even when tests were available. That is free-market rivalry and exclusion at work, and the results are not rational or responsible—they are downright grotesque.[3]

Public health is not a mere product that can be delivered through an unregulated free market; it is a public good. The difference between the public health demanded by citizens and the products created for consumers is absolutely critical when it comes to our water supply, the safety of our food, and our public health. Antipublic advocates of privatization will always try to convince us that we are mere consumers of the products we need for our own individual health and our very lives. But in reality it's only when we work together as citizens that we can obtain the public health we deserve.

Not on the Menu: Public Health on the Free Market

Theories of free-market supremacy tell us that the hands-off approach to COVID testing should have reduced costs, improved quality, and enforced efficiency. Instead, we got jacked-up prices, inaccurate tests, and thousands upon thousands of faxes. "Picture the image of hundreds of faxes coming through, and the machine just shooting out paper," Dr. Umair Shah of Houston's Harris County Public Health Department told a reporter. The faxes were COVID-19 results coming from small labs that hadn't really interacted with public health centers before the pandemic. Each piece of paper contained information that a patient was desperate to receive and that public health officials had to have in order to work toward larger public health goals. But each piece of paper was added to a growing pile awaiting manual data entry days, if not weeks, later.[4]

A free and unfettered market should have incentivized small labs to give up their fax machines and join the rest of us online. It should have ironed out inefficiencies, leaving those who did not evolve in the dust. This never happened. During COVID-19, as the price of test processing skyrocketed, small labs took on as many tests as they possibly could. Tests that would normally cost $100 to evaluate could suddenly garner $500 or $900 or in one case $2,315 for a single test. There was a gold mine out there, and the market was doing what markets do, regardless of the impact on public health.[5]

So small labs had plenty of market incentives to get into COVID testing. But at the same time they had zero incentives to use some of their obscene profits to actually improve on the quality of their products. Why bother with a $5,000 investment in technology when your $150 fax machine will also get you paid?

The market failed during the pandemic because the testing companies were not selling the same product that the larger public was trying to buy. The labs were selling individual test results. The public was trying to buy timely public health data, but the public did not take control of this public good. Early in 2020 the federal government set aside money for testing and made sure insurance companies were covering it, but it did not enforce the quality of the results. That would have "shrunk the market." That would have been too much regulation, too much red tape. Too much of the "iron fist of bureaucrats," as Milton Friedman would say. So, many testing companies were incentivized to get into COVID testing but were not incentivized to meet the need for timely public health data.

Unfortunately, our elected officials have stubbornly resisted taking control over public health for quite some time, even when receiving ample warnings that a pandemic was inevitable. "I want to emphasize the certainty that a pandemic will occur," Gregory Poland of the Mayo Clinic told Congress in 2005. "It's not a matter of 'if,' but 'when,'" epidemiologist D.A. Henderson told columnist Dana Milbank in 1999. The H1N1, or swine flu, crisis of 2005 was another warning, many public health experts told us. And yet our political leaders went the other way.[6]

In 2019 the Public Health Emergency Preparedness program was funded at $617 million—less than half of what it had to work with in 2002 (in inflation-adjusted dollars). The Centers for Disease Control saw cuts of 10 percent over a decade. Following the financial crisis of 2008, public health departments serving states and regions reduced their staffing by one quarter. The National Institutes of Health received special scorn from budget cutters: the archconservative Republican Study Committee wanted to see it plundered by 40 percent in 2011. During the Zika outbreak of 2016 President Barack Obama asked for $1.9 billion; the Republican Congress gave him about half of that, more than half a year later. As we maintain throughout this book, the defunding of public goods is privatization; it leaves the public hamstrung and at the mercy of the market. And that's often the real motivation behind the starvation of our public programs.[7]

Public health is not cheap, but neither are bank bailouts. As former secretary of labor Robert Reich pointed out in March 2020, "Late last week the Fed made $1.5 trillion available to banks, at the slightest hint of difficulties making trades. No one batted an eye. When it comes to the health of the nation as a whole, money like this isn't available." This is more than just oversight, and more than just a preference for Wall Street over all else. A hardened core of conservative politicians and commentators are actively hostile to the very idea of public health.[8]

Public health is not "what most people think it is," opined Pierre Lemieux, writing for the strident pro-privatization Reason Foundation. "Although some of its experts and activists cloak themselves in the mantle of science, many might be surprised to learn that it is mainly a political movement with a specific ideology." Lemieux's attack on the very idea of public health was hitting all the check marks in the conservative playbook. After he dismissed the science behind public health as just politics through other means, he claimed that public health workers' motivation wasn't merely health; it was "social justice." Ideologically, this puts them in the same boat as "community organizers" and antifa street fighters. Lemieux then sounded the alarm: "In the public-health vision, social justice can justify government interventions in virtually any private choice." Thus public health officials, who seemed to most of us to be largely concerned with keeping people alive during the pandemic, became not just partisan hacks but social justice warriors. They were the enemy. Their sin, of course, was in how they limited individual choice by requiring masks or asking people to stay home.[9]

Such think-tank musings may not have been read by the antimasking crowd, but they certainly filtered down as public health officials faced protesters who turned up at their homes to call them Nazis, socialists, and communists. One protester with Freedom Angels explained why she was on a public health official's lawn in California: "They're coming to *our* houses. Their agenda is contact tracing, testing, mandatory masks, and ultimately an injection that has not been tested." Dr. Amy Acton, Ohio's popular and effective state health director, received home visits from armed protesters along with a barrage of anti-Semitism. She resigned.[10]

To those opposed to public solutions, this merely cleared the way for the private solutions they preferred. In early 2020 the FDA, reacting to criticism that it had moved too slowly, actually tried what the conservative commentators had suggested. The agency's emergency deregulation declared that instead of the FDA performing a rigorous evaluation of new testing products, a test manufacturer simply had to affirm it had done its own validation. Within months some two hundred companies had tests on the market. And yet somehow the market failed to work its magic. Instead, according to Representative Raja Krishnamoorthi, who was investigating the FDA's actions, "fraudulent tests flooded the market. Hundreds and hundreds of tests taken by hundreds of thousands, if not millions of people." Public health officials doing their own evaluations found that tests they'd ordered in bulk had an accuracy rate of something like 20 percent. Laredo, Texas, put its drive-through testing plans on hold because their stocks of tests were worthless. This is the obvious reality of an unregulated market, as explained by Krishnamoorthi: "When you open the floodgates to virtually any product being sold by anybody, well, guess what? Shysters, scam artists, and people who are preying on unsuspecting consumers enter the fray."[11]

Staying true to Dr. Birx's promise to keep the response "centered fully on unleashing the power of the private sector," the administration privatized our public health through a combination of deregulation, lavish no-bid contracts, and prioritizing the reopening of businesses over the preservation of life. But not only did the free market fail to produce solutions, it often rewarded people and companies that were manifestly incompetent.[12]

One was once a telemarketer who had previously faced charges of making illegal automatic calls, posing as a nonprofit credit counseling service, and making unauthorized withdrawals from victims' bank accounts. But that was in 2012, and in 2020 his company, a soda-bottle manufacturer named Fillakit, won a $10 million contract from the Trump administration's Federal Emergency Management Agency to make vials for testing kits. It had never produced medical supplies before, and it showed. ProPublica reporters watched as "Fillakit employees, some not wearing masks, gathered the miniature soda bottles with snow shovels and dumped them into plastic bins before squirting saline into them, all in the open air." One employee told them, "It wasn't even clean, let alone sterile." What's more, the tubes weren't the standard size. "They're the most unusable tubes I've ever seen," a state public health official told them. "They're going to sit in a warehouse and no one can use them. We won't be able to do our full plan."[13]

ProPublica investigators found that the Trump administration's focus on the private sector had delivered some $2 billion to contractors who'd never done government contracting before. Many of them had never produced medical supplies before. These novices received about 13 percent of the total contracts. This haste and lack of due diligence created problems across the board. Swabs for collecting samples that should have been individually wrapped were delivered unwrapped in boxes of 180, meaning 180 chances for contamination as health care workers reached in. Another contractor shipped supplies using transport media that produced deadly cyanide gas. In Rhode Island a hazmat team had to clean up the mess.[14]

An NPR reporter asked the administration's testing czar, Admiral Brett Giroir, about some of these failings, "and he basically dismissed their complaints as kind of bellyaching." The admiral seemed oddly focused on the swabs, but his answer speaks volumes about how he and Trump saw public health:

> Now, yes, there are some labs that say, I would prefer a different type of swab. We are not in a menu situation where everyone can have filet mignon on the menu. You're going to have to have the chicken dish or the salmon because we do not have all of a single type of swab.

This is someone who sees public health as nothing more than a series of consumer products. This is someone who sees government as essentially having no role when it comes to what the market will produce. The public's needs simply aren't on the menu. If the market produces bad swabs, then that is what you shall have—at a hyperinflated price.[15]

Having defunded government health programs, vilified public health professionals, deregulated drug and testing approvals, and left planning itself to the whims of private corporations, our leaders handed us nothing but a series of market-approved products. This is not public health. This is no way to deliver a public good.

We know there is a way to establish and maintain public control over public health, because we have done it before. And it wasn't part of a tyrannical government overreach; it was the result of citizens demanding safe food and water as a public good.

The People Created Public Health: Privatization Is Tearing It Down

In 1884, twenty-two years before Upton Sinclair exposed the Chicago stock houses in *The Jungle*, the Ladies' Health Protective Association, made up of fifteen neighbors from New York's Beekman Hill neighborhood, levied a series of attacks on the city's slaughterhouses, which dominated the cityscape from 43rd to 47th Streets along 1st Avenue. Their concern was not only for the safety of the food that emerged from the filth, but also for the environmental hazards, which included a stockpile of manure thirty feet high and two hundred feet long, destined to be sold as fertilizer once it had "ripened."

When the association won a surprise victory against the manure's politically connected owner, a city official warned them to "go home" and to "not meddle any more in matters that did not concern them." Instead, they persisted and expanded their membership and reach, forcing the slaughterhouses to clean up their operations inside and out.[16]

The same pattern emerged in most major cities, with women often leading the charge. Temperance activists got involved with food and drug safety issues because many tonics, soothing syrups, and even foods were altered by adding narcotics, which the activists saw as paving the way to a lifetime of alcoholism and drug addiction. It took decades, but a combination of protests by these associations, advocacy by doctors, and exposés by muckraking journalists created enough public pressure to compel Congress to pass the 1906 Food and Drugs Act. Decades later, it passed the 1938 Food, Drug, and Cosmetic Act. The year 1958 saw the passage of the Food Additives Amendment, and we now live in a country where food is assumed to be safe rather than suspect. But it's still hard to imagine just how much of an impact the women who started this had. One researcher examined nineteenth-century death records, extrapolated them into a hypothetical twentieth century that never passed these laws, and estimated that we save nearly 1.8 million lives per year by holding food producers and drug companies to account.[17]

Corporate interests have resisted every step of the way. Speaking out against the 1906 act, an attorney for the cattle industry told Congress that labeling meat with a packing date did no one any good, that it would be an "unnecessary expense . . . ultimately borne by the public." The 1938 act would "put thousands of men and women out of work . . . close dozens of manufacturing plants and hundreds of stores. . . . It will hurt thousands. . . . It will help none," or so said the New York Board of Trade. Others fretted about "such a sweeping grant of autocratic power being placed in the hands of any bureau or department of government," and the counsel for the National Association of Retail Druggists told Congress that the 1938 bill "could wreck the industry of pharmacy." All of these hyperbolic and easily disproven lines of attack should be familiar; they emerge, zombie-like, each time the public takes a step toward ensuring safe food and public health as a public good.[18]

This is to be expected; corporations act in their own interests. Some champions of business and unfettered markets, such as Milton Friedman, who insisted that the notion of a "socially responsible" corporation was a dangerous myth, will openly admit this. And yet, each time the public asks for better food safety, the answer from the industry is the same: we can self-regulate; we can privatize this public responsibility and do away with public control. In the 1990s, the industry turned to privatization of food inspection as a tool of their quiet counterrevolution. In the new century, its effects began to be felt.

In 2010 AIB International, a for-profit food production auditor, gave an Iowa egg farm an inspection and a "Recognition of Achievement" for fulfilling safety standards. But after the Centers for Disease Control discovered a nationwide salmonella outbreak, and after health workers traced it back to the same Iowa farm, the Food and Drug Administration stepped in to do an inspection themselves. They easily found the cause of this public health disaster, which poisoned nearly two thousand Americans and forced the recall of over a billion eggs: piles of chicken manure rising up to eight feet high, rodent burrows and feces, and "live and dead maggots too numerous to count."[19]

Are FDA inspectors just as prone to error as for-profit inspectors? Might they too have missed what AIB missed? Perhaps, but the reason AIB missed these obvious signs was because they inspected only areas that their "client," the farm itself, had asked to be inspected. Obviously this would never include the piles of excrement out back.

This problem is systemic. It's not about human error; it's a function of privatization. AIB has a board of directors that includes high-ranking managers of some of the nation's largest food companies and followed a set of standards created by food industry associations rather than by public agencies. AIB sees the farms it inspects as clients. This is what happens when the public gives up control. The public is no longer the client. The public merely bears the consequences. In 2011, for example, thirty-three people died after eating melons contaminated with listeria monocytogenes. The farm that grew the tainted fruit had passed inspection, conducted by a private for-profit company, with flying colors.[20]

On poultry and hog farms the counterrevolution in food inspection has been even more sweeping. In the late 1990s, during the era of Clinton's government downsizing and deregulation, the Department of Agriculture started pilot programs for meat inspection that would effectively allow producers to use their own employees as inspectors. USDA inspectors, who once had the power to shut down a production line, were shunted aside.[21]

The goals became speed and efficiency. The USDA foresaw speeding up production lines by 25 percent while eliminating 40 percent of their inspectors. The poultry inspectors who remained had to examine chicken carcasses at the rate of 2.33 per second, and they were largely reduced to advisory roles. Undertrained employees took over as nominal inspectors, and were placed in the terrible position of having to decide to stop production if they suspected unsafe food was getting through; essentially, they had to choose between the health of a consumer they'd never meet and a boss who saw stoppages as cutting into profits. The industry was anticipating saving $256 million a year in overhead and looking forward to production lines humming along at 175 birds per minute.[22]

We know the results of these experiments only because of FOIA requests filed by consumer advocacy organizations. The inspectors on the pilot programs reported an error rate of 64 percent for failure to detect issues like organ parts, feathers, bile, and glands on carcasses ready to ship. An inspector described in graphic detail an intestine wrapped around a spinning paddle, spreading fecal matter across every bird that passed through it. A hog inspector claimed, in an affidavit, that the meat he saw coming off the line was not "wholesome or safe to consume." Another bluntly stated, "It's no longer meaningful for consumers to see that mark indicating that their product has been USDA-inspected."[23]

Why then did this program go nationwide? Why was there so little public input into a process that is undoing a century of popular and highly successful legislation?

In the free-market frenzy of the 1990s, global forces overcame our own careful regulations. In order to freely trade food products with nations that had already gone down the road toward privatized self-inspection— or that had never instituted high standards in the first place—the United States agreed to recommendations from an international commission that allowed it to import food that had not been through the same process as our own domestically produced food. That then became a powerful privatization argument for our own food producers, who wanted to be allowed to experiment with our health and well-being while finding cheaper ways of getting food past the inspectors. Ron Leonard, a former special assistant to the secretary of agriculture, referred to the result as a "race to the bottom" on a global scale.[24]

Food is a consumer product; public health is not. While the free market in food has done amazing things for consumers in terms of variety and price, the market will never on its own deliver the kind of safety we've come to expect. When food inspectors see the producer as the client, rather than the public, inspection itself becomes just another service and the client, rather than the public, is the one who has to be protected.

Keeping our food safe and our communities healthy means that we the public cannot allow private interests to blur the line between product and public good. Tests for virulent diseases and vaccinations are good for us as individuals, but they also protect our neighbors. Food may be a product, but as a potential carrier of disease it has a public facet as well. The market will have something to say about how tests and vaccines and food get made, and private corporations will make a profit by selling these things. But when it comes to the public health aspects, the public must retain control.

4
"They Just Have to Pay"
Privatizing the Public's Water Supply

"CUSTOMERS WANT THE LOWEST RATES POSSIBLE ON THE PLANET," COMplained a pro-privatization water commissioner as he spoke to a meeting of private water companies. He then went on to liken affordable public water to welfare, and encouraged his colleagues to use their power to teach people a lesson: "We live in a nanny state; we live in an environment where everyone needs to be a victim of some sort. Don't let them be a victim," he told them. "They just have to pay." His tough-love stance echoed the notorious statement from Nestlé CEO Peter Brabeck when he complained on camera about charitable organizations that "bang on about declaring water a public right" and how it was "extreme" to believe that "as a human being you should have a right to water." It is better to treat water like a "foodstuff," he continued, better to treat it just like any other product, "so that we're all aware that it has a price."[1]

Many observers thought that Brabeck's musings denied that water is a human right, and there was an appropriate outcry after his statements went public. He later "clarified" his position, but his company continued to act as if water were nothing more than a consumer good. During one of California's more intense droughts, when water was rationed and lawns withered, an enraged pitchfork-wielding crowd in Sacramento shut down a Nestlé bottling plant. The pitchforks were plastic and the crowd was nonviolent, but the anger was real. Nestlé had been pumping municipal water from the drought-stricken region, bottling it up, labeling it as "spring water," and shipping it far away.[2]

Just because corporations *can* package water and sell it at a profit doesn't mean we should accept that this public good—one absolutely essential for life—should be treated as a product. When it comes to basic needs, we are right to question whether private corporations should be in control of setting prices, just as they do for bottled water or soft drinks (or COVID-19 tests or medical swabs). Piped-in water, whether public or private, is not free, but that does not mean that it's delivered to us for the same reasons one would deliver to consumers a product or a "foodstuff."

Our commitment to public water, and the fact that virtually all communities in the United States have pipes running through them, is largely due to the relationship between safe water and public health. But if you ask an executive of a private water company, or an adherent of privatization, they will claim that municipal water happened because of consumer demand. The public wanted this service for their own purposes and convenience, and big government provided this "product" to them at below-market rates.

The real reason we have this amazing and near-universal infrastructure of water and water disposal is because we as citizens decided that such things are public goods deserving of public access and, more important, that they promote public health. The access part of this story has ancient roots; the public health part is more recent. But neither one follows the logic of the market.

Public Water: Moral, Patriotic, Necessary

"Let all you who thirst, come to the water," reads the Book of Isaiah, reflecting a common rule that humans have embraced across cultures and epochs: those who need water for their survival should not be denied. Wells may have been dug on private land, rivers may run through land that is privately held, but community members, and even strangers, have universally been granted access for basic needs. When the Romans built aqueducts and brought water into their cities, they built public need into their waterworks by allocating a certain amount of water for public use in public fountains. They provided for nonessential uses as well, like extra water for wealthy private homes or the communal baths, but the public portion of the water supply had its own rules and even its own infrastructure. It followed its own logic. Some water and some uses could be treated as products, but there always *had* to be a portion preserved for thirst, basic survival, and basic hygiene.[3]

Manhattan in the late eighteenth century was less organized when it came to the water supply. There were a few 150-year-old wells that supplied most of the water, but it wasn't very good. The wealthy bought drinking water bottled at nearby springs, and the less well-off tried to purify the well water with liquor. The situation limited growth, and Alexander Hamilton jumped into city council debates in the late 1790s over bringing more water to the population. Thanks to a big push by Aaron Burr in Albany, New York City got a largely private solution: the Manhattan Corporation, which was chartered to pipe clean water into the island.

The Manhattan Corporation was brilliant at raising funds and soon had over $2 million in assets. But under Burr's guidance, only about one in ten of those dollars went to water development; the rest was invested in Manhattan business interests. The Manhattan Corporation eventually dropped the charade, left the water business, and became Chase Manhattan Bank. But even though it always had little interest in providing water, it saw great benefit in using its state-sponsored monopoly to bankrupt smaller for-profit suppliers. As a result of this private approach, New Yorkers faced even fewer choices than before.[4]

Philadelphia, on the other hand, started the United States' first big public water system in 1799. Following several severe outbreaks of yellow fever, and believing that polluted wells were the cause of the disease, Philly's citizens petitioned the city for piped-in water. Appealing to the government as "Fathers of the City, as Guardians of the Poor, and the health and prosperity of their Fellow citizens in general," the citizens' petition insisted that "there is no object of use or ornament to which a liberal proportion of the city Funds can be more acceptably applied . . . even if no return of interest on the capital were to be expected." The petitioners felt certain the city leaders would approve public water, and the higher taxes that would make it possible. "We have full confidence in the patriotism of those we address," they explained. Providing public water wasn't about setting up a nanny state; it was patriotic.[5]

The citizens were wrong about how yellow fever is transmitted, but their new water supply still improved sanitation, and was a clear benefit when cholera, which *is* waterborne, hit the east coast of the United States in 1832. In New York the death toll was 3,500; in Philadelphia it was 900. That stunning difference finally convinced New York City that new water infrastructure had to be public—in both funding and control. Before long, New Yorkers were drinking clean water from upstate.[6]

For most of human history water has been treated not as a mere product but as a public good—both because it is simply immoral to deprive thirsty neighbors of the right to drink and because providing water dramatically improves public health. The common good, not the desire for convenient access to a consumer good, has driven the development of public waterworks. Public water is not just another government giveaway. The public needs these waterworks for reasons of survival.

By the 1890s, 70 percent of cities with populations over thirty thousand had invested public money in public systems. By the end of the decade, 82 percent of the fifty largest cities had public waterworks. New projects were coming online with intense regularity: the nation had only 244 water systems in 1870, but 9,850 by 1924. These remained mostly in cities until the New Deal's Works Progress Administration started expanding them into rural areas. By 1940 the nation had some 14,500 waterworks. And by the end of World War II, the number was 15,400. Twenty years later, we had over twenty thousand water systems with 20 billion gallons of water running through them every day. Eighty-three percent of these were publicly owned. This is a real achievement, and it happened because of public will and public investment.[7]

Government Neglect Is the New Oil

Those 20,000 community water systems in 1965 are now 51,356. One million miles of pipes devoted to drinking water crisscross the United States. Virtually all of them were designed as public projects.

The public accomplished all this. It was not a power play by an autocratic government; typically, government stood on the sidelines until the public demanded action. But now, unfortunately, our elected officials are returning to the sidelines and letting the public's investment crumble.

Neglect of our water system was evident before the 2008 Great Recession and has only accelerated since. Federal spending has remained flat, while state and local spending on water systems plummeted between 2009 and 2014, dropping 22 percent. This happened at exactly the wrong time. Pipes that were laid up to one hundred years ago are now leaking six billion gallons of water every single day—that's as much as 18 percent of the total amount of water that the United States treats and pumps on a daily basis.[8]

Each year we replace a mere 0.5 percent of our water systems' pipes. If we continue at that rate, we'll finish the job two hundred years from now. And that doesn't account for the fact that, according to the American Society of Civil Engineers, we will need to spend $1 trillion over the next twenty-five years just to create *new* infrastructure to meet new demand.[9]

During the early twentieth century, the public rose to the challenge and created a public good. Today, we are being told that we are powerless. A New Jersey legislator, for example, reacted to the alarming news about our water systems by throwing in the towel, declaring that the water systems were "beyond government capacity to restore."[10]

This makes no sense. The public built these systems, and the public can repair them. It is a matter of public and political will.

When residents of Madison, Wisconsin, discovered that their water had lead levels of 16 parts per billion—the EPA limit is 15 ppb—they looked at the standard options, like using chemicals that might prevent lead pipes from leaching into their drinking water, but found these would also pollute their lakes. And while this might reduce the levels of lead to just slightly below the EPA's limit, it wouldn't get rid of it entirely. What, in this case, would be in the public's best interest? Joe Grande, the city's water quality manager, summed up Madison's answer: "The safe level of lead is zero."

Getting even close to zero meant replacing every single lead pipe in the water system. It took ten years of digging, $20 million, countless disruptions and inconveniences, and cooperation from several thousand home owners. It was a big political risk on the part of the mayor and the utility. It has happened on this scale in only one other place—Lansing, Michigan, where it cost $40 million.[11]

Fixing our waterworks is not easy, but it is not beyond the capacity of the government or the public. It is also not the sort of decision that can be made by a for-profit business interest. Madison and Lansing won't profit by this act made for the common good, at least not in ways that can be explained to shareholders.

Madison and Lansing are exceptions. In most cities, we are keeping water cheap by not paying for the necessary upgrades and repairs, even when it puts citizens in danger. Flint, Michigan, found this out after its lead levels soared to as high as 13,200 ppb, more than twice what would be considered toxic waste. In the case of Flint, local decision-making had been stripped away and handed to state-level conservatives looking to cut corners so they could cut taxes. Flint's citizens didn't have the choices that wealthier cities like Madison and Lansing enjoy. But even when citizens retain local control, they often feel their budget woes have painted them into a corner, and that's when private-equity firms and multinational conglomerates swoop in.[12]

An overstretched city facing a water system on the brink of collapse faces a set of politically unpopular choices: raise taxes, float a bond, or raise water prices. At that point a private corporation shows up with an enticing offer—sell us the entire system, let us worry about everything from repairs to billing, receive an influx of cash, avoid a tax increase, and get out of the water business. These corporations promise that their practiced efficiency and massive scale will result in lower water prices, better customer service, and improved delivery. The politicians don't have to raise taxes, the citizens get to deal with a nimble corporation instead of a bloated bureaucracy, and the corporation turns a profit. Everybody wins, or so they claim.

There is so much interest in the privatization of water, from both the corporations running the systems and the private-equity partners backing the takeovers, that one mayor, beset by offers to take his system off his hands, quipped that water is the "new oil." That was a few years out from the financial collapse of 2008. Wall Street was bursting with capital, but cities were still struggling to recover. As noted earlier, desperate government is a great opportunity for these investment firms. After 2008 there were a lot of desperate governments, and they stayed desperate for a long time.

In fact, according to Michael Pagano, director of the University of

Illinois at Chicago's Government Finance Research Center, many cities and counties had "only recently returned to where they were in 2006 and 2007" when COVID-19 hit in 2020. If the pattern holds, they might "be in another ten- to fifteen-year trough." By June 2020, some seven hundred cities had scrapped important infrastructure plans—including improvements to water infrastructure—just to close up budget shortfalls. The federal aid packages passed to that point were no help because the Trump administration had pointedly stated the money could not be used as a budget remedy. Meanwhile, the Treasury Department made sure the investment banks (every privatization scheme needs at least one) were flush with cash. Senate Majority Leader Mitch McConnell (R-KY) suggested cities should simply declare bankruptcy, which would make their assets prime targets for investors. All this created a recipe for a privatization fire sale.[13]

And if this were not enough, it seems that Senators Tammy Duckworth (D-IL) and Mike Braun (D-IN) were determined to make sure that the next wave of water privatization would be unprecedented. In 2020 the senators advanced the Voluntary Water Partnerships for Distressed Communities Act by tossing the long-lingering legislation into an infrastructure bill. The act incentivizes privatization by letting water systems avoid federal environmental regulations for 180 days if the system is moving toward a public-private partnership and then letting them off the hook for three years if the partnership is finalized. For private water companies considering purchasing a distressed public water system, this is a huge incentive—it's permission to provide unhealthy water for three years and avoid costly improvements. Nearly three hundred community and environmental organizations quickly condemned the legislation. "Truth from the Tap," the private water industry's PR outlet, lavishly praised it.[14]

Squeezing, Squeezing, Squeezing: Water Privatization and Rate Hikes

What then, might these takeovers look like? In cash-strapped Coatesville, Pennsylvania, Pennsylvania American Water purchased an ailing water system in 2001, and the city (which once had a booming steel industry but was by then struggling to maintain a median income of $35,000) invested the $40 million it received, hoping to forever reap the benefits of the sale in the form of dividends and interest. Now, the city leaders thought they had money to cover fiscal emergencies, investment income, and cheap water.[15]

But ten years later, it had none of these. Three-quarters of the money was gone, repeatedly tapped by the city council to cover budget shortfalls. Pennsylvania American Water tried to force a 229 percent increase for wastewater treatment, and Coatesville had to spend its own money, some $40,000, fighting the increase in court. Even after they settled on a much lower increase, Pennsylvania American Water went back to the proverbial well, hiking water rates by 13 percent while claiming it had to cover the costs of more infrastructure improvements.

"They're squeezing, squeezing, squeezing us," Paul Trizonis, owner of a three-unit apartment building in Coatesville, told a local paper. Landlords like Trizonis, when faced with these sorts of increases, do what they have to do—they raise rents. And so the problem of how to pay for water was never really solved; it just flowed downhill. The residents paid for the system's upgrade through their bills and rents instead of their taxes. The big difference, the really tragic difference, is that they were funding an upgrade to a now-private system that once belonged to them. And under the new arrangement, Pennsylvania American Water would ultimately profit even further from the improved efficiency bought with residents' money.[16]

The profit expectations of these corporations are high; many are publicly traded or backed by private equity. They don't like to see profits dithering around the rate of inflation, and the only way to get a bigger return on investment is to raise rates. The town manager in Apple Valley, California, reflected on his town's own private water supplier, which charged rates 50 to 100 percent higher than the publicly owned water utilities next door: "What gnaws on people most is that when they go through a downturn, they don't get a guaranteed rate of return. They trim, they struggle. But even in bad times, these rate increases just kept coming." Apple Valley saw rate increases of 68 percent over thirteen years of private ownership and in 2015 was bracing for another 30 percent hike. These came courtesy of the Carlyle Group, a massive private-equity fund that was already boasting of 12 percent annual profits when its subsidiary, Park Water, demanded the rate hike.

During the 2015 California drought, most residents responsibly cut back on water use, and most were rewarded with lower water bills. But in Apple Valley, conservation cost more. Residents like high school teacher Lance Arnt, who ripped out his lawn to cut back on water, got hit with a 5 percent surcharge for using less water. Asked about this, Park Water's CEO explained "the reality" of the water business in simple terms: "With declining unit sales, you almost have to raise rates." The reality behind that "reality" was that Park Water had raised rates when there was no drought *and* when there was a drought, when times were good *and* when times were bad. Really any excuse to raise rates would do.[17]

In Rockland County, New York, United Water demanded a 28.9 percent rate hike at a time when inflation was virtually nonexistent. They settled for 13 percent. Then an investigation of their expenses revealed that United Water was covering its executives' kids' private school tuition—$80,000 worth—and had rented the CEO a second home (or was it his third?) for $16,000 per month. Other expenses included a lavish brunch for executives' spouses and an assortment of embarrassingly large liquor bills, but the $6,000 spent on golf balls was especially brazen.[18]

These executives are a far cry from the city fathers of Philadelphia, the ones citizens called patriotic for acting as "Guardians of the Poor" and for acting on behalf of "the health and prosperity of their Fellow citizens in general." Those pioneers established a public water system that made life better and saved lives during epidemics. Their example spread for nearly two hundred years. Now lawmakers are telling us that the problems with the water system are beyond the ability of our governments to handle. They aren't. We certainly need to pay for our water systems, but the government has shown that's possible without handing control and profits over to the private sector.

5

The Stuff of Life
Reclaiming Public Water

THE PUBLIC MUST RETAIN CONTROL OVER WATER BECAUSE IT IS ESSENTIAL to public health and to life itself. We also know, on a deep level, that applying market rules of exclusion and rivalry to water is morally repugnant. In an unfettered market, someone will always get left behind. When water is treated like a product, public health falls by the wayside.

Water is one of those things that's easy to not think about, and this has allowed privatization to advance well beyond where it should have. But when citizens do turn their attention to matters of quality, price, and who controls their water supply, they seem to instinctively want to take it back. Sometimes this happens only through hard-fought battles and relentless organizing, but it can also happen very quietly. It can happen as a rebellion against the restrictions water companies place on conservation and infrastructure policy, or it can happen because city managers simply run the numbers.

Public Water Pragmatism: When Privatization Costs More

As they craft their budgets, cities and towns often realize that they can manage their water more cheaply and do a better job. And they often find that even after paying the penalty to get out of their contracts with private companies, they still save money.[1]

In Donna, Texas, population 16,448, the city let its contract with CH2M Hill-OMI expire after watching the private company steadily raise the cost of its water management contract, from $1 million annually in 2001 to nearly $2 million in 2015. And as prices went up, the quality went down: the state environment commission dinged Donna four times in five years with water-quality violations. The city's analysis projected ten-year savings of $4.5 million from taking over, even after the city hired an additional seven employees to rebuild the cost-slashing, profit-enhancing understaffing typical in these private contracts. The city looked forward to passing those savings on to the residents or investing in upgrades, and City Manager Fernando Flores added a note about intangible benefits accruing to the city as well: "I think sometimes it's just about taking ownership. You do it, why not operate and manage it on your own? That's the big underlying factor. That way you can get a better feel for things and adjust better."[2]

Coeburn, Virginia, opted to take over from Veolia Water North America after comparing its $1.47 million town budget to the annual cost of the contract—$1.41 million. "When we ran the numbers ourselves, it was about $400,000 cheaper," Mayor Jess Powers explained. With barely over 2,100 residents and a median income of $25,000, Coeburn had cut its spending by reducing police and town manager hours and freezing staff salaries. Taking over from Veolia was a matter of survival for Coeburn, but once it had regained control of the water system, it discovered that its assets had not been well maintained. Veolia, according to the town manager, "never actually cleaned [the system] and so here we are six years later having to pay for them now."[3]

For these small communities, making the rational decision to take control of operating and maintaining their own waterworks was straightforward; they had not taken the more drastic step of actually selling their infrastructure to a for-profit corporation. For communities that did transfer these vital assets or entered long-term contracts, the road is much harder or at least more expensive.

Atlanta, Georgia, gave United Water a twenty-year contract but ended it after four years. As is typical in these cases, United Water's profits came from cutting corners—in this case they dropped half of Atlanta's waterworks staff. Residents soon noticed orange and brown discoloration in their tap water, and the city had to hire its own inspectors (at $1 million) to get straight answers. Atlanta and United Water finally parted ways under a court settlement that awarded both parties much less than they'd originally sought.[4]

Indianapolis also got stuck in a bad contract—it took the city $29 million to get out ten years early, but it may well have been worth it. One million of the city's residents got alerts telling them to boil their water during Veolia's tenure. Former city water-workers' pensions evaporated. A federal grand jury looked into allegedly fraudulent water quality statements. Bills went out for "estimated" rather than actual usage, a practice that unsurprisingly led to overbilling and that skirted the state's utility oversight commission. Unbeknownst to most residents, however, the water company was threatening to walk unless the city rewarded its poor performance with an additional $1.9 million per year, because it wasn't showing enough profit. If it weren't for a class-action lawsuit and dogged reporting, the company might have gotten away with it.[5]

Between 2003 and 2019, seventy-one U.S. communities took back their water, following a global trend that saw 2,400 cities in fifty-eight countries bringing water and other essential services under public control. The experiences of Atlanta, Indianapolis, and others have served as object lessons to cities like Baltimore, which stopped privatization in its infancy after a sustained public outcry. Only after Baltimore residents obtained documents under the Public Information Act did they learn how Veolia had met in secret with their city council members to propose an incremental, under-the-radar takeover of water services. Baltimore's community organizations quickly responded in 2014 with facts and figures from previous Veolia debacles. They packed meeting halls, council sessions, and street corners, and they partnered with national organizations for research support. More than forty organizations got involved, and the pressure on the city's elected leaders, many of whom were accused of having connections with the international water giant, was irresistible. As one resident wrote to the *Baltimore Sun*, "They say you can't fight City Hall, but we did. . . . We can come together to prevent abusive corporations from gaining a foothold in this or any other city."[6]

The Long Haul: How Missoula, Montana, Got Its Water Back

Arthur Laffer was Ronald Reagan's director of management and budget and a driving force behind the president's adoption of supply-side economics. While he is widely credited with the Laffer Curve, a paradoxical and widely discredited notion that tax cuts will lead to increased revenue because of increased economic activity, he is also a leading advocate of privatization. In 2016 he praised Turkey for its privatization efforts, ignoring the widespread corruption and oppression that followed, and said he wished he could trade President Obama for Turkey's autocratic president, Recep Tayyip Erdoğan. But in 2015 he was in Missoula, Montana, as an expert witness on the ownership of its water system.[7]

Missoula was fighting in court for the right to purchase its waterworks from Carlyle Group, one of the largest private-equity funds in the world. The value of Missoula's Mountain Water Company amounted to a tiny sliver in Carlyle's total of $194 billion in assets, but it was apparently a sliver worth fighting for—so much so that Carlyle thought it worthwhile to bring Laffer to Montana and pay a rate of $15,000 per day for him to lecture a judge on how marketplace magic was a blessing for Missoula's water consumers.[8]

Laffer started with the familiar refrain that "water is a product." Water was markedly *not* like the fire and police departments, Laffer argued. As a product, water "lends itself" to private ownership. He added, according to the court records, that because of the profit motive "private companies are far more concerned about water quality than municipalities." According to Laffer, a distant private-equity firm under pressure to produce returns for investors cared more about water quality than did the public servants who actually drank it. Laffer's free-market fantasy blithely ignored what every investor knows—you don't have to be good to get rich—and was equally myopic in how we judge quality. He couldn't seem to fathom the larger issues at play.[9]

Missoula was an anomaly in Montana; it was the only municipality that did not own its water system, and this was due to a historical quirk and some long-standing bad blood. A local family had originally owned the system for generations and fought with the city in state courts and the court of public opinion over its ownership. When the family decided to unload this bulky asset, it went not to the city but to Park Water, a regional company. Then Carlyle became interested in Park Water as a part of a grander scheme that involved repackaging several different waterworks from across the country and selling them off—a Canadian company looked like a likely buyer.[10]

Carlyle, knowing that it had to face Montana state regulators to approve the purchase, courted Missoula mayor John Engen, who came to believe that his town would have a chance to buy Mountain Water from the equity firm. Even then, Carlyle made it clear that it was interested in this water system only for the short term. And Engen claims that Carlyle told him it was more interested in Park Water's California assets than in anything having to do with Montana. He backed the deal believing Carlyle would carve out Mountain Water from the larger package, and that his tiny town would get favorable treatment.

You can call his belief naive, but handshake deals and relationships built on trust still have currency in places like Missoula. Engen remembered how Carlyle executive Robert Dove took him to a tony Washington, DC, restaurant, gave him a friendly side hug, and asked, "Mayor, are you ready to buy a water system?" That, for the mayor, counted as a deal. The public letter they issued said only that Carlyle would consider the city's offer in good faith, but to Engen there was a solemn promise behind that bland and noncommittal statement. Missoula backed Carlyle in its purchase of Mountain Water, and one of the world's largest equity firms suddenly controlled Missoula's drinking water.[11]

Missoula, which prides itself on inspiring *A River Runs Through It*, had a population of seventy thousand and a budget of about $116 million. The very notion of taking over a water system was daunting, but over 70 percent of residents, in a poll commissioned by the city, supported spending public money on the purchase. Significantly, this was not because Mountain Water was doing a bad job in terms of the service. Most residents polled agreed that their needs were being met. As consumers, they saw no problem with private ownership.[12]

But when they approached the question as citizens, continued private ownership posed numerous problems. First and foremost, the system was losing water at an astounding rate. Leaky water mains were dumping over 50 percent of the water that had been treated and pumped. Mountain Water's private owners saw no problem here, but Missoula's citizens saw this as unsustainable and wasteful, even if it had minimal impact on their water bills. Next, Missoula was planning on infrastructure improvements; it didn't own its water, but it *did* own its sewers—the other half of any water system. Long-range planning on how these two halves would work together was needlessly complex as long as Missoula didn't know who would actually own its water, much less what the next owner's plans might be.[13]

So Missoula offered $50 million after Carlyle agreed to entertain offers in 2011 for the water system. When Carlyle refused, Missoula offered $65 million. Twice. Again, Carlyle shot them down, claiming Mountain Water was worth at least $120 million. Mayor Engen began to realize he'd been played. The sale of Mountain Water wasn't a priority for Carlyle; it had its eyes on increasing the value of Park Water, on squeezing as much profit out of that scheme as possible.[14]

Engen was indignant: "This isn't 'Flip This House.' This is the stuff of life." Missoula moved to take control via eminent domain. For the next several years, the legal bills piled up: the city had estimated a $400,000 fight, but it ended up costing them $1.9 million. Carlyle, confident it would win, agreed to sell Park Water, which included Mountain Water, to a Canadian company for $327 million and the assumption of $77 million in debt. A local columnist worried about the mounting expenses and the prospects, criticizing the city for getting into "a high-stakes game against an aggressive bluffer with many, many more chips."[15]

At the heart of any eminent domain case lies the belief that there is a public good and the public has a right to control it. By bringing Laffer in to testify, Carlyle hoped to undermine that argument, offering in its place an assertion that water is a mere product; therefore, all the public's demands can be met through market incentives. Justice Townsend saw clearly that this was bigger than the fight between Missoula and Carlyle, and that water was more than a consumer good: "Dr. Laffer's testimony did not address the critical nature of water supply and its inextricable link to the public health, safety and well-being of the community," she wrote in her decision. And then she went on:

> Under municipal ownership, important financial decisions regarding the Water System can be based on promoting pub-

lic health, safety and welfare rather than on decisions regarding returns on investments for a large and growing utility conglomerate.

. . .

Short term investments for the benefit of investors are incompatible with long term planning and investment needed to ensure the reliable delivery of clean water.

. . .

Protection and promotion of the public health, safety and welfare is the fundamental duty of a municipality. Private corporations have no duty to protect and promote the public health, safety and welfare.[16]

In other words: Water is a public good. The public good is best served by the public. Private corporations have no responsibility to the public and cannot be expected to act to their benefit.

Carlyle did not accept this ruling, and kept up the fight long after the decision came down. Ultimately it found every legal avenue closed, and Missoula paid $83.87 million for Mountain Water, a court-ordered price that Carlyle fought to the end. As the sale went through and the city took possession of the water infrastructure, the local newspaper celebrated even in the face of the challenges ahead: "For the first time in our town's history, ownership of our water system—its pipes, pumps, wells, water rights, wilderness lakes and dams—finally landed where it belongs: in the hands of the people, to be managed for the public good, for all time."[17]

As Carlyle itself had admitted when it purchased the considered opinion of Laffer, America's premier supply-sider, this was bigger than Missoula. As the court fight dragged on, the town's leaders and activists heard other horror stories, including one that involved Carlyle. Apple Valley, California, had just experienced a round of drought pricing—a 35 percent increase—under Park Water. Missoula's Engen reached out to Apple Valley's manager, Frank Robinson, who immediately recognized they were "having the same issue." Missoula activist Hermina Harold, who had long supported the use of eminent domain, had a similarly broad view: "If we can set a legal precedent that helps other communities win control of their water, it will make the City's efforts even more worth it." Apple Valley and Missoula quickly established a partnership to share strategies and support, both recognizing that water is, as Robinson put it, "essential and meets the basic needs of human life." As such, the citizens of both cities started to "have a hard time believing that our water should be owned from afar by a private corporation."[18]

Water, when treated as a public good and not as a product, can create and define communities. Our feeder pipes and water mains connect us to each other, as does the ancient and very human belief in our right to access water for our basic needs. For most of the twentieth century, we in the United States got so good at meeting this need that we forgot about what we had accomplished and started taking our water for granted. We used up the life span of our pipes that had been paid for by previous generations, and we failed to pay it forward for our own children and grandchildren. We even, in some cases, let our water become a product and a profit-making machine for corporations with no attachment to the communities that pay them.

Now our water systems are failing and we face a choice. We can abandon our values: the idea of a right of thirst and its ancient roots; the idea that public water is patriotic, as the citizens of Philadelphia demonstrated; and knowledge that public water serves public health. Or we can take this opportunity to rediscover water as a public good and the active, inclusive communities that form around it.

Most of us live in cities and towns that own their waterworks, but the issues of water privatization affect us all, and will affect us more as the infrastructure crisis deepens. As the examples of Missoula, Apple Valley, and Baltimore show, citizens can win the coming fights over water when they accept responsibility for paying for it, when they elect civic-minded politicians who side with the public over the multinational corporations, and when they insist on treating water as a public good and refuse to accept that it is a product.

This means also that it is time to broaden our thinking about public health as a public good. While the struggles over water have often had encouraging outcomes, the fight over safe food rarely takes on such local intensity. The activists who fought for public health against the New York meatpacking district could make their presence felt—they just had to walk a few blocks. Now the food producers are tucked far away from population centers while the regulations are obscure and easily manipulated. Too often our answer to unsafe food is to make consumer choices, like shopping at high-end specialty stores, rather than citizen choices, like pressing for safe food for all.

Resistance to the privatization of food inspection, an utterly obvious attempt to let the fox guard the henhouse, has to take on aspects of the fight for public water. The issue is less local, but it can be localized. The issue lends itself to consumer thinking, but it can be recast into the realm of the citizen. Our federal food laws started with local actions; even if we don't live next to a slaughterhouse, we likely live near a grocery store.

Polls taken during the 2020 pandemic revealed strong majorities that prioritized shoring up public health over resuscitating the economy. The protesters opposed to the lockdown failed to make a dent in this public attitude, but many politicians—most of whom followed the president and desperately sought his approval—still went the other way, and we all paid the price. All it took were the decisions of a few public figures and a noisy minority of constituents to take public health out of public hands. Had we been more serious about public health before the crisis—had we built up public structures, institutions, and capacities—it would have been much more difficult to wave away the experts and continue on our self-destructive path.

If we don't want to relive this nightmare the next time a novel virus appears, we the public must establish firm democratic control over the levers of public health. This will mean treating individual health, not just public health, as a public good. And it will mean having a plan to quickly realign the private sector to meet the public's needs as the next crisis emerges.

Part III

THE PUBLIC GETS US THERE

Transportation, Communication,
and Economies That Work for All

PUBLIC HEALTH AND WATER ARE PUBLIC GOODS BECAUSE WE NEED THEM TO live; transportation and communications infrastructure are public goods because we need them to help create economies that allow us to live well. Thinking like a citizen about water and health leads us naturally to realize that both should be spread as widely as possible, not treated as mere products. The same goes for roads, bridges, airports, mail service, and access to the internet. These are not mere conveniences or responses to consumer demand. They are essential for getting people to work, moving products, and spreading knowledge. They provide the framework for modern economies, and, as President Joe Biden has explained, public investment in infrastructure "builds a fair economy that gives everybody a chance to succeed."[1]

Placing these public goods in private hands grants those hands immense power to shape economic destiny to their own ends. Keeping them in public hands allows democracy to shape economic destiny for the good of all—even for those fellow citizens who live in rural, out-of-the-way towns. Connecting these members of our national community with roads and data networks expands the range of what they can do to participate in the economy, and that benefits all of us.

Protecting these public goods is about the economy, and it's also about the money. Who pays for infrastructure and how financing is arranged often determine whom it will serve and how. It's also about responsibility—the Indiana Toll Road is a case study in what can go wrong when politicians convince the public that turning things over to private investors will mean a free ride. And it's about our rights and freedoms; we have a right to travel. No one else should own the journey, and we should always have a right to find another way when someone has placed obstacles in our path.

In other words, thinking like citizens about roads, bridges, buses, trains, and fiber-optic cable opens up new possibilities for building a stronger, more diverse, and more equitable economy. Conversely, letting them go to private companies that will treat us as mere consumers of their infrastructure guarantees that our economies will serve narrow interests and that many of us will be left out.

6

Economic Destiny and the Pitfalls
of the Public-Private Partnership

PRIVATIZATION FOLLOWS THE MONEY. WHEN WE LOOK TO PRIVATE CAPITAL to help solve infrastructure funding problems, those private interests putting up the money will inevitably guide public projects to the places that are most profitable for them. This leaves out vast sections of the country and ultimately narrows what kinds of economies those places will have. If we want to have an economy where innovative businesses and ideas can thrive regardless of zip code, if we want an economy that works for all, we need a public willing to invest where corporations won't.

Infrastructure is economic destiny, so we need to pay attention to who is calling the shots; typically it's those who are putting up the money. Iowa joined the union in 1846, but it took railroads to fully tie the state to the nation and create economic opportunity. In the 1850s Iowa tried to develop a dense network of railroads that would serve local interests. A state with such rich agricultural resources would thrive if it had both regional hubs and access to markets in the east. But Iowa's constitution tightly restricted the state's ability to take on debt, so what projects did arise were driven by the market; they were short, haphazard, and sometimes rerouted to satisfy a higher bidder.

Finally, Congress stepped in with land grants—this was an early privatization scheme that handed public lands over to private companies with the understanding that they would build and operate railroads. But no one back east was interested in completing the railroad network that Iowa planners asked for, one that would promote a diverse economy in Iowa, one that would include financial hubs where commodities could be traded and manufacturing could thrive. Especially not the eastern railroad companies. Instead, they built railroads that served established financial and manufacturing interests in the east.[1]

Iowa got five railroad lines. None of them ran north to south. All of them fed into the east. According to historian and political scientist Zachary Callen, this had the effect of "limiting Iowa's economic growth to primarily agricultural goods" and demonstrates "how early choices about infrastructure established an economic relationship that, through continual reinforcement, lasted for decades." The project served the purpose of linking the East Coast to the frontier, it served the purpose of getting Iowa's crops to hungry mouths in the east, and it served mid-Atlantic manufacturing, but it did not serve Iowa's economic development outside of agriculture. Long before the state would joke about being a "flyover state" it was designated a "ride through" state and a satellite to the eastern establishment's economic core.[2]

Now, there's nothing wrong with choosing to remain a primarily agricultural state, but Iowa didn't make that choice. The choice was made for it by private interests because Iowa had chosen to avoid state-level public funding of infrastructure. And perhaps no one realized how far-reaching the outcomes of these choices would become for the state's economy long into the future. With the benefit of hindsight, we can look at examples like this and recognize that infrastructure is destiny. Those who foot the bill control that destiny; they get to determine infrastructure's contours, purposes, and risks. They also get to decide who should benefit.

Iowa resisted raising taxes or taking loans to build infrastructure, but public funding came more easily in states that saw private interests for what they were. When citizens of Pennsylvania petitioned the legislature for a canal in 1825, the choice was clear. It was, they claimed,

> a truth well established that all power granted to corporations is so much deducted from the sovereignty of the people; and that consequently the creation of such bodies, or the increase of power to those already existing, should be deemed, in general, impolitic, dangerous, and contrary to the true spirit and genuine principles of republican government.[3]

Pennsylvania got it right. Power over infrastructure given to corporations is power taken from the people. The underlying supports for transportation and communications are public goods and will serve the public only if they remain under public control.

P3s and Public Power

When Ronald Reagan spoke approvingly of privatization in 1987 he mentioned the Homestead Acts, which evoke the image of the small family farmer doing on his own what bureaucracies can never do. He failed to mention the massive transfer of land from public hands to private railroad companies that started in 1850 and helped define the latter half of the nineteenth century. In Texas alone, private rail companies received acreage equal to the size of Indiana. Reagan's romantic version of privatization was one of government simply standing aside, and it obscured some incredibly complex arrangements. Today, the obscuring is handled by the term *public-private partnership*, or *P3*, a slippery phrase that applies to an ever-widening circle of infrastructure contracts and agreements and evokes an enticing promise of citizens and corporations working hand-in-hand. In practice, the public often finds the partnership to be less than equal.[4]

So what is an infrastructure P3? Creating or improving public infrastructure typically involves five main activities: designing, building, financing, operating, and maintaining. During the twentieth century, especially after the New Deal, we got used to the idea of the public performing all of these except for building; rarely does it make sense for a government to function as a construction company on major infrastructure projects, so this function has typically been contracted out. But more recently we've seen the rise of "design-build" arrangements, a form of public-private partnership that can raise significant issues of public control and oversight, whereby one contractor is responsible for both functions. And finally, there are P3s centered on financing (which may also privatize one or more other activities), where all the problems inherent in traditional contracting arrangements are amplified and public control becomes directly pitted against investor control.[5]

Big projects need big piles of money up front. State and local governments don't typically have that kind of cash lying around, and so the traditional public solution involves floating a tax-exempt bond to raise the money. A wide variety of entities, from pension funds to individual investors, buy these bonds, and they have to be paid back. This means taxes and tolls, but these can be spread out over time and made equitable. The benefits and burdens can be shared. The people get a completed project; contractors get paid on time; the bond buyers get safe, predictable returns; the public retains control over a public good that has a measurable impact on their lives; and the overall economy, for both workers and business owners, improves. Spreading the benefits like this, creating "wins" in many different columns, is something the public can do, and traditionally has done, incredibly well.[6]

But from the perspective of Wall Street, the most enticing piece of the infrastructure puzzle is financing, and it is on this hinge that public projects typically become P3s. Companies that seek out P3 investment opportunities follow a new model: they are infrastructure companies that act like investment banks, or they are actual conglomerates of construction, management, and investment companies. They are often multinationals, and in most cases the finance segment of their corporate structure is dominant. In the Chicago parking meter fiasco, it was Morgan Stanley with its army of analysts that saw huge returns where the city of Chicago did not. In Missoula, Montana, it was the Carlyle Group, the world's largest private-equity firm, that saw opportunities in buying up, carving up, and reselling small-town municipal waterworks. In most cases, the P3 is led by a company that's not in the business of making roads or making bridges, but is primarily in the business of making money. These new beasts are another example of the financialization of corporate America—the ever-increasing use of Wall Street financial instruments to maximize profit.

Their wizardry is beguiling; if they can make money on Wall Street from virtually nothing, they are worth listening to, some policymakers conclude. Their pitch goes like this: You don't need to raise taxes for your infrastructure project. We will pay for it. We will make our money back down the road, and most of this will come from improved efficiencies. The cost to taxpayers will be next to nothing.

If these corporations put up the money, however, they will want to safeguard their investment, and that's where the financing hinge swings into the other parts of the project where the public has an interest—operations and maintenance. The private company will insist on having a say in, if not outright control over, how the completed project is run and how it is maintained. And here is where it's important to keep in mind that, in the end, we are still talking about a public asset.

P3 projects are still owned, ultimately, by the public. If the public gave that up, it would be a private project, not a public-private partnership. Common business sense might say that private companies shouldn't take responsibility for someone else's asset, but if they can control operations and maintenance for a set period of time, they can get their money and get out. They don't have to be worried about being saddled with a depreciating asset with increasing maintenance costs. The operator of a toll road built on public land might have the right to collect tolls for sixty years. They have an interest in maintaining that road for just that amount of time so they don't lose customers or get sued for negligence. They will also have calculated just how little they can get away with. They will know that it's cheaper to maintain a road when it is new. They will, toward the end of that sixty years, let certain things slide, knowing full well that it will not impact their bottom line, even if it does ultimately impact the public.

If a private company puts up the money for a P3, it will want control over how that public asset is run, managed, and maintained. It will obtain control through contract clauses and will defend its rights in court. It will tailor its operations and maintenance toward the narrow interest of return on investment rather than the broader interest of improving either the infrastructure itself or the economy for the common good. It will have leverage to do all this because it is putting up the money.

These sorts of concerns do little to dissuade P3 adherents. Donald Trump's secretary of transportation, Elaine Chao, said there were "trillions" of dollars in investment capital waiting for partnerships with "a bold new vision" and claimed, "We all know that the government doesn't have the resources to do it all." Visiting a project in Miami, Trump's housing and urban development secretary, Ben Carson, opined, "Public-private partnerships work because there's almost unlimited money in the private sector."[7]

These former senior cabinet officials speak as if they don't know how either government or the private sector actually works. Governments don't pay for these projects out of pocket; they almost always rely on bond sales, and they can get incredibly good deals that simply don't exist in private financing. At the time Trump entered office and started devising infrastructure plans, the federal government had the ability to borrow at the rate of 2.4 percent. In mid-2020 the rate on municipal bonds was also low—between 2 and 4 percent.[8]

To financial institutions looking to invest in public infrastructure with high returns, that low rate of return represents unfair competition. One of the little-noticed proposals in the 2017 Trump tax reform was a bid to eliminate the income tax deduction for those who purchased some classes of municipal bonds. This is a long-standing goal of pro-privatization think tanks because without the tax break these bonds are less attractive to investors, which means they have to entice those investors with higher interest rates. This means higher taxes and fees all around, but for the otherwise tax-adverse pro-privatization crowd that's okay if it means P3 financing looks a little more attractive.[9]

The difference between public and private financing is vast. Governments can finance projects at rock-bottom rates of less than 4 percent; private companies consider a healthy rate of return to be anywhere between 10 to 20 percent, making P3s a promising source of profits. Their returns may come from fees, tolls, or charges to the government, but in the end it is always the public that pays. A government that enters a P3 with one of these companies may avoid the appearance of public expenses, but its citizens always end up paying. What's more, they also lose public control over assets that should be public goods and could even lose the economic benefits that these projects are supposed to provide.[10]

When Iowa failed to put up the money for its railroads, it got railroads that served the narrow interests of those who financed the project. As a result, it got an economy that served those interests before serving the interests of Iowans, who wanted a more diverse economy. Infrastructure gave Iowa opportunities, but it was really infrastructure financing that called the shots.

Today, most transportation officials in rural states recognize this and look at P3s with skepticism. Early in the Trump term, the transportation departments of North Dakota, South Dakota, Montana, and Idaho sent Wyoming's director and CEO of the state's transportation department to Capitol Hill with a message intended to tamp down some of the privatization fervor that the president had stoked. The director had a simple message: his states would be left out of a national infrastructure plan that relied on private financing. P3s that rely on big returns on investment, he claimed, "are not a surface transportation infrastructure solution for rural states." The states he represented just don't have enough cars on the road to generate the revenue to pay back the debt to the private financiers.[11]

P3s on the Road Well Traveled

Despite all the talk about how the private sector is innovative and adventurous and the bureaucracy is stagnant, the truth is that private capital will typically seek out safe returns on investment. Risk-taking capitalists are the exception to the rule, but they are the ones who get the headlines and the laurels when their gambles work out. When it comes to infrastructure projects, grand visions and game-changing projects have long been the domain of the public.

Citizens of the early U.S. republic thought quite a bit about what we'd call infrastructure and what they called "internal improvements," but they and their politicians had vast disagreements about how to plan them and pay for them. Many in Congress and most in the White House believed the federal government had no constitutional authority to plan or fund roads, bridges, or canals, and they shut down attempts to develop a coherent national plan, leaving the states to set their own agendas and come up with their own funding. State by state, the results were strikingly different.

At first, Virginians assumed that their wealthy, slaveholding planter class would plan, fund, and execute the big projects. This class had won the Revolutionary War, framed the Constitution, and largely ran the state government. They claimed to be always acting on behalf of the common good, and the public largely believed them. Nevertheless, the most-hoped-for improvement projects—including locks and dredging on the James River up to Richmond and beyond, and a canal through the Great Dismal Swamp—faltered for decades in spite of their impressive ability to draw investors.[12]

By 1816 Virginians were ready to accept some government involvement, and settled for what they called a "mixed-enterprise" model. But the resulting system left pretty much all of the initiative in the hands of the private sector. The state could consider *only* projects that wealthy investors brought forth. Virginia would then back those projects with a state engineer, surveys, and public investment (up to a set percentage). But although the state would be a shareholder, it would also subsidize the private shareholders by waiving its portion of dividends until private capital had turned a profit of at least 6 percent.

The widely held assumption was that if the state stood aside, the private sector would spur existing proposals to completion while garnering new ones. This proved overly optimistic by far. The James River project stalled at Richmond, and investors resisted the state's calls for improved technology on the route. The investors were already earning large dividends, so why take on substantial risk and few rewards in a complex system of new locks, dams, and turnpikes leading to Ohio? A publicly controlled project might have seen it serving the greater good of the commonwealth, but this group of private investors did not.[13]

Part of the problem was that much of the tidewater planters' wealth was tied up in people held in slavery. With little cash on hand, they predictably resisted both large investment and increased taxes. This was a significant factor in the long, drawn-out effort to put a canal through the Great Dismal Swamp. Many investors sent slave labor as part of their investment, but it wasn't in their interest to send those who were healthy and strong. The resulting labor pool skewed toward the old and infirm, who suffered terribly while making little progress on the canal.

Self-interest also ran up against broader public interests because many of the investors in the project owned land within the swamp that would soar in value if the swamp were drained. So this became a priority, not for engineering reasons or because the public demanded it, but because that was where the money was. Meanwhile, a canal through the swamp, a comparatively simple project, languished. Settlers on the other side of the swamp, who yearned to be connected via a canal to people and markets on the coast, were a secondary concern. Ultimately the canal was completed only after direct investment by the commonwealth.[14]

A year after Virginia settled into its mixed-enterprise model, the New York State legislature, in 1817, passed the Erie Canal Bill, embracing the public model that Virginia had so studiously avoided. New York planned to pay for the canal through loans and planned to pay back those loans through tolls on Erie Canal traffic and taxes on salt, auctions, and land along the canal route (but the canal was so successful that these land taxes ended up being unnecessary). The state planned to handle the money through appointed commissioners, and other commissioners would oversee construction. This was, they said, an appropriate function of the state, as such large sums as those expected would be handled "more economically . . . under public authority, than by the care and vigilance of any company." The key difference between New York's initiative and Virginia's was public control over the project—including financing.[15]

Among those most opposed to this project were those who would, ironically, benefit the most in the end. All of the delegates from New York City voted in unison *against* the Canal Bill. Wealthy New York City residents studiously avoided taking part for the first two years of the project, seeing it as a risky venture with modest returns that would serve only a howling wilderness. What's more, the project eschewed private control. What these investors didn't see is how the project would bring to New York City more products, goods, and people, cementing it as a center of global trade.

It was the small investors, banks, and towns along the route that loaned the state the money for the project, and within a couple of years, once it was clear that the canal would be a success, the big money from New York City followed. The canal was an astounding success; its tolls alone covered the construction costs in just nine years. But beyond the return on investment and the effects on Manhattan, the canal transformed life in western New York State. Small manufacturing boomed in places like Rochester, Syracuse, and Buffalo, as did their populations. A middle class was born in formerly small towns in New York's hinterlands. Opportunity expanded, wealth increased, and the public advanced together. None of this would have happened if it had been left to Manhattan's wealthy investor class to decide on which infrastructure projects should move forward. It took a democratic body—in this case the state legislature—to recognize, fund, finance, plan, and build this public good.[16]

Up in the Air: The Never-Ending Effort to Privatize Air Traffic Control

We're a long way from reliance on canals, but many of the same principles hold. It's the public that's willing to take risks and include rural areas and smaller cities in economic development. Despite what antigovernment activists will tell you, it can do this really well. Public air traffic control, for example, made commercial aviation possible; it now handles 42,700 flights per day and 944 million passengers per year, with a nearly flawless safety record. The system is remarkably efficient, requiring only 14,500 air traffic controllers and 6,000 technicians who handle over 5,000 airports, many of which are active twenty-four hours a day. And these public employees have, over the seventy-five-year history of federal air traffic control, built a vibrant culture of service, dedication to safety, and professionalism. The system, like America's interstate highways and waterworks, is a towering public achievement that boosts the economy and improves our quality of life.[17]

But since the 1970s, air traffic control has been a target for privatization. The big airlines have spent some $16 million on lobbying for legislation crafted to meet the needs of an extremely narrow interest group, and one that methodically locks out the public.

The most recent proposal aimed to sever the publicly controlled Air Traffic Organization, which operates air traffic facilities, radar equipment, and airport control towers, from the Federal Aviation Administration; transform it into a nonprofit corporation; and establish a board of directors dominated by large commercial carriers to oversee its operations. The legislation would authorize this board to create its own bylaws, acquire and own property, set its own budget, negotiate its own contracts, and borrow money. But its most significant power, perhaps, lies in its ability to set, charge, and collect fees for "any individual or entity using air traffic services provided by the Corporation." These fees would not have to be cleared by Congress. The nonprofit corporation might not benefit directly, but it is designed to favor large commercial carriers.[18]

President Trump loved this idea. During a fake signing ceremony in the Oval Office, where he signed a pair of nonbinding memos, not actual legislation, he claimed that "this new entity," meaning the air traffic corporation, "will not need taxpayer money, which is very shocking when people hear that. They don't hear that too often." He was wrong. We hear that quite often because it's the same promise of something for nothing that privatization advocates offer every single time. It's an empty promise; the fees don't go away. Make no mistake: the public will pay one way or another. The questions are who decides and how the bill gets settled.[19]

What should our broad public objectives be when it comes to air traffic? Like the railroads and the interstate highways, our airports and air routes link us together as a nation. As a nation we should value not only the hubs but also the small cities and out-of-the-way areas that use their airports as vital links to the nation's larger centers of population and power. Infrastructure privatization, on the other hand, follows the road well traveled, and the same holds true for privatization of air traffic. Some of the most vocal opponents of the ATC privatization plan are mayors of small and medium-size cities—both Republicans and Democrats—and 117 of them signed a letter of opposition warning of the "dire ramifications of eliminating congressional oversight of this public air transportation infrastructure."[20]

One of those who signed was Jeff Longwell, Republican mayor of Wichita, Kansas. His city is not a big hub for airlines, and Longwell feared that runway fees for cities like Wichita would go up so the privatized air traffic corporation could lower fees for the moneymaking big airports. But Wichita is also the nation's largest manufacturer of small aircraft, and this vital industry could easily see a downturn if big airlines jacked up fees on smaller aircraft.[21]

The public's level playing field has allowed industries like this to grow in cities like Wichita, creating diverse economies in a broader range of places. Public control of infrastructure means a broader economy for a wider slice of the country; this was true when New York funded its famous canal and it's true today with air traffic. If it is a public good, it requires and deserves public control.

7
Toll Roads at America's Crossroads

WHEN MIKE PENCE WAS GOVERNOR OF INDIANA, HE HELPED SOLIDIFY privatization's grip on the Main Street of the Midwest, also known as America's Crossroads, also known as the Indiana Toll Road (ITR). This critical public asset fell into private hands in 2006 with a lease of seventy-five years; it will not revert to public control until 2081. Pence trumpeted the deal as he made his way to the vice presidency, and he used his first foreign trip as VP to promote his old Australian friends at IFM Investors—a key player in the Indiana Toll Road saga. Whenever Donald Trump made one of his unserious promises to invest trillions in infrastructure through privatization schemes, Mike Pence could point to the alleged success of the lease.[1]

The ITR deal can be considered a success in the same way Trump's pre-presidential real estate debacles were a success; they both sold the public on outlandish promises and limped along in spite of bankruptcy. Instead, the ITR's privatization should serve as a cautionary tale. Our nation is in desperate need of very expensive infrastructure improvements, and every time our governments attempt to tackle them we hear the same refrain: there is no money, so we should let private corporations handle it. The Indiana Toll Road stands as a monument to this refrain and what it ultimately means.

Money Moves: Crafting the Toll Road Deal

The story of the ITR is one of influence and behind-the-scenes maneuvering, and this continued as Pence moved to Washington. IFM's interests in the Indiana deal were represented by Bose, McKinney & Evans LLP, a major donor to Pence's gubernatorial campaign. After Pence assumed the vice presidency and made his voyage to Australia on behalf of American infrastructure, Bose formally declared that it would lobby in Washington for IFM and filed paperwork naming Pence as a contact in its campaign to influence the formation of Trump's infrastructure plan.

Two other foreign firms involved in the toll road deal, Australia's Macquarie Group and Spain's Cintra SA, ponied up for expensive lobbyists to promote "private company financing" or "support for the greater use of public-private partnerships" in Trump's infrastructure plan. These lobbying groups were pushing on open doors. D.J. Gribbin, a White House infrastructure adviser, was formerly with Macquarie. The then-director of Trump's National Economic Council, Gary Cohn, was formerly president of Goldman Sachs, which advised Indiana on the toll road deal. All the big influencers were involved; even with Trump out of office and Pence in the warm embrace of the private sector, what happened in Indiana will not stay in Indiana.[2]

The 157-mile Indiana Toll Road provides a vital link between Ohio and Illinois. By supporting the toll road, the state of Indiana remains an attractive headquarters for shipping and logistics companies. But in the early '00s the road was not paying for itself for a simple reason: no one had taken the politically risky move of raising the tolls since the 1980s. Some estimates claimed that the toll booths were not paying even for themselves, much less for maintenance and improvements on the road. In 2005 Governor Mitch Daniels, who had been George W. Bush's budget director and whose marquee policies included school vouchers and laws to undermine labor unions, backed a move to lease the toll road for seventy-five years to the highest bidder.[3]

The proposal came soon after his inauguration; it was likely something that had been developing for some time, and it was carefully wrapped in a statewide infrastructure package called Major Moves. Daniels claimed that by leasing the toll road and taking the full payment up front Indiana could use the money for infrastructure expansions and improvements across the state. The road had been built with public funds for public benefit, but Daniels was proposing to place it in private hands for several generations in exchange for an up-front payment.

Daniels enlisted Goldman Sachs to manage the bidding and provide financial advice. The investment bank, which ultimately raked in $20 million in fees from Indiana for its advice, managed to score a bid of $3.85 billion from a consortium formed by Cintra and Macquarie—which was $1 billion higher than the runner-up's bid. The Daniels administration, leaning heavily on Goldman Sachs for advice, claimed that the road, if left in public control for the next seventy-five years, would take in only $1.92 billion. Little known at the time was the fact that Goldman Sachs was, through its Australian subsidiary, investing in the Macquarie Infrastructure Group at the same time it was providing advice on whether Indiana should lease this public asset.[4]

The winning bid looked like a windfall for the state, like a perfect example of the win-win of free-market magic. Daniels proposed to use most of the money for the ten-year Major Moves initiative and promised to sock away $500 million in a "Next Generation Trust," which would be invested and grow over time to meet future infrastructure needs. He claimed that the road's new landlords would treat this public asset like their own, providing upgrades and much-needed maintenance. And he hammered away on his main talking point, one that President Trump repeated endlessly: all this was happening without additional taxes.[5]

At this point it would have been reasonable to ask why two experienced players—Cintra and Macquarie—would be willing to pay up front more than double what Indiana thought the road was worth *and* take on all the costs of maintenance and improvements. And with the hindsight benefit of knowing that Goldman Sachs was playing both sides, why would it advise Indiana that this was a fantastic deal for the state at the same time its Australian subsidiary was expecting to make such a large pile of money on the other side of the deal as investors?

This story holds many lessons, but perhaps none is more important than the need to scrutinize the estimates. The Daniels administration, in its enthusiasm, didn't set up an independent analysis until the deal was nearly done, and it turned out that the initial rough estimate of $1.92 billion in revenue was far from the mark. This estimate worked only under the assumption that tolls would practically never rise, but that was a faulty assumption: everyone knew that they had to go up at some time. Estimates that took into account increased tolls and more efficient toll collection—possible through electronic tolling—looked radically different.

While the Daniels administration was lamenting that public management would bring in a mere $1.92 billion over seventy-five years, Macquarie and Cintra went looking for investors (they each put $374 million of their own money and borrowed the other $3 billion from seven European banks that they would service with predictable toll revenues), quietly promising that they would make back the $3.85 billion outlay in a mere fifteen years. That meant sixty years of toll collection would be almost all profit—and all private. An economist at the University of Notre Dame who specialized in long-term valuation took into account reasonable toll increases and discovered that the road could easily take in $11.38 billion over seventy-five years. If he's correct, Indiana's blunder could take some $7.53 billion from American wallets and ship it overseas.[6]

The Public Pays: Toll Hikes and Shunpikes

Those who included toll increases in their estimates were proven right in at least one regard even before the deal went through: a politician did finally raise tolls. In fact, it was the same politician who had touted the estimate without toll increases. The contract gave the winning bidders the freedom to increase tolls themselves—and everyone knew they would—but their increases were limited to certain percentages of the existing tolls. The formula could not result in profit-making toll increases because the tolls the consortium inherited had been in place since 1985—they had not even been adjusted for inflation since then.[7]

So just prior to the lease signing, Indiana gave the ITR Concession Co, LLC the gift of a whole new base rate upon which to build. The cost of a passenger car paying with cash traveling from one end of the ITR to the other suddenly jumped from $4.65 to $8.00. Shorter trips increased by an even greater percentage. Then, in order either to lessen the pain or to obscure the reality until after the next election (take your pick), the legislature insisted on taking some of the $3.85 billion Indiana received from the consortium and using it as a ten-year subsidy for drivers who paid electronically, insulating them from the rate hike and insulating themselves from driver anger. So $278 million that the state had just received from the consortium *went right back to the consortium* as the state picked up part of the tab for certain drivers.[8]

To Democratic lawmakers who opposed the deal, the motivation was clear. Indiana representative Scott Pelath said that the subsidy merely "did some favors for the people who enacted it. It kicked the can down the road past a few elections." The Daniels administration responded that new projects and improvements had gotten started "with no new state debt and no increase to taxpayers." And yet, tolls were already rising, and the state was paying for it.[9]

Drivers who were not subsidized, especially commercial truckers, faced toll increases of up to 76 percent over the first seven years of the lease, and they did what you'd expect consumers would do in a free-market economy—they found cheaper routes. Some businesses and residents along byways had worried about this when the lease was being debated, and their concerns were dismissed. A few years later, traffic surveys showed that traffic had increased on alternate routes "with a spike around 2007 after the lease of the Indiana Toll Road."[10]

Traffic on the toll road declined at the same time by 21 percent as truckers' online forums openly discussed how to avoid the higher tolls by using US 30 and US 20, two roads not up to interstate standards.[11]

These truckers were following a long American tradition of shunning the turnpike, or "shunpiking," which has long complicated road privatization. The collective decision of shunpikers points to a larger issue of managing traffic while balancing the public good against private profit. If you are selling something, you can make money by charging a little and selling lots of it, or by charging a lot and selling to a select few who can afford it. The ITR Concession clearly decided that a high-price, low-volume business model would work best for them, especially since some of its customers were subsidized and wouldn't feel the pain of higher tolls. Their decision is a popular one in the world of P3s, as evidenced by the spread of "Lexus lanes" that promise a quick commute for a high price.

In the general economy, one company's decision to go for the high end of the market—aiming for the lucky few who can pay thousands of dollars for a designer handbag or a new watch—has no negative impact on the rest of the market. But if the item is a public good, the public and its tax dollars will be swept along. When those truckers decided to shun the ITR's new tolls and take other roads, they added substantial maintenance costs on the byways while forcing the state to consider widening those side roads and bringing them up to interstate standards. Those who lived along those roads faced longer commutes, increased danger from trucks trying to barrel across the state, and increased noise and pollution. They were forced to live with the results of the ITR's decision to raise tolls by as much as it possibly could. The decision had a wide impact on the public, but the public was not allowed to have a say.[12]

To make matters worse, any attempt to lessen the impact on the side roads risked running afoul of the noncompete clauses in the ITR lease. For seventy-five years Indiana has to avoid creating roads that might take traffic away from the toll road, or pay a penalty. So in many circumstances, even if shunpiking traffic makes a side road practically unusable, the state cannot step in to do what's best for its own citizens. Indiana's hands are tied, and it is contractually committed to helping a private corporation squeeze as much profit from its narrow band of concrete as possible.[13]

The ITR Concession had other priorities than the common good or the needs of the citizens of Indiana, and if that wasn't clear in the first year of their operation, it certainly became clear in fall 2008. After a disastrous storm flooded sections of northern Indiana and closed most major roads, Governor Daniels declared an emergency and ordered tolls waived on the ITR so residents could evacuate and supplies could get through. The consortium went along, but also insisted that it be reimbursed. In the end, the state had to pay $447,000 to make up for the lost revenue. Margie Stewart, who worked on the toll road and served as a Teamster's Union representative, was incredulous: "Why should the taxpayers pay for this? The company is making plenty of money. It was a disaster here. They could have helped." These are fair questions, but then again, the leaseholders had creditors and investors to answer to. And when you're focused on the bottom line, it's hard to feel sympathy for disaster victims in Indiana while sitting in an office in Spain or Australia.[14]

A Bad Deal Gets a Do-Over

Eight years after it took over, and with Mike Pence as governor, the ITR Concession Company declared bankruptcy. For at least two years before it filed for Chapter 11, it was clear that something was amiss. Drivers noticed decaying roadways and vented online about unsanitary and sketchy rest stops. Word leaked out that a European bank that had helped finance the privatizing consortium was trying to shed its ITR-related debt, letting it go for sixty cents on the dollar. When the bankruptcy came, some things became clear. The consortium had shamefully gambled on its $4 billion in debt through a series of interest-rate swaps. With this exotic financial instrument, it had in effect placed a bet on a floating interest rate. The consortium lost its bet, which had little to do with the road running through Indiana, and now was an additional $2.15 billion in debt. In June 2014 it failed to make a payment of $102 million, and within months it was in Chapter 11.[15]

The leaseholder's filings made that much clear, but it was still unclear who now owned the toll-road debt, although most signs pointed to hedge funds and vulture capitalists willing to take a short-term risk on a sale of the lease. And their gamble paid off. While the ITR Concession Company withered away under its crushing $6 billion debt, new investors lined up with even more stunning bids than the original eye-popping $3.85 billion.

Mike Pence was at this time halfway through his first term as governor. Buried in the original contract was an option for the state to take over the road in the event of a bankruptcy. Here was an opportunity to reverse what was clearly a poor decision and return the road to the public. Against the advice of Indiana's U.S. senator Joe Donnelly, Pence decided instead to let the lease continue and take new bids. It was a decision as inexplicable as it was uninformed, but it paled in comparison to what came next.

Into the new round of bidding came the two Indiana counties most affected by the toll road's privatization, the ones that had used the road to evacuate during the 2008 flood and that daily suffered the consequences of higher tolls as shunpiking trucks rolled through their backyards. Their proposal offered a respectable but not astronomical amount of cash, sweetened by appeal to the common good and the promise of public control. It was a return to normalcy that offered steady hands in place of the reckless chase for profit through interest-rate swaps and other Wall Street shenanigans. But it had to stand up against a newly invigorated push for privatization, namely a $5.72 billion bid from Australia's IFM Investors.

If the original bid of $3.85 billion was a surprise, this new bid should have set off alarms in every corner of the state. What was this road really worth? Why was a savvy group of investors willing to pick up a lease that had already led to a bankruptcy? The original lease granted the governor power to approve a sale in the event of bankruptcy, and Pence promised to evaluate the proposals thoroughly. He commissioned a report from KPMG, the consulting and accounting firm, but it was one that the public never got to see—Pence locked it down under a FOIA-proof "deliberative materials exemption." Not even the lawyer representing the counties that wanted to have their bid fairly considered got to see it. The road went to IFM rather than back to the public. Almost all of the $5.72 billion went to pay off the ITR Concessions' debt rather than to the State of Indiana. But a big chunk—$2.45 million—went to five executives of the bankrupt firm as bonuses for unloading the road at such a high price.[16]

Lurking behind all this is a comparatively modest sum of $116,000. That's how much Mike Pence's political campaigns have received from Bose, which represents IFM. But there's a clearer explanation of why Pence utterly dismissed two opportunities to regain public control over this public asset. According to the lawyer who represented the bid by Lake and LaPorte counties, "Pence believes in this religion—the magic and mystery of markets is solving all the problems." As is too often the case in these stories, ideology trumped common sense.[17]

After becoming vice president, Pence pitched his ideas about infrastructure in the White House. Meanwhile, the toll subsidy set up by Governor Daniels expired and motorists saw tolls go up by as much as 126 percent. All of that increase was already there; it had been hidden from citizens by the subsidy. Then, in July 2017, just one month after the subsidy expired, the new leaseholders added another increase, as they were allowed to do under the terms of the contract. These increases, made without public input and without regard for the public interest, will continue until the lease finally expires and control reverts to the state in the year 2081.[18]

Driving Our Values: What These Deals Say About Us

When Indiana faced a shortfall between tax revenues and the cost of new, improved, and repaired infrastructure, it faced a choice between competing sets of values. One set of values said that raising tolls, floating bonds, or raising taxes had to be avoided because they make government too powerful. Better, in that case, to cede control to a private entity that would act in accordance with the rules of the market—especially when that choice included a massive cash infusion that obscured a significant loss for Indiana citizens. Another set of values accepts that the public is responsible for paying for what it uses and resists kicking the can down the road.

One set of values accepts the idea that we can make decisions for future generations and burden them with the costs of our decisions; another set of values insists that we should pay our own way and even leave future generations the gift of functioning infrastructure. This stark choice was convincingly outlined in a paper by economist and political scientist John B. Gilmour, who calls the ITR lease an "intergenerational cash transfer." This is a polite and academic way of saying that such deals amount to stealing from our children and grandchildren.

The key problem with the Indiana Toll Road deal, which Mitch Daniels established and Mike Pence perpetuated, is that it proposed to fund a ten-year infrastructure project—Major Moves—with a seventy-five-year lease. The current generation will enjoy all of the benefits; the next several generations will pay the costs through the ever-increasing tolls. If future citizens of Indiana also want to improve or repair their infrastructure, they will not be able to use tolls from the ITR to do so. In deals like this, we get the benefit, our children pay the costs.[19]

Bonds are the more traditional means of funding projects like Major Moves, and most states limit the terms of these loans to twenty or thirty years because this term more exactly coincides with the term of benefit and helps prevent intergenerational theft. Long-term leases on existing public infrastructure to private corporations (also known as "asset recycling") are not tightly regulated and can get around this restriction. Some observers feel, with good reason, that the whole point of these elaborate leases and P3s is to get around the limits on intergenerational theft. Others point out that there's a fiscally responsible argument for bonding as well—one estimate demonstrated that the state of Indiana could have made four to five times more than its $3.85 billion through reasonable toll increases and a series of twenty-year bonds. The citizens would have retained control of the road, and future generations would have been given the freedom to make their own decisions.[20]

The religion of the free market often convinces our leaders, however, that it's best not to give citizens those choices. They often worry about the supposed impulse to accept government "giveaways," and they look for opportunities to head off the possibility of citizens choosing public over private. The Indiana Toll Road lease, an utter debacle from a fiscal standpoint and bad for transportation planning, nevertheless had the effect of locking the public out for seventy-five years. For an antigovernment activist, that's an added benefit that makes it worth the cost.

Public values impel us to do our best to hand something down to future generations, including the ability to make their own choices. Gilmour points out that the Hoover Dam was designed to last a thousand years. The public had cheaper ways to do it, but the generation that undertook this massive project chose to make it a gift to future generations and to pay for it out of their own revenues (which in the 1930s were meager indeed). When we selfishly refuse to pay for our own infrastructure, we are not only shortchanging our children, but also dishonoring our parents and grandparents, who in many cases were much more committed to passing on a fully lit torch.

8

Who Owns the Journey? Recentering the Public

FAILING TO TREAT TRANSPORTATION AND COMMUNICATION INFRASTRUC-
ture as a public good rubs against our identity as a free people. If the
road belongs to someone else and they make our way forward prohibi-
tive, the public will inevitably try to find a shunpike—a way around. In
Indiana, the toll road conglomerate anticipated this reaction and locked
the public into an agreement that prevented it from improving nearby
roads. This is a typical reaction from privatizers. Turns out they don't
really want free-market competition; they want the guaranteed profits
that come with monopolies.

We could save ourselves a lot of trouble if we let the public own the
journey, but this requires a shift in thinking. We correctly put a significant investment into public transit, but then we also charge riders as
they board. Rider contributions are typically a small part of transit budgets. Why do we reflexively treat them like consumers? We've hailed
the broadband revolution as a way to shrink space and bring economic
opportunity to rural areas. So why do we so often depend on private telecom companies to get the job done? We the public can do away with barriers to free movement and full participation. We can find a way around.

No Property in Public Travel

After the federal government largely stood aside from infrastructure
development in the early nineteenth century, private turnpikes seemed
to be the only recourse. Turnpike corporations were chartered by the
state and held by a board of directors that raised money for a road from
investors and hoped to get it back through tolls. They also often had
sweeping powers. The turnpike designers, not the public, laid out the

route. The company typically got to choose the location of the fare gate. The state did little to enforce general maintenance. The corporation often had permission to take raw materials from the surrounding landscape, even from private property. The corporations often didn't have to ask the communities served for permission or give public notice of their intentions. And they weren't cheap to use. In Connecticut a man on a horse paid four cents for two miles, but if he was in a four-wheeled carriage the charge was twenty-five cents. Average daily income for a manual laborer was about a dollar.[1]

Many, like the writer who went by "Civus," saw the turnpikes as tending "to make the rich richer and the poor poorer" and "to divide the community." Some may have been willing to "rather enjoy LIBERTY and EQUAL RIGHTS under some inconveniences, than sacrifice them at the shrine of Monarchical improvements." But this didn't mean stopping travel. It meant making a new road that shunned the turnpike—a shunpike. This was not individualized toll dodging; it sometimes involved the repeated use of an alternate route to the point where a road formed. Sometimes it involved a community getting together to create free alternative byways. Either way, it hit the turnpikes hard. One Massachusetts turnpike owner complained that his revenues would be 60 percent higher if not for shunpiking. In New York one turnpike complained so loudly that it got a charter amendment that inverted the rights of those accused of shunpiking—the accused, not the company, was saddled with the burden of proof.[2]

"There cannot be any property in public travel," declared the Supreme Court in 1837, too late to help legitimize what the shunpikers had done in the 1800s and 1810s, "because no one is under any obligation to pay toll, unless he passes the bridge, and that is an optional act." The case was *Charles River Bridge v. Warren Bridge*, and it was a curious one. The Charles River Bridge linked Boston to Charlestown and was wholly owned by a private company chartered in 1785 and given the right to charge tolls for forty years; later this was extended to seventy.

The project's early investors had done well. The initial cost of the project was about $46,000, and the first shares sold for $100. Over fifty years the bridge tolls had brought in over $1.2 million, and by that time shares were selling for $2,000. But the owners had no incentive to ease the toll, improve the bridge, or do anything about the logjam of traffic waiting on either side every day. So the city and state chartered a new bridge, one that would be free and would revert to public control after just six years. The original bridge owners sued, only to ultimately find themselves before a Supreme Court in a surprisingly pro-public mood.

The court could have decided on narrow grounds; there was nothing in the original charter that explicitly prevented the city and state from building a new bridge. The court could have simply told the Charles River Bridge owners that they should have gotten a better contract, but instead the court went further: "While the rights of private property are sacredly guarded, we must not forget, that the community also have rights."[3]

This was a lofty principle, and it has typically stayed that way—in the clouds and rarely applied to actual situations. And this attempt to balance private ownership against community needs still fell short because it's easy to ignore the fact that the community has a right to travel and communicate. For example, a company can simply get a contract that includes noncompete clauses, or one that treats citizens like customers, with private toll roads and Lexus lanes. Pro-privatization politicians have been more than willing to do this, time and again. The public, however, is more reluctant to give up its shunpiking rights, and has started applying them to both public mass transit and broadband as a public utility.

Owning the Journey with Prepaid Public Transit

One of the authors of this book used to work as a teacher and program manager in a small adult learning center in southeast Washington, DC. The clients were working strenuously toward their high school diplomas. Most were unemployed, some were on probation, all were living on the margins. They worked with urgency, and not just when a case worker or probation officer was monitoring them from afar. They earnestly believed that a high school diploma was the first step toward a more empowered life.

Despite that urgency, a big chunk of these clients quickly bolted from their studies at the two- or three-hour mark, apologizing on the way out the door. The issue was that most took the bus to get to class. Back then, a DC bus fare bought you a paper transfer that was good for four hours. If the riders could make it back before that time expired, they cut their transportation costs in half. So students' sessions were often rushed, with this artificial timeline hanging over their heads.

How much more could they have accomplished if they didn't have to worry about making that bus? What if we didn't charge a toll at the fare box? What if public transportation was just there, like schools and side-walks? The idea seemed absurd.

But the absurdity was always on the other side. Why should we charge for use of public transportation at all? Every city, and even most medium-size towns, has to have a public transportation system. They benefit all of us. They save us from significant road repairs and expansions, they reduce pollution, keep traffic down, and let people get to work, which provides all of us with services we need and also increases the tax base. If the bus is the only way or the preferred way for some people to travel, and if their decisions benefit the rest of us, why put additional barriers in their way by charging them a fee? Change perspective a bit, and charging per ride starts to look even more absurd. "You don't have to insert coins to light individual lamp posts on your way home at night, or pay for every minute spent in a park or library," Wojciech Kębłowski, a postdoc at Université Libre de Bruxelles, pointed out. Such things are just there.[4]

We have been ignoring the fact that public transportation is a public good, and instead we have been treating it like a consumer product. Our consumerist impulses have led us into thinking that each ride must be exploited and treated as a cost to be recouped rather than a benefit to be encouraged. We could go further. "It's not really a transport issue at all," said Adie Tomer, an infrastructure expert at the Brookings Institution, when asked about doing away with rider fees. "It's about making sure people can get around so that they are full participants in the regional economy and regional society." In other words, it's not about this ride or that bus line. It's about enabling and empowering citizens.[5]

Kansas City, Missouri, eliminated fares on in-city trips in 2019, and fully embraced a new way of thinking. The Kansas City Area Transportation Authority's own president and CEO, Robbie Makinen, signaled the shift: "We got to stop acting like we're in the profit business, because we're not. We're in the people business. It's our job to take care of people, and this [doing away with fares] is doing that." Others have spoken about how eliminating fares opens us to "a completely new way to look at the city," including how we tax and how we relate to each other. It helps us establish movement as a right. And it expands freedom by providing choices; private transportation will not go away, but it will adapt, and we will become more aware of its true cost. We will not be tied to one path. No one entity or industry will own the journey.[6]

The city council vote to make transit fare-free in Kansas City passed unanimously, making it the largest city in the United States to embrace this approach. Olympia, Washington; Lawrence, Massachusetts; and Ozark, Arkansas (with a population of 3,500 and two bus lines) had already taken this step. As of fall 2020 Denver, Colorado, and Atlanta, Georgia, were considering it. In the case of Kansas City, the decision came when that shift in thinking forced the city to look at what fares actually meant to the city. They amounted to less than 10 percent of the system's budget. "Not a ton of money," said one council member. In Lawrence, Mayor Daniel Rivera found transit fares brought in just $225,000 a year. Not a difficult hole to fill, and besides, "It's a public good."[7]

Advocates often talk about these proposals as "free" public transit, but it is not free. "We look at it as a pre-paid fare program," said Brian Litchfield of Chapel Hill Transit in North Carolina, which eliminated fares in 2002 and saw ridership double. There's a case to be made for covering the lost fares through property taxes and vehicle registrations, since both home owners and drivers benefit from good public transit even if they don't use it. There's another argument in the fact that it costs money to collect fares: elaborate electronic ticketing systems need maintenance, quarters have to be hauled to the bank, and enforcement has to be deployed. The Metropolitan Transit Authority in New York City vowed in 2019 to pay for a $249 million expansion of the transit police, including the hiring of five hundred additional officers, with a crackdown, by many of those same officers, on turnstile jumpers, who cost the system $200 million a year. Step outside this circular logic, and maybe it makes more sense to collect the necessary funds in a way that doesn't commit the city to an intensive assault on petty crime that invariably hits youth and minorities the hardest. Take steps toward thinking of the public good first, and the fact that transportation accounts for 30 percent of our greenhouse gas emissions—more than any other sector—comes into view. With that in mind, why would we want to charge people who are helping avert this crisis and treat them as criminals when they don't pay? In the end, pay-per-ride makes sense only if we think of public transportation as a product to be purchased rather than as a public good to be provided.[8]

While support for fare-free public transit has been quietly building, a somewhat louder campaign has been building on the other side of the issue, attacking public transportation every chance it gets and proposing long-shot private options instead. Most prominent in this campaign has been the Koch-funded Americans for Prosperity, which helped kill a public transit ballot initiative in Nashville, Tennessee, through extensive, targeted, and highly efficient campaigning. They've undertaken similar efforts in Arizona, Arkansas, Michigan, and Wisconsin.[9]

In Phoenix, during the early stages of a rail project, transit planners were dealing with the demands of local opponents when a flood of outside money entered the city; suddenly what had been a demand to leave certain roads at capacity became an extremist ballot initiative: not just a "no" to the planned project, but an absolute ban on all future light rail construction in the city. The mayor said she'd "never seen this kind of outside group come in and write an initiative." Local rail skeptics turned against the extreme direction the campaign took, with one saying the outside influence "dirtied the movement." Voters soundly defeated the light rail ban, with 62 percent opposed to what the Koch-funded campaign had proposed.[10]

This is, however, a well-funded and well-organized effort, and it will not go away. It has a distinct advantage in that highway funds are often baked into state and federal budgets, while new or expanded public transit typically has to go before the voters in a ballot initiative. The price tags appear high—it's difficult to show the lasting benefits and savings that will accrue over time. And the message of Americans for Prosperity, when they knock on doors, is exceedingly simple: taxes are already too high; you don't want another tax, do you?

As a free-market alternative to public mass transit, the Koch-funded Americans for Prosperity and Cato Institute propose to get us off our buses and into Ubers. They say we are wasting our money on public bus and rail because ride-hailing companies, which allegedly offer a pure free-market solution, can get us there. This distorted vision has nothing to do with where we are now, and has little to do with anything resembling a free market.[11]

The ride-service companies Lyft and Uber are sleek, individualistic, utterly nonunionized, and largely unregulated. In those aspects they are a libertarian's dream conveyance. But in other ways they are an odd choice for those who believe in rational markets. They are not profitable companies; they are hype machines designed to attract capital, and their sagging IPOs indicated that investors have realized that their business model isn't sustainable. As it stands, each ride is effectively subsidized by investors; the companies are keeping the service artificially cheap to get the number of rides up. This cannot last, and they know it. So they've set their sights on competing with buses and trains as a "massive market opportunity." Uber even told investors in an April 2019 public filing that it wanted to completely replace public transportation, only to back off after receiving a dose of bad press.

But the public relations messaging shift foreshadowed new strategies to increase market share and close the profitability gap: public-private partnerships and contracting directly with public transit agencies. This happened in Tampa and St. Petersburg, Florida, where Uber offered $1.00 "last mile" rides for short trips to transit hubs. Taxpayers picked up the rest. By the middle of 2019, Uber had twenty partnership agreements with government agencies of different types, and Lyft had fifty.[12]

Calling this a free-market solution is pure fantasy. Uber and Lyft didn't win in the transportation market, they won in the investor market. Now they want to win against truly public options as well and grow profitable on public money by "attracting consumers to our platform and away from personal vehicles or public transportation." If they do, they'll succeed in diverting money from mass transit while adding even more congestion to roads (even more than privately owned cars since much of their drivers' time is spent deadheading to the next fare). They'll succeed in creating more traffic and fewer options—less freedom, to put it in Americans for Prosperity's favored terms.[13]

The public should have the right to mobility. Cars are not going away, and ride services will likely limp along. But when these private options are prohibitively expensive or stuck in gridlock, the public needs other options. And no private company should be allowed to own the journey.

Owning Economic Destiny with Public Broadband

Connecting rural America—whether through roads, airports, electricity, mail service, or internet—is not a profitable venture. If we want our fellow citizens in the exurbs and countrysides to have a shot at creating their own economic destiny, we have to support public roads, public control over air traffic, and a fully functioning postal service. All of these represent expanded choices and greater self-reliance for rural America, but in the twenty-first century they are not enough. Full control over economic destiny now depends also on fast, reliable broadband.

Residents of the small town of Tullahoma, Tennessee, population eighteen thousand, saw in the late 1990s that the telecom giants were unlikely to link them to the broadband revolution, so they went it alone. The town's municipal broadband project began to offer download speeds of one gigabyte per second, eighty times faster than what AT&T offered. The investment paid off; new businesses got started or moved in because of the cheap, reliable service. Agisent, a start-up software company, relocated from South Carolina because its business—providing document management to far-flung police departments, courts, and prisons—depended on a fast, dependable link.[14]

The free market had failed to improve quality and failed to meet a demand, so the public stepped in. It should have ended there, but this and similar stories caught the telecom giants' attention. Their free-market ethos and thirst for competition should have led them to pay attention to customers while expanding and improving service. Instead, they flexed their political muscle to stop the movement from spreading. In 1999 the state passed a very strange and specific law that banned any city or town that offered broadband from selling the service to any customer who did not already receive electrical service from that city or town. Small businesses just outside of Tullahoma were out of luck. State Senator Janice Bowling, representing Tullahoma and surrounding areas, had watched her rural constituents patiently wait for AT&T or Charter (or anyone) to bring broadband to their door. Bowling is a Republican in her sixties who notes, "I believe in capitalism and the free market." But she came to understand that the free market isn't always interested in small markets like hers: "When they won't come in, then Tennesseans have an obligation to do it themselves."

Bowling proposed legislation to allow Tullahoma to expand service beyond the utility service limits and watched as the telecom giants threatened to pour millions into an opposition campaign. In what she thought was a cordial meeting, a representative of a major telecommunications company leaned over the table to say, "Well, I'd hate for this to end up in litigation." Support for Bowling's bill evaporated.[15]

Just outside of Tullahoma, Matt Johnson pieced together a homemade signal booster; it was an attempt to squeeze a little more out of his slow and expensive connection. Johnson's business is in manufacturing gauges that monitor engine performance, and because Bowling's bill had been killed, he couldn't buy service from Tullahoma. Johnson's business has clients as far away as China and South Africa and needs broadband as much as it needs roads and electricity. The competition is using automation, 3D printing capabilities, and connected machinery; a dependable internet link is an absolute necessity. For entrepreneurs like Johnson, a public investment in broadband means economic independence and room to innovate. But not only are the telecom companies not providing this needed service, they are blocking public efforts to provide what they won't.[16]

Forward-looking city managers and planners have started looking at broadband as simply another public good, an extension of services they already provide. "At this point, who would go to a city that doesn't have electric utilities?" Grace Simrall, chief of civic innovation for Louisville, Kentucky, asked. "Who would go to a city that doesn't have water, or access to highways? Fiber is that type of infrastructure plan." Or, as San Francisco's chief marketing officer put it, "It's one of those fundamental things. We fill potholes, we clean the streets, and yes, now we provide wifi. And our citizens expect that." These aren't isolated sentiments. According to the Institute for Local Self-Reliance, over 130 cities and towns in the United States offer municipal broadband. Most of them are small or mid-size, and they got into broadband because commercial internet providers saw their markets as too small.[17]

Nineteen states have laws that severely restrict the creation or expansion of municipal broadband. These are state-level laws that punish towns and cities for trying to serve the public. North Carolina's law prevents cities from offering their services to anyone outside the city and then goes further by taxing municipal services as if they were a business. It demands that all cities look to private-sector partnerships before attempting a public option. And perhaps most significant, North Carolina's law forces cities to pay for the construction of networks with general obligation bonds, which put all of the risk of things going wrong on taxpayers, instead of revenue bonds, which share that risk with bondholders. North Carolina's effort to put the burden on the taxpayer, which has been duplicated in many states, is one of the more insidious ploys to tie the hands of municipal governments, but all of these add up to a strategy by states to throw as many hurdles as possible in the way of municipal broadband—an idea that seems to be becoming more and more inevitable and scares the hell out of the telecom giants.[18]

South Carolina passed similar legislation a year after North Carolina. Missouri took on a law that both required a voter referendum and banned the use of the city's own revenues from other services for the construction of networks. In Kansas, a law essentially banning the creation of any municipal broadband networks came before the legislature with no elected sponsors—it was introduced directly by the president of the Kansas Cable Telecommunications Association, which represents the interests of Comcast, Cox, Eagle Communications, and Time Warner Cable. This bill and others either copy directly or borrow heavily from model legislation created by the American Legislative Exchange Council, the "Municipal Telecommunications Private Industry Safeguards Act."[19]

The fight against municipal broadband is a fight for the free market, according to the broadband industry and the politicians it supports with generous campaign funding. "It's inappropriate for public tax dollars to be invested in competitive businesses," a telecom executive told the *Rocky Mountain News*. According to Rocky Miller, the sponsor of Missouri's anti–municipal broadband bill, his intention was merely "to even the playing field and eliminate socialized/non-commercial services provided by municipalities." But a few things get missed in these arguments. For one thing, there is little to no competition in most markets when it comes to broadband. In general, internet providers run as monopolies, especially in rural areas and small cities, and the corporations that run them are steadily consolidating. Second, the idea that small cities and towns are so powerful that the telecom giants need a level playing field is absurd, not only on its face but especially in light of the cozy relationships between state-level politicians and this multibillion-dollar industry.[20]

Miller, who called municipal broadband "socialized," received $4,700 in campaign funds from telecom interests. When Tennessee went to court against the FCC and its own city of Chattanooga, it hired Wiley Rein, a law and lobbying firm that was founded by a former FCC chairman and has represented AT&T, Verizon, and Qwest. And North Carolina, also objecting to the efforts of its own city of Wilson, had its anti-broadband law enforced by an attorney general who received $35,000 from the telecoms for his 2012 campaign. In Tennessee politics, these companies loom large: AT&T has given $1.3 million to political interests, while Comcast has chipped in $500,000. North Carolina's 2014 election cycle alone saw $870,000 pour in from the telecom industry. But all this was overshadowed by the vast sums that went toward the attempted defeat of a local ballot measure in Colorado.[21]

In 2005 Colorado became one of those states doing its best to stop its own citizens from building broadband networks. A state law passed that year required a local vote on any attempt to even explore the possibility of municipal broadband. In 2009, Longmont, Colorado, voted to move ahead with its plan, and within a few years it was offering gigabyte service not just to its ninety thousand residents, but to its libraries, schools, and businesses as well. In 2017, Fort Collins asked its citizens if they wanted something similar. The industry players campaigned against the measure through "Priorities First Fort Collins," an astroturf organization funded by the Colorado Cable Telecommunications Association, which ended up spending some $900,000 trying to defeat the measure. Its main opponent in the election was the Fort Collins Citizens' Broadband Committee, which spent $15,000 on campaigning and advertising.[22]

When the dust settled, the voters approved the broadband plan by 57 percent. Elsewhere in Colorado, nineteen other cities and counties voted to opt out of the 2005 state law and start exploring their options; their citizens voted in favor of municipal broadband by 61 to 90 percent. Residents in Denver, Berthoud, and Englewood approved opt-out in 2020, with Denver voters passing the measure by 83.5 percent. There's a shift happening, and the big telecom and cable industries will not like it. Health care providers need broadband service to share patient and public health data and to conduct telemedicine. Libraries use broadband connections to serve their communities, and knowledge-based businesses use it to share data, models, and presentations. Teleworking helps reduce time spent in traffic, and measurably improves quality of life. Universal access to internet connections helps address inequality by helping people find jobs, providing training, and linking to public services. And as the 2020 pandemic showed, whether or not you can access broadband sometimes determines whether or not you can go to school.[23]

Cities would be foolish to leave something so essential to monopolistic entities beyond citizens' reach. Yet this is exactly the opposite direction from the one privatization advocates want us to go. In the 1970s, antipublic activists thought they could target city services like trash collection and utilities first. Privatize these, and more will follow. Instead, we are moving the other way. As we've seen, citizens are increasingly eager to own their water. And as the citizens of Snowmass Village, Colorado—where 90 percent of voters approved a municipal broadband ballot measure—have made clear, citizens want control over their information infrastructure and local economy as well.

*   *   *

Infrastructure is more than roads, rails, and bridges; infrastructure is economic destiny. Decisions about how and where to invest have lasting consequences on local economies, and from there they shape local lives.

So what questions should we ask when creating infrastructure priorities? We should ask first what it is we value. Do we value the national marketplace above the rights of communities to shape their own economies? Should corporations far removed from the community make such far-reaching decisions for that community?

Do we value the right of our children and grandchildren to make their own decisions about how to use public assets? Should we pay for projects that benefit us here and now with money that would otherwise be available to them?

Do we value the diverse economies that thrive when they have access to infrastructure that was established for the public instead of for narrow profits?

Do we value the middle class and the entrepreneurs who can succeed only in those diverse economies?

And finally, do we value democratic control? From the Erie Canal to Tullahoma, we find that when a broad group of citizens is involved in making decisions, and when a broad group has a chance to speak and invest in those decisions, we get better results.

Privatization is anathema to these forms of democratic decision-making and governance. The market may seem free in P3-type arrangements, in that there is some semblance of competition, but corporate control over public assets obscures an undoing of democratic process and civil rights. In this section, we've seen just that in the loss of local control and the willingness of some politicians to give corporations power over public goods. In the next section, we will see how much further privatization can go toward the undoing of democracy.

Part IV

PRIVATIZATION'S SLOW COUP

The Undermining of Democracy and Justice

IN 1837, IN *CHARLES RIVER BRIDGE V. WARREN BRIDGE*, THE U.S. SUPREME
Court asserted, "There cannot be any property in public travel." In 2020
the court declared that "no one can own the law." These may seem like
utterly obvious statements, but privatization forced the issue in each
case. Private interests wanted to own public travel, and in Georgia private interests wanted to own the law.[1]

In Georgia, if you have a legal question you should look at the Official
Code of Georgia Annotated. There's also an official unannotated code
of Georgia, but without the annotations you'd not see which laws have
been overturned or which ones are no longer being enforced. When the
Georgia legislature passes a new law it votes on "an act to amend the
Official Code of Georgia Annotated." In 1982 that legislature enacted
the annotated version as the law of Georgia. When the courts apply and
interpret the law, they use the Official Code of Georgia Annotated. So do
Georgia prosecutors.[2]

A good bit of work went into annotating the code, but despite its
importance, it's work that the Georgia legislature didn't want to pay for.
So it outsourced the work to LexisNexis. This for-profit publisher did not
charge the state, but it didn't do this important work pro bono. It expected
to recoup its investment by charging users. And Georgia backed up its
contractor by holding and enforcing an exclusive copyright on the entire
Official Code of Georgia Annotated.

So if you wanted to know the law in Georgia, you could have expected
to pay $385.94 for online access or $1,259.41 for a copy on CD. As the
U.S. Supreme Court later pointed out, this created two classes of users.
The court even imagined a situation where "states would be free to offer
a whole range of premium legal works for those who can afford the extra
benefit. A State could monetize its entire suite of legislative history. With
today's digital tools, States might even launch a subscription or pay-per-
law service."

Georgia's arrangement was challenged in 2015 by PublicResource.org,
a nonprofit transparency advocacy group, which went ahead and published the annotated code—all of it—and encouraged users to make
copies, distribute copies, and create "derivative" works. Surprisingly, a
lower court supported the cease-and-desist orders that PublicResource

received, arguing that if the law was freely available, if paywalls were removed, "the State of Georgia will be required to either stop publishing the annotations altogether or pay for the development of the annotations using state tax dollars."[3]

Making sure that all citizens have equal access to the law seems like a good use of tax dollars, but Georgia's legislature apparently disagreed. And by avoiding paying for the creation of a written and annotated law, it agreed to limited citizenship and diminished democracy.[4]

Privatization limits public access to essential public goods like public health, water, and safe food, and it interferes with public goods like infrastructure that create strong economies. It also undermines the public's civil rights and limits access to democratic institutions and policymaking. Private interests can use the logic of contracts to trump civil rights—on a private street you accept the owner's terms, which may include warrantless searches. Private business interests have no interest in transparency or in providing open access; they consider information to be proprietary. And when private interests get involved in the delivery of public goods, they suddenly have a stake in policy—skin in the game—and will muster their ample resources to influence laws and regulations. It's rare that their interests will actually align with the public's or with preserving democracy.

In an era of unbridled privatization, we are facing the privatization of everything. That includes some of our most important institutions—courts, prisons, the criminal and civil justice system, and the law itself. Private corporations that take up public services invariably embed themselves in our policymaking and governance; their policy preferences serve their own interests, not the common good. Privatization, sold to us as a way to avoid intrusive government, in fact actively creates distant, unaccountable, and inscrutable centers of power. This can only make our country less democratic and less free.

9

When the Contract Is King

How Privatization Trumps Democracy

PRIVATIZATION HAPPENS BECAUSE IT'S PART OF A BROAD POLITICAL STRATegy, because of unequal access to power, and because of plain, simple greed. Privatization also happens when rights, freedoms, and democracy get in the way.

In 2017 Kansas City, Missouri, faced a serious problem with gun crimes and gun violence in the popular Westport district. Legitimately concerned over an uptick in firearms incidents (not all of them involved a shooting), business owners wanted a cordon placed around one particularly problematic intersection, running a block in each direction, that would prohibit entry unless patrons agreed to a search for weapons. That was the only way they could think of addressing the violence.[1]

What the businesses wanted was plainly unconstitutional: you can't stop people on a public street for weapons searches without probable cause. But what if the streets weren't public? On an 8–5 vote, the city council gave a consortium of restaurants and bars ownership of the streets and sidewalks in question. For free. The public space became private property, allowing businesses to block the streets and require all who entered to submit to a search by a private security force. The city agreed to continue to maintain this private space with its full array of municipal public services—road repairs, water lines, sewer lines—all at public expense. But if the city wants its streets back, the agreement stipulates, it will have to pay $132,784.[2]

Faced with a public problem, this elected body focused on a solution that used privatization as a wormhole to negate the rights of its own citizens. This city council is not the first to have dealt with nightclub-related violence; it is, however, likely the first to throw up its hands and claim that privatizing public streets is the only solution.[3]

Entering the privatized zone in Westport, one moves from the set of rules that we all had a hand in creating to a set of rules created by the district's new owners. We move from a set of reciprocal and mutual arrangements to a top-down arrangement. We move from a social contract to a set of individual contracts. We move from being a citizen with rights to a consumer who has entered into an agreement with a business—in this case one that demands we be searched. This is where privatization takes us, and it runs counter to our nation's struggles to expand democracy and civil rights.

The Freedoms We Made

Over a hundred years ago, in the last quarter of the nineteenth century, the wealthy residents of several cities—New York, Chicago, and Cleveland, to name a few—partnered with the government to construct armories in the middle of wealthy enclaves. The rich paid for them, but the military manned them, and they were designed to serve as redoubts for the wealthy if the masses rose up. Chicago's armory was surrounded by opulent homes and paid for by its residents, who also chipped in to supply the police force with cannons, hundreds of rifles, and a Gatling gun. New York's new armory on the Upper East Side had William Astor as head fundraiser and placed amenities fit for a millionaire—a mahogany library and a "Veterans' Room" designed by Louis Comfort Tiffany—inside walls fit for a siege.[4]

During this time of unchecked industrialization, the fears of the wealthy and powerful over the working masses surged, and they began to doubt whether America was really all that different from Europe, where class warfare was right on the surface. The problem, they decided, was too much freedom. Too much democracy. Racism and xenophobia also played their familiar roles; it was easier to believe in the ability of "the people" to govern before that body included freed slaves and an unprecedented number of immigrants. And so the elites took several steps to limit democracy and freedom after decades of watching them expand.

Democracy narrowed dramatically in the South as freed slaves lost the franchise under Jim Crow. Citizenship opportunities narrowed as anti-immigration laws targeted supposed undesirables. Rights and freedoms came under assault, primarily for the benefit of the new plutocrats. And private industry became more than just a way to make a buck; it became a tool for organizing society.[5]

While many citizens clung to the idea that they had a right to organize labor unions, protest unfair practices, vote in elections, and not be lynched, the plutocracy and the politicians under its wing tightened the definition of freedom to protect property rights above all else. This was couched in the *right of contract*—the right to enter into a binding agreement. This right was, supposedly, all that the citizens needed in a capitalist society. Therefore, laws and group actions limiting what contracts can do interfered with freedom. In fact, government itself was barely needed since we could all be governed by contracts—between employer and worker, buyer and seller, husband and wife, government and business. This amounted to a wholesale privatization of government, in which its only role was to defend the contracts and the wealth they created—from behind armory walls if necessary. As the influential Yale sociologist William Graham Sumner asserted at the time, all we should expect of government is that it protect "the property of men and the honor of women."[6]

In the late nineteenth century, the nation's courts largely embraced the idea that property should be protected and the people were on their own. In Illinois, the state supreme court said laws limiting the workweek to forty-eight hours were unconstitutional—the employers were free to require any number of hours they wanted, and workers were free to either work those hours or find work elsewhere. The employment relationship was a private contract between company and worker, and the public had no right to interfere. Kansas passed laws trying to stop employers from discriminating against union members; the U.S. Supreme Court said the law was an attack on the liberty of the company and the individual worker to enter into a contract. It was the same for West Virginia's attempt to stop employers from paying in company script rather than actual money. Companies were free to pay however they wanted, and workers were free to accept or find work elsewhere.

The infamous Supreme Court decision in *Lochner v. New York* held that any attempt to legislate limits to the workday was unconstitutional. And workers who attempted to improve conditions through unions rather than through legislation were equally an affront to freedom, according to the logic of the times: the courts handed down some two thousand injunctions against strikes and organized labor boycotts between 1880 and 1931, all in the name of "freedom." The activist Florence Kelley, who had seen her efforts to improve working conditions for women and children dashed by the courts, observed how "under the guise of republican freedom, we have degenerated into a nation of mock citizens."[7]

The masses never stormed the millionaires' armories, but they did not let the millionaires' vision of democracy and freedom stand. Well before FDR articulated his Four Freedoms, the people had begun to redefine freedom on their own, and to make their redefinition felt. In the letters that poured into the office of the new president and his appointees, suffering Americans reframed freedom as much more than the right to sign a contract to work for someone else: "I believe that this country owes a living to every man, woman, and child," a New York woman argued. "If it can't give us this living thru private industry it must provide for us thru government means." That right to survive, she insisted, was "an inalienable right of every person living under this government."[8]

The right of contract had not made the public free; it had enslaved them. The workers were "slaves of the depression," claimed one correspondent. Another saw an opportunity for Roosevelt to "be another Lincoln and free us from the slavery that we are in." Still another concluded, "Truly, there is such a thing as economic slavery." These workers were arguing the flip side of the long-standing (and it stands to this day) assertion that government has us all on the "road to serfdom," as put by laissez-faire cheerleader Friedrich Hayek. The citizens who appealed to FDR were insisting that without government intervention to protect their rights, they were more like slaves than citizens. By the middle of the decade, Roosevelt was echoing the claims of these workers, proclaiming that while the "royalists of the economic order . . . have maintained that economic slavery was nobody's business," he would "stand committed to the proposition that freedom is no half-and-half affair. If the average citizen is guaranteed equal opportunity in the polling place, he must have equal opportunity in the market place."[9]

Today conservatives refer to the New Deal, something created by American workers and the officials they elected in landslide after landslide, as a form of tyranny. They want to drive a wedge between the idea of an active government and its very real links to citizenship, democracy, responsibility, and freedom. But the rise of an active government was not a series of dictatorial decisions made for the sake of expanding socialism; it came about because of expanding awareness of freedom and through ever larger groups of people taking part in democracy. The New Deal was imperfect, especially in how it too often excluded minorities, but over time it lit a path. The people created a democracy that embraced certain values—transparency, freedom, public policy for the public good—and a government that protects freedom. But this public push has always had to contend with private interests that are hostile to all of these values.

Democracy and Privatization Don't Mix

After the New Deal, few could deny that freedom ought to include economic self-sufficiency—freedom from want—but the Reagan era successfully turned FDR's contribution on its head. Now unions and government, rather than the monopolistic corporations, were the oppressors. It wasn't the right of contract that created servitude, it was taxes.

Still, Reagan's economic advisers and his libertarian fellow travelers recognized that they would never succeed in convincing the voters to give up on basic government services. With privatization as their tool, they didn't have to. Robert Poole, a founder of the Reason Foundation, described a gradual approach of privatization "dismantling the state step by step" instead of "waiting until the majority of the population is convinced of the case for a libertarian utopia." Stuart Butler, writing for the Heritage Foundation, saw that the "beauty of privatization" and the "secret of privatization" were in how "the demand for government spending is diverted into the private sector. . . . Instead of having to say 'no' to constituencies, politicians can adopt a more palatable approach to cutting spending." There's quite a bit of deception in this approach, and the leading lights of economic conservatism were unashamed of it. Honoring the will of the people was dangerous; democracy had made taxes necessary, therefore it had failed to protect property rights. Some antipublic economists lamented the "failure of democracy to preserve liberty." Historian Nancy MacLean sums up this antigovernment world-view neatly: democracy is messy and politics is governed by "exploita-tion and coercion." But the realm of economics is one of liberty and free exchange. This view holds that the freedom associated with capitalism, free markets, and the right of contract is not inexorably linked to democ-racy; it is democracy's victim.[10]

So while politicians and the private sector offer privatization projects as a cheaper, more efficient alternative, the real reason for privatization is the slow forced march toward dismantling democratic control. Even if privatization is not cheaper, faster, or better, it helps serve a bigger agenda. Privatization's failures must be hidden away because the people might vote in favor of the public taking control. That is one reason why transparency is typically the first casualty of privatization—openness is bad for the movement.

This secrecy is closely related to how privatization narrows control and dodges accountability, and all this undermines the cornerstone dem-ocratic principle of separation of powers. When we privatize a public good several things happen: Contracts often trump legislation. Execu-tive branch political appointees become empowered to circumvent public servants. This weakens legislative and judicial oversight. Decisions and money flow along a corporate path, far from public accountability. The result is a further-empowered executive branch that operates through cutting deals with unfettered private corporations. As UCLA law profes-sor Jon D. Michaels wrote, the end result is not smaller and less powerful government, but *more* state power:

> What's really happening is that the government is being trans-formed. There is no denying that the State today is bigger and more potent than ever before. It just happens to look very different—a consequence of it being privatized, marketized,

and generally reconfigured along decidedly businesslike lines. In short, Reagan didn't, and couldn't, kill the Nanny State. But he did replace our old familiar nanny with a commercial upstart, a nanny corporation as it were.[11]

This privatization of democracy portends extensive loss of rights and freedoms; many of our most important freedoms no longer exist when we are on private property or if we have given them up in a contract. Along with these often vanish the right or even the ability to participate in public decision-making.

It wasn't until the Voting Rights Act and the Civil Rights Act that American law finally recognized the broad definition of freedom and the broad definition of the public that the Constitution had hinted at. American democracy is still imperfect (and is still under attack today), but it is well-enough admired that those who want to deny public demands for public goods are resorting to privatization as a stealth tactic. Their slow march has created a government that is more distant from the people, an executive branch that is more powerful, a policymaking process that is further obscured, and a public that is less free.

10

Democracy in Darkness

Privatization's Shadow over Transparency

MAXIMUS INC. IS A PUBLICLY TRADED COMPANY THAT PIONEERED THE privatization of welfare case management in the 1990s. In 2013 the company won a contract with the State of Connecticut to provide a call center for the state's health care exchange. Maximus boasted that it had secured a three-year contract worth $15 million.

But what exactly were the taxpayers of Connecticut getting for this $15 million? How many calls would be handled and at what cost per minute? Was this a good deal? A local public radio station tried to find out by submitting a public records request to see documentation of the breakdown of expenses, and this is what it received:

Maximus defended its "release" by claiming that if "one of our competitors learned of how we priced . . . then they have an advantage that they have not earned." This happens all the time when private companies take over public services. Suddenly, something that used to be public information as a matter of course becomes a trade secret to be protected—even though it is bought with public money.[1]

Transparency Makes for Bad PR

The operators of charter schools often fall back on secrecy, and in a sector where the product is knowledge, these attempts to claim trade secrets quickly become ridiculous. In Ohio, considered a dangerously unregulated wild-west environment even by charter school advocates, the for-profit school management company White Hat set up several nonprofit schools and then won contracts to manage them. This is a fairly typical shell game that charter organizations use to get around laws that try to stop profiteering, but White Hat's own schools went rogue and sued the management company over ownership of materials. They quickly found they could not get any information about how White Hat was spending public money. This generated a lot of bad publicity for White Hat, but it seemed to make the decision that releasing information on its spending would be even worse. White Hat evoked the defense that this information was a "trade secret." Under questioning by a judge, however, their lawyer made clear what that really meant:

The Court: I'm asking you why does [the information] need to be protected?

***

[White Hat's Counsel]: Okay, Your Honor, because it will disclose information that these Plaintiffs have exhibited an ability to disclose out of context of this Court's pleadings improperly.

The Court: You don't make any sense.

[White Hat's Counsel]: And for the wrong purpose.

The Court: What's the wrong purpose here?

[White Hat's Counsel]: To convince someone, Your Honor, you read the
press, to convince someone that the White Hat Management Companies are doing something improper.

Here a private, for-profit manager of publicly funded charter schools
claimed that its operations were trade secrets because the public might
object to these operations and attack the company for "doing something
improper," thereby making White Hat less competitive and less profitable. Or, as a White Hat representative explained to a disbelieving court,
the private company's interests here must be protected, not the public's.[2]

Fighting Transparency with the Reverse FOIA

When a private company makes a promise to the public and gets something in return, it should be a given that the public can check to see if the
promise was kept. And yet private companies often insist on closing the
books. In 2013, New Flyer of America, Inc. (a U.S. subsidiary of a Canadian bus manufacturer, NFI Group, Inc.), won a $500 million contract
to build up to nine hundred compressed-natural-gas buses for the Los
Angeles County Metropolitan Transportation Authority (LACMTA),
in large part because it promised to create 69 jobs locally and in the
United States and pay living wages and benefits for the project. Based
on the dollar value of those wages and benefits, New Flyer was given an
$18 million credit on the contract when comparing its cost to other bid-
ders, giving the company a cost advantage. The principle is clear: millions of dollars in public money should do more than simply buy buses. It
should tackle other public problems like growing economic inequality—
and it certainly shouldn't worsen inequality by creating low-wage jobs.
An LA-based advocacy group, Jobs to Move America, wanted to see if
New Flyer had kept its promises and so requested the contractor reports
from LACMTA. This should have been a non-issue; the company was
required to submit quarterly reports with the job data. But before the
agency complied with the information request, New Flyer immediately

filed a "reverse FOIA," a lawsuit to prevent the release of information requested under the Freedom of Information Act or its state equivalents. LACMTA backed down and refused to defend their belief that how much New Flyer spent on labor to build a bus was a trade secret—even though it was a key factor in awarding the bid.

Jobs to Move America and a coalition of open-government organizations, including In the Public Interest, Project on Government Oversight, Food & Water Watch, the Center for Media and Democracy, Open the Government, Corporate Accountability International, and Californians Aware, stepped in to fight the reverse FOIA. A judge agreed that there was obviously a "substantial public benefit in ensuring transparency" on the issue of whether New Flyer had kept its promise to the public. Even further, a judge agreed that Jobs to Move America had acted as the public's attorney because the transit authority had left a vacuum when it failed to defend the public's right to know. The labor advocacy group therefore was entitled to have its legal expenses paid by New Flyer. It was an unequivocal and stunning victory, but it took three years from the time Jobs to Move America first inquired about seeing whether New Flyer had done what it promised to do, for justice to be served and the public's interest to be protected.[3]

The victory went further than that individual contract to create new policy and practice. After the case was settled, LACMTA determined that wage and benefit information will no longer be considered a trade secret in future contracts. Standard practice at the agency now is to disclose job and wage data in publicly available contract-compliance data.

When Public Policy Becomes a "Trade Secret"

"Sunlight is said to be the best of disinfectants," Louis Brandeis noted in 1914 while arguing that publicity and openness were the best ways to address corruption and "social and industrial diseases." Ohio lawmakers acknowledged that open government is essential to democracy when they passed the state's robust sunshine laws guaranteeing public access to information about public institutions. But when private corporations like White Hat and New Flyer perform public functions, it can take a drawn-out court case to bring essential information in from the shadows.

In the case of JobsOhio, the privatized version of an office of economic development, powerful interests avoided both transparency and inconvenient court cases by simply exempting themselves from the law. JobsOhio, according to Ohio law, is "not a public office for the purposes of the Public Records Act." Not many public agencies in Ohio get that sort of exemption. The Department of Job and Family services, child fatality review boards, and the Organized Crime Investigations Commission get exemptions for privacy and safety reasons. So JobsOhio, which sets up tax breaks and incentives for corporations, gets to enjoy the same level of secrecy as agencies that investigate mobsters and child abuse.[4]

Governor John Kasich created JobsOhio in 2011 to replace the Department of Development. He devised it as a public-private partnership and staffed it with hand-picked business leaders. The mandate of JobsOhio is to identify tax breaks and grants for Ohio businesses to keep them happy so they won't leave for another state or another country. JobsOhio claims that it does not formulate policy, only recommendations, but the separate panel that approves the recommendations has apparently never used its veto power. There is little question that JobsOhio drives public policy. But its very structure and scope, and the promises made by Kasich to provide a cheaper-faster-better policy machine, have driven JobsOhio to avoid the public eye.[5]

In its first year the organization moved quickly to hand out tax breaks and loans, granting public support to 154 companies. But how were decisions made? How were companies chosen? What formula determined whether a particular tax break or grant would be a good deal for the taxpaying citizens of Ohio? JobsOhio's answer was that the process was a trade secret. If it were public, other states could use it against Ohio and draw businesses away. Since JobsOhio was more private than public, it didn't have to tell the public much of anything.[6]

For example, it didn't have to say who contributed to its pot of $6.9 million in private donations in 2012. Secret donations were going to a secretive body that largely decided, in secret, how much public money to give away to Ohio businesses. You don't have to be terribly cynical to see the problem here. In addition, investigative journalists found that of the board's nine members, six had personally benefited from state subsidies (some prior to joining the board). The state's ethics commission in 2013 flagged possible conflicts of interest for nine out of twenty-two JobsOhio employees. The CEO and president received a salary of $516,458 in 2017, and employee compensation averaged $142,000. By this time the operation had expanded to a staff of eighty-one. And that's just the salary—JobsOhio did not release additional information on benefits. It didn't feel it had to.[7]

After the state auditor made clear that he would not be deterred by JobsOhio's attempts to keep its records private, Kasich moved rapidly to introduce legislation to stop him. The governor's spokesman explained that secrecy had to be maintained "to prevent a chilling effect on job creation caused by a mistaken, overly intrusive interpretation of the auditor's duties." The state legislature passed the bill just hours after it was introduced. The state auditor said it was an obtuse and "complex" bill with "numerous exceptions" and "somewhat dense language," leaving him "uncertain as to all its legal implications."[8]

Other implications are more certain. JobsOhio is a rejection of democracy. It asserts that decisions about public money and Ohio's economy cannot be left to the people. The people should not even know how those decisions are made. Their proper role is to accept what's decided for them by the wealthy and well connected.[9]

Opacity is a private-sector reflex. When you are locked in competition to sell a car or smartphone, you don't want the competition to know too much about your operation. But it is exactly the wrong model for a democratic public sector, which relies on a flow of information from the executive branch to the legislative branch, and by extension to the citizens who are paying the bills. When organizations withhold how they make decisions and refuse to show how those decisions play out, power further accrues to our leaders and away from our voters. From there, it's a simple matter to drive policy away from the public good.

11

Skin in the Game

Environmental and Planning Policy in Privatization's Grip

THE CONTRACT IS KING. ACCORDING TO THE IDEOLOGY THAT EMBRACES property rights above all else, according to those who wish to limit government and thereby limit public input, the contract can override public-policy choices and even the common good. Privatization contracts can remove public control over public goods by locking in a policy and forcing democratic governments to adhere to that policy for generations into the future.

Environmental policy is especially vulnerable because to be effective it needs to be long term, flexible, and balanced against many trade-offs. So these policies often run headfirst into privatization contracts, which are geared toward narrow interests and deliberately limit what the public can do. The looming environmental catastrophe of global warming, one that can be addressed only through a cohesive public commitment, does not figure into these contracts. Nor do public health, the public's preferences, or democracy in general.

Locked In: The Power of "Compensation Events"

When Chicago leased its parking meters to Morgan Stanley, the city agreed to compensate this multibillion-dollar behemoth for any public decision to take any meters offline for any period of time. The contract term for this is *compensation event*; such events include street fairs, removals for improvements, and temporary closures of parking lanes for roadwork. Morgan Stanley has been merciless in squeezing the city for alleged loss of revenue, and won $61 million in a court battle over closed streets. It didn't end there; compensation events totaled $21.7 million in

2017 and $20 million in 2018. Concerns over triggering a compensation event now factor into every effort to alleviate traffic or introduce new and cleaner modes of transit. The contract has an outsized role in driving policy to reduce pollution and greenhouse gases (among other things) and is often at odds with what is best for the city.[1]

Chicago once had a vision for twenty Bus Rapid Transit (BRT) lines. These are attractive, inexpensive options for congested streets, but they involve closing the curb lane. After the parking meter deal went into effect, the city had to either provide Morgan Stanley with new meters in a new location when it introduced a BRT or pay for lost revenue for the life of the lease. The city's long-term plans are now in jeopardy.

Chicago once had a plan for 645 bike lanes and cycle tracks by 2020. But these often involve moving parking meters, removing parking spaces at the end of the block for a longer turn lane, and taking some parking offline for construction. Now these plans are tied up in red tape. A frustrated planner behind the project explained, "If we didn't have this deal, they could remove the parking meter space and get it done today. . . . It's so easy to accomplish this but our hands are tied."[2]

The lease was never as simple as letting someone else maintain the meters: "The parking meter lease creates a new jurisdiction over the streets," one city transportation planner noted. "The city gave up the freedom of future management options," said another. The contract's compensation events granted Morgan Stanley a de facto authority over what happens in Chicago's streets and parking lots, introducing an unelected and unaccountable power into public decision-making.[3]

The corporations on the other side of P3 deals generally want the opposite of what the public wants and what the public knows to be sustainable. These corporations want more cars on the road, more parking, and less public transit. Private water companies want more consumption and less conservation—and are in a position to charge their customers for *not* using water. Privatized trash-disposal companies want more trash. It's easy to see why a private company that specializes in getting rid of our trash would want to see more waste and less frugality. But some private disposal companies have taken it even further with private incinerators.

Burning Up: Ensuring Incineration with "Put or Pay"

Put or Pay is the name for the contract clause that forces a municipality either to give a company a certain amount of trash or to pay a fee. Put or Pay comes up a lot when an incinerator company hopes to burn trash for electricity. Lake County, Florida, started its tangled relationship with the Okahumpka incinerator, owned by Covanta Energy, in 1988, when the county helped build the $79 million trash-burning monster—the company would own it, but the county floated low-cost municipal bonds to finance the project. In 2004, to keep the revenue flowing to Covanta, the county promised to feed the incinerator 160,000 tons of waste each year. If all went well, Lake County stood to receive a little over $500,000 a month from energy sales, which it could use to help offset fees paid to Covanta and payments on the bond debt.[4]

The delicate balancing act did not anticipate the depths of the 2008 financial crisis and how it forced people to buy less and hold on to what they had. In one quarter, trash volume fell by 16 percent. Falling below 70 percent of the promised volume of trash in any given month would mean a total loss of the $500,000 share in energy sales. So Lake County went on a trash hunt, sending officials to nearby towns to, in the words of one reporter, "implore them to dump their garbage at the Covanta facility." One Lake County manager insisted, "We're looking all around to find what waste we can. . . . Not doing this will be very, very costly." And while they got seven different cities to help them feed the beast they'd created, a Lake County official noted, "We're also not promoting recycling in a big way right now."[5]

This local government was lured into a free-market bear trap with the promise of trash for energy. Incinerators create the illusion of an alignment of interests between public and private, but what they really mean, in this case and elsewhere, is that a local government gets locked into a long-term commitment and an incentive to avoid recycling. As it happens, material that burns hottest and creates the most energy also gives us the best returns on recycling. Creating new paper, for example, takes three to five times more energy than recycling old paper for new uses.

Burning that paper for electricity recaptures only a fifth of what went into making it and converts much of it into greenhouse gases.[6]

For the public there's little financial or environmental incentive to continue with incinerators, and yet they persist. Detroit was saddled with an albatross of an incinerator built back in the 1980s inside the city limits that provided heat to downtown through a steam loop. Although the city had issued $478 million in bonds to get the plant built and running, it sold it to a private company for $54 million just two years after it opened. Over twenty years of interest and upgrades added up to a cost of $1.2 billion for Detroit. With no money left to spend on finding alternatives, Detroit could afford no other options and signed a put-or-pay arrangement that guaranteed a revenue stream for the private operator. Still, with all the money residents poured into this facility, it ended up costing Detroit some $172 per ton of waste. At the same time that this plant was helping to bankrupt the city, the facility was taking trash from Detroit's wealthier neighbors and charging them as little as $10 a ton.[7]

Detroit owned the land that the incinerator occupied, but had "no direct authority over its operation," according to a city official. Unaccountable and apparently indifferent, the incinerator company took some 70 percent of Detroit's waste, and the city remained hampered in its ability to promote recycling, with one estimate finding a recycling rate of just 7 percent, compared to the national average of 34 percent. Meanwhile, health problems associated with the neighborhood near the incinerator, a place the Michigan Department of Community Health called an "epicenter of asthma," where childhood asthma rates were four to five times higher than statewide, represented another cost. Finally, the threat of an environmental lawsuit, with evidence of hundreds of violations, forced the incinerator's owner to close suddenly in 2019. Detroit was free of this disaster but left in the lurch. It had no other solid waste disposal plan in place.[8]

Indianapolis, Indiana, also has a power-producing incinerator that needs to be fed, and a similarly low recycling rate. The incinerator, owned and operated by Covanta, had been burning trash since the 1980s and in 2008 managed to lock in a ten-year contract with a put-or-pay provision to ensure the delivery of 300,000 tons of waste per year. The terms also gave the mayor the ability to extend the contract without city or county council approval. Once again, the contract displaced democratic decision-making. The city repeatedly failed to produce enough waste to hit this mark and burned through $2.3 million dollars in compensation payments by 2015—again, that's money spent for not providing the incinerator with enough trash.[9]

Covanta was growing increasingly unpopular as the end of its contract neared, so it remade itself as a recycling company; it would sort through all of Indy's trash for recyclables and burn what it couldn't recover. The city got a break on the put-or-pay requirement, but it had to make new promises to keep Covanta's investment in recycling profitable. For the next ten years (until 2028), the mayor promised, Indianapolis would not undertake or even promote any new recycling or allow the small existing program to grow by more than 5 percent. If it did, the city would pay up to $4 million per year until the contract ended. Now the city could be penalized both for not producing enough trash to burn and for recycling too much.[10]

This is how privatization ties the hands of policymakers and stands in the way of democratic decision-making. And the way in which this contract was approved is particularly egregious. The mayor's office claimed that this was merely an extension of the old contract. This ignored the fact that it involved a whole new facility, new penalties, new restrictions on future policy decisions, and $4 million in tax breaks, handed quietly to Covanta while both the corporation and the mayor claimed the new recycling program was costing the taxpayers nothing.[11]

The deal was bad through and through, but it came undone because it was also undemocratic. The Indiana Court of Appeals overturned the contract because it had flaunted public bidding and participation. The city had argued that because the new facility was privately owned, it was exempt from public scrutiny. The court, quoting an amicus brief, decided the opposite was true: "The fact that the decision to create the facility might have originated with the private corporation—motivated, at least in part, by a desire to increase profits—simply underscores the importance of an open and transparent decision-making process."[12]

Back Rooms and Fake Crowds:
Winning the Contract, Undermining Democracy

An open and transparent process, along with multiple opportunities for public input, is exactly what privately run municipal services do not want. And when they can't get around it, as they tried to do in Indianapolis, they'll resort to tactics worthy of autocracies. Entergy, a corporation with annual revenues of $11 billion, wanted to build a gas-fired power plant in New Orleans, Louisiana. It anticipated grassroots opposition at the city council meetings and hired a PR firm to attack the opposition. This firm went to an outfit called Crowds on Demand that offered an amazing astroturfing solution. Crowds on Demand boasts on its website, "If you need to hire protesters, we can get a crowd on the street, sometimes within 24 hours time. If you need speakers to present at a council meeting, we can provide talented and well-spoken individuals to advocate for the cause." In New Orleans they packed city council meetings with paid "protesters" wearing bright orange shirts that read "Clean Energy. Good Jobs. Reliable Power." Some of them received $60 dollars just to cheer loudly for the plant and boo whenever someone mentioned wind or solar energy alternatives. Others were professional actors who auditioned for speaking roles and delivered prepared speeches. One later told a reporter he thought he'd been hired to appear in a commercial, adding, "I'm not political. I needed the money for a hotel room at that point."[13]

The strategy wasn't merely to influence the opinion of the public and the council members. It was also to pack the room early, so those opposed to the plant couldn't get in. In other words, it was part of their plan to suppress opposing views, to drown out public voices, and to thwart the democratic process. And it was disturbingly effective. The council voted in Entergy's favor. One of the council members, after learning about the rent-a-crowd scheme, which she described as "morally reprehensible," claimed that "it had a phenomenal impact on public opinion."[14]

What we do with our trash and what we put into the air affects us all. We have to start thinking about water, air, and land as limited resources that are removed from public use—actually consumed—when a corporation pollutes them. Retaining public control over these resources isn't about restricting profits or restricting freedoms; it's about enforc-ing corporate and individual responsibility for the consequences of their choices. That's hard to do, however, when our elected representatives agree to contracts that are expressly designed to put private corporations' bottom line before public demands for a cleaner environment and better city planning while removing any exposure to financial risk. "Compen-sation events" and "put or pay" are not just clauses in contracts, and they are not just bad for the environment; they are shackles on democratic decision-making.

12

Freedom Has a Price

Privatization's Assault on the Justice System

IN COLORADO AT THE END OF THE '00S, POLICYMAKERS TOOK NOTE OF A
miraculous drop in crime—down over 30 percent over ten years—and
saw that they had more prison beds than prisoners. This called for a reas-
sessment, and, in 2012, the state initiated a study to help decide which
prisons to close and which to retain.

Colorado, however, was home to three private prisons run by the Corrections Corporation of America. CCA did not want the prisons closed
and delivered a strong-arm threat: it wouldn't wait for the study—it
would immediately shutter one of its prisons, leaving the state in a bind.
That got the governor's attention, and CCA was rewarded with a lopsided
negotiation that took place in back rooms, far away from inconvenient
public input.[1]

CCA managed to introduce into its new deal the industry's favorite
mechanism for reducing risk and calming stockholders—the bed guarantee. This is the private prison industry's version of the incinerator's
put-or-pay schemes and is very similar to the Chicago parking-meter
deal's "compensation events." The guarantee is for state payments covering a certain number of prisoners, whether there are actual "heads in
beds" or not. It is a way to reduce risk and secure profits, and it also has
the effect of tying the hands of the public and redirecting public policy.[2]

When Colorado first let CCA set up shop in the state, policymakers
had intended to use the private facilities for overflow; they were a stop-
gap. But with the bed guarantee in place, the private prisons took precedence. The outcome was exactly the opposite of the public policy, and the
reversal took place without public discussion or input. It all unfolded in
the realm of the contract.

What happens in the contract, however, never stays within the contract. If you are a lawmaker and you have empty beds that you've already paid for, do you support justice reforms allowing early release for nonviolent prisoners? Rehabilitation programs? Expanded use of parole or probation? Reform of the bail system? Or do you settle for policies that have already been covered in your state's tight budget? One independent organization estimated that Colorado lost $2 million in the CCA deal. That's $2 million less to spend on other options. The private prison industry's very existence creates pressure to lock people up for profit and creates conditions where other options become ever more expensive and impractical.[3]

If we accept that we will be ruled by contracts rather than by public decision-making, we will end up accepting significant losses of freedom at the hands of private prisons and private probation companies. And even if law-abiding citizens feel unaffected by these developments, they cannot escape the forced-arbitration clauses embedded in everything from employment contracts to credit card agreements, which amount to an across-the-board privatization of civil law. Privatization advocates have embraced the right of contract as the right that trumps all others, even as corporate exercise of this right makes the public less free.

Locked Up: Undermining Democracy with Privatized Prisons

Colorado's experience is not unique. A 2013 study by In the Public Interest found occupancy guarantees in 65 percent of the prison contracts it was able to obtain. These contracts committed states to pay for 80 to 100 percent occupancy, no matter how many prisoners were actually present. In Arizona, all the private prisons were compensated as if the facilities were 100 percent full, even if they weren't. So if crime rates fell, these states would not see significantly diminished expenses in their spending on incarceration.[4]

In 2016 the private prison industry had a brush with oblivion; the Justice Department announced that it would not renew its contracts, the Democratic presidential candidates promised to end them, and public opinion turned against them. Donald Trump, meanwhile, claimed that private prisons "seem to work a lot better." It's unclear where he got this idea, unless it was from the private prison political action committee that donated lavishly to his campaign.[5]

Private prisons simply do not "work a lot better," and we know this because both public and private studies have shown the opposite to be true.

They are not cheaper, according to studies undertaken by the National Institute of Justice, the General Accounting Office, the University of Utah, the Arizona Department of Corrections, an audit in Georgia, and the Mississippi Department of Corrections, to name just a few. In most cases, they are more expensive.[6]

They are not safer. The Department of Justice noted "serious or systemic safety and security deficiencies at contract prisons" when compared to public Bureau of Prisons facilities, and found a higher rate of violent incidents at private prisons, including a 38 percent higher rate of attacks on staff. Assaults were three times more common in Mississippi's private prisons, and four times more common in Idaho's.[7]

They are not better at rehabilitation. While some focused studies have found little difference between public and private, broader approaches have found significantly higher rates of recidivism associated with private prisons. A Minnesota Department of Corrections study ran results through twenty different statistical models and reported private prisons had "a greater hazard of recidivism" in all of them. An Oklahoma study found private prisons increased the chance of recidivism by up to 17 percent. Recidivism represents another cost to the taxpayer while presenting a business opportunity to the private prison owner. A repeat offender is a burden to the state and to society, but to a private prison company he is a repeat customer.[8]

Private prisons are not more secure. A study by the U.S. Bureau of Prisons' Office of Research and Evaluation found a higher escape rate from private prisons: during the survey period the bureau experienced just one escape from a population 17 percent larger than the private prison population, which experienced eighteen escapes from inside their prisons and five escapes during transport.[9]

A full list of the bloodstained scandals and horror stories set in private prisons could fill volumes, and they would include the Idaho Correctional Center (ICC), a facility that was host to more violent assaults than all the rest of Idaho's seven state prisons combined. The ICC's nickname, Gladiator School, came not only from the horrific level of violence, but also from the fact that much of the carnage was instigated and calmly observed by the correctional officers.[10]

A full list would have to include the Walnut Grove Youth Correctional Facility in Mississippi. The facility—run by the GEO Group, the nation's second-largest private prison company—flaunted the recommended inmate-to-officer ratio of 12-to-1 with a much more economical ratio of 60-to-1. The result was what one former inmate called "the deepest depths of hell": near anarchy, unchecked contraband, sex between guards and inmates, predatory gangs, and generalized brutality involving guards and inmates alike. All of this was treated with what the U.S. Department of Justice called "deliberate indifference."[11]

The list would also have to include Ohio's Lake Erie Correctional Institution, the first state prison to be sold to a private corporation. When CCA took over, it promised to revitalize the local economy with good jobs; instead the porous security invited smuggling. The nearby town of Conneaut saw stunning increases in crime as the contraband pipeline into the prison opened up. In the first year of CCA ownership, local police found themselves responding to crimes related to the prison four times more often than they had in the five previous years combined.[12]

There was simply no basis for candidate Trump's claim that private prisons seem to "work a lot better." They have failed on every level. Their profitability and persistence is not due to winning a free-market competition with a superior product; it's due to salesmanship, lobbying, campaign donations, and shrewd contract negotiations.

The rise of private prisons required certain social conditions. The government had to be in the hands of people who saw privatization as a good in itself. Public apathy toward prisoners had to be firmly established. And a new class of businesspersons, people who saw how to use influence and ideological arguments to secure contracts, had to emerge. Their opportunism is a direct descendant of those who saw profits in prisoners during Reconstruction. In this tragic historical moment, southern landowners realized they could replace slaves with convicts and thereby avoid having to negotiate with free laborers. The widespread convict leasing system became known as slavery by other means and faced its own moment of reckoning; in 1887 Congress stepped in and banned the leasing of federal prisoners. By the turn of the century, most prisons and the treatment of prisoners within them were back in public hands. But policies of mass incarceration, promoted by the prison industry, have brought us full circle.[13]

If you want to make money in prisons, you have to engage in politics and shape policy. You have to bend the social definition of punishment, and it helps if your prisoners are largely minorities. Then you have to lobby. When asked by a reporter about his company's lobbying efforts, the GEO Group's vice president for corporate relations claimed, "We do not take a position on, nor advocate for or against, criminal justice or immigration policies such as whether to criminalize behavior, the length of criminal sentences, or the basis for or length of an individual's incarceration or detention." CoreCivic's director of public affairs likewise claimed a "strict policy" of not lobbying on issues that would affect anyone's incarceration or detention.[14]

And yet the industry spends quite a bit of money advocating for something. It often seems to be most generous to politicians who advocate for longer prison terms and who help award contracts to private prison companies. It has also been especially active in the American Legislative Exchange Council, which helped write tough-on-crime legislation. The Corrections Corporation of America held a membership in ALEC for more than twenty years and was among its top contributors. CCA's representatives wormed their way into key committees like the Homeland Security Committee and the Public Safety Task Force (where they even served as co-chairs). During this time, these committees drafted and advanced model legislation on mandatory minimums, three-strikes sentencing laws, and "truth in sentencing" legislation that would limit or eliminate parole.[15]

Eighty-five pieces of model legislation having to do with crime and punishment emerged during CCA's deep involvement with ALEC. Yet

CCA claims it did not vote or even remark on this legislation. It wanted us to believe it was merely in the room but took no position on policies that would add millions to its bottom line. Okay. But we should notice another pattern here: these laws deliberately tied the hands of judges and courts. This tough-on-crime movement represented an undoing of due process and the balance of power. Like "heads in beds" or "put or pay," it represented another opportunity for business to guarantee profits, while eliminating risk by restricting our rights.

The spread of harsh sentencing laws and the booming prison population ultimately did not insulate the private prison industry from the drop in crime in the early twenty-first century. What was clearly a blessing for society as a whole was a threat to the industry's profits, and its stock prices sagged. The industry had to find new populations to imprison, and it focused on immigrant detentions as a growth area. Here again, its fortunes were closely tied to policy decisions, its targets were largely nonwhite, and the public-policy process became warped by its efforts.

In 2009, Arizona state representative Russel Pearce—a man full of "paranoia and bigotry" to an "astonishing" level, according to the Southern Poverty Law Center—took an idea to ALEC's Public Safety Task Force, which included representatives of Corrections Corporation of America. From the meeting emerged State Bill 1070, the infamous attempt by Arizona to require all levels of law enforcement to demand proof of citizenship based on suspicion alone. Opponents of the bill lambasted it for permitting racial profiling and for essentially requiring citizens to always carry their papers—a birth certificate or a passport.

Once this secret meeting was reported, CCA naturally denied any role in drafting the model legislation that emerged. But it wasn't just at that meeting. Governor Jan Brewer, who enthusiastically signed the legislation in 2010, employed two key advisers who were former private prison lobbyists. Thirty of the bill's thirty-six co-sponsors all received generous campaign contributions from CCA and GEO in the months that followed the bill's introduction. With SB 1070 moving forward, with other states taking up the model legislation, and with the federal government adopting zero tolerance, GEO president Wayne Calabrese promised investors that "those people coming across the border and getting caught are going to have to be detained and that for me, at least I think, there's going to be enhanced opportunities for what we do."[16]

Before the private prison boom, the capacity of federal prisons was largely determined by need. The number of people caught and jailed told policymakers how many prisons to build. But in 2006 Congress changed the conversation. In February of that year, several members of Congress from Texas met with the chair of the House Subcommittee on Homeland Security and the assistant secretary of Immigration and Customs Enforcement to complain about "hundreds of empty beds" and "detention facilities . . . that are only one-third full." In 2009, legislation demanded that DHS provide for "not less than 34,000 detention beds," and hard-line members of Congress began insisting that Immigration and Customs Enforcement treat this as a mandate to fill those beds. The absurdity of this was captured by a former ICE director who'd faced the pressure to go find people to put in the system's prisons: "Having a mandate out there that says you have to detain a certain number—regardless of how many folks are a public safety threat or threaten the integrity of the system—doesn't seem to make a lot of sense. You need the numbers to drive the detention needs, not set an arbitrary number that then drives your operation." Yet his commonsense approach became further out of reach as the private prison population increased and private prison companies started building more facilities *in the hopes* of filling them. By 2017 almost three-quarters of all immigrant detentions were in for-profit prisons.[17]

The Trump administration will forever be associated with putting kids in cages, and the stain of that scandal should adhere to the private prison companies as well. They paved the way for Trump's anti-immigrant push by enabling and backstopping politicians who used immigration as a political wedge. They saw fortunes in the new policy of incarcerating asylum seekers. The value of their contracts and stock went up under the policy of child separation, and went up again when Trump changed his policy to one of family incarceration. They were prepared for the influx because they had been adding new facilities on the principle of "if you build it they will come," so when the government needed new jails they were prepared. When they ran out of space, they constructed substandard tent cities and then shrouded the resulting inhumane conditions in secrecy. The government had many policy choices, but the private prison industry made the worst choice the most feasible and easiest to implement. Then they shielded friendly politicians from public scrutiny of the outcomes. In doing so, they made a killing.[18]

After Trump was elected, GEO Group's stock price shot up by 63 percent and CoreCivic's by 81 percent. These are solid returns on a relatively small investment in friendly politicians, and they followed on a political season that embedded the private prison industry deeply into the marrow of the Republican party. In 2016 the industry gave 85 percent of its political contributions to Republicans. This is not something other industries do; most businesses cynically play both sides. But this particular industry clearly sees its fortunes tied to the success of just one party and the spread of its most racist and inhumane ideologies. The private prison companies then use their profits to further solidify their influence in back rooms, far from scrutiny and other inconveniences of democracy.[19]

Let Loose: For-Profit Probation Companies

Judicial Corrections Services perfected the privatizing siren song of something for nothing, and the town of Greenwood, Mississippi, listened. Judicial Corrections offered to run the town's probation services at no charge. The probationers would pay, and the company would manage the probation. In a town with a meager tax base and an average income of $14,000, this made ample sense, at least for a moment.

Within eight months almost 10 percent of Greenwood was on probation—not because the town was full of criminals, but because fines for minor infractions could result in probation and additional fees from the profit-seeking probation company. Judicial Corrections, meanwhile, was raking in $48,000 per month or more, leaving Greenwood on the verge of a major economic crisis. This town of 15,000 had 1,200 residents beholden to a private company, with three hundred facing possible jail time for failure to pay, and $48,000 of their collective income being spent on probation each month instead of being spent locally on groceries, rent, or baby formula. Greenwood was lucky. It was able to cancel the contract.[20]

The best customer is the captive customer; that's why private probation companies are so successful and why they are so bad for individual rights and freedoms. Private probation represents an infection in our justice system that actively restructures the DNA of justice in order to create captive consumers and tiered systems—exactly the opposite of what probation should provide. When we grant a citizen probation as a punishment, we are honoring their ability to self-correct and following the idea that society is a better influence than prison. Probation is supposed to be a chance at rehabilitation with achievable goals and a clear end point, all of which are defined by carefully balancing the common good against an individual's rights. But several states have privatized probation, and thereby transformed it from a second chance into an indentured servitude.

Private probation rests on the idea that offenders should pay for their own rehabilitation. The court then hands the offender over to a private company to monitor the probationer and collect any fees and fines. Of course, the private probation company also wants to make a profit. So instead of focusing on the rehabilitation of the probationer and the prevention of future crimes, these companies act more like payday lenders, bleeding their victims for as long as possible. A typical scenario might involve a misdemeanor offender—a first-time shoplifter or someone who was arrested for public intoxication—facing a fine. An offender who can't afford to pay the fine up front might be given the opportunity to pay it off during probation, with the end of probation contingent on the payment of the fine.

But more costs creep in as soon as the private company takes over. It will place a service charge on top of the fine. It will add in the cost of regular background checks. It will add in the cost of drug testing even if the original offense wasn't drug related. If the court wants the probationer to attend anger management classes, that's another billing opportunity. If the court wants location monitoring, that means the private probation company provides the high-tech equipment and charges the probationer, adding on a cut for itself. One company even hit its probationers with an extra fee to complete court-mandated community service hours. These fees are where struggling probationers get snagged. An investigation by Human Rights Watch found many more cases of citizens being jailed for failure to pay for these extras than for failure to pay the original fine and probation fees.[21]

Cindy Rodriguez, who was under the supervision of Providence Community Corrections, a private probation company in Tennessee, lived on disability payments due to a back injury and started her probation owing the court $578 in fines and fees. Then Providence added its own fees, and, like a payday lender, applied payments to those fees rather than to the original debt. After a year, Rodriguez had paid Providence almost enough to clear her original debt, only to find that they had taken almost all of it for themselves; the court still demanded $512. Human Rights Watch found how an original fine of $750 could metastasize into $2,465, where private companies could cultivate a penalty of $250 into a bumper crop of $2,231. All good for the corporations' bottom lines, but devastating to the folks caught in their undertow who face jail time and loss of a job, an apartment, or custody of children if they don't pay.[22]

The consequences of privatizing probation filter up as well, corrupting court systems and proceedings from above while shattering lives from below. Our court systems have the ability to waive probation fees when they recognize an insurmountable burden. This is unlikely to happen when a for-profit probation company is involved, according to judges and defense attorneys interviewed by investigators. One striking reason lies in judges' fear, which they admit to in interviews, that "waiving private probation supervision fees would negatively impact the companies as they rely on these fees to operate." The scales of justice apparently can be tipped by the need to keep these bottom-feeding companies profitable and available.[23]

Tipping those scales past the point of absurdity, courts in Missouri and Tennessee, according to investigators, regularly reached out to private probation officers for testimony in hearings that decide whether or not a citizen remains on probation. Let that sink in: the court welcomed testimony from an employee of a corporation *that profits from continued probation* in deciding whether to terminate probation.

Crystal Bradford was arrested for shoplifting from a Walmart in Tennessee after her friend pocketed a bottle of infant cold medicine and the cashier missed the case of water under the cart. Bradford was given probation just shy of twelve months—the maximum allowed. The judge explained to Bradford that during this time she would have to pay $100 a month to recoup court costs and $50 per month to cover her supervision. She was on disability due to an autoimmune disease and unremitting pain and told the judge she wouldn't be able to make the payments. The judge told her to take it up with the private probation company.

The private probation officer, Bradford recalls, was downright cheerful while threatening her: "If you don't have all of your fees paid by the end of the month or at the end of probation, then just let me know and we'll just sign the arrest warrant." The probation officer also wanted drug testing, which had nothing to do with her original offense. When Bradford explained that her medications might produce a false positive, her probation officer, already aware that she was barely scraping by, sent her out for even more expensive hair-follicle testing.[24]

Probation is supposed to be a punishment that leads toward rehabilitation. It comes from a justice system that is supposed to serve the common good by carefully restricting freedoms of those whose actions damage others. But private probation restricts freedom in the pursuit of profit, and its ability to exert pressure on the whole system leads to two-tiered justice, corruption of judges' rulings, and a voice for special interests when it's time to decide the fate of the accused or convicted. When privatized, probation ceases to protect freedom and becomes its antithesis.

Signed Off: How Forced Arbitration Is Remaking American Rights

We are in the midst of a quiet revolution against our justice system. In the words of one federal judge, the Reagan-appointed William G. Young, it is "among the most profound shifts in our legal history." This is not overstatement; businesses have constructed an entirely private ersatz legal system, one where basic constitutional rights do not apply. The conservative bloc in the U.S. Supreme Court has sanctified this alternative legal system with rulings against consumers and employees. Now, Judge Young warned, "business has a good chance of opting out of the legal system altogether and misbehaving without reproach."[25]

The mechanism is deceptively simple. A consumer signs a contract set in minuscule type that goes on for pages and pages. Or a new hire receives an employee contract that's a condition of employment. Within each lies a clause stating that all disputes must be settled in private arbitration. The consumer signs because he is too busy to read through the mind-numbing fine print. The new hire signs because she needs the job. Both have now waived their constitutional right to seek justice in a public court.

In 1992 the arbitration clause was a novelty—only 2 percent of workers labored under forced-arbitration clauses. In the early twenty-first century 25 percent of them did. In 2018, 56 percent of nonunion private-sector employees could be denied a day in court if they fell into a dispute with their employer. Consumers face similar certainty that their rights are being stripped away. Just over half of all credit card companies demand mandatory arbitration, but it gets worse for financial products used by lower-wage Americans. Eighty-six percent of student loan companies require arbitration, 92 percent of debit cards require them, and virtually all payday lenders (99 percent) force resolution of all disputes through arbitration. It seems that the more powerful the company and the more vulnerable the consumer, the more likely it is that forced arbitration will replace the public justice system—for example, it's estimated that 90 percent of large nursing homes force arbitration in their admissions paperwork.[26]

Unlike a civil trial, an arbitration proceeding will typically be run by an individual or a for-profit corporation selected in advance by the corporate defendant. The proceeding may be in a city far removed from the plaintiff's home. It may take place in the offices of the corporation's lawyers. It may be overseen by a retired judge, it may be presided over by a corporate lawyer, or it may be someone with no legal expertise—some arbitration agreements force plaintiffs into faith-based arbitration run by religious leaders.

The stripped-down procedure will involve no rules of evidence, discovery, or respect for the consumer or employee's rights. Who decides how much or what type of evidence the plaintiff can present? The arbitrator. Who decides how much evidence the corporation can withhold? The arbitrator. "What rules of evidence apply?" asked one arbitration company's FAQ webpage. "The short answer is none," it admitted. This apparently was a selling point.[27]

Judges are bound by rules and ethics. Arbitrators in the privatized system are not, and the results can shock the conscience. When Sister Irene Morissette, an eighty-seven-year-old nun, reported to police that she had been raped in her nursing home, officials collected significant physical evidence but were unable to name a suspect. She and her family wanted to sue the home for negligence—among other things, the family's request that the facility preserve security video footage was ignored—but they were bound to settle for arbitration. There, they were forced to endure hearsay testimony speculating that the victim masturbated so often that she herself caused the violent wounds detailed by the medical examiner, not her rapist.

Such a line of questioning, based on rumor and speculation, would have had little chance of seeing the light of day in a public courtroom, but in these for-profit hearings no such rules applied. In a public courtroom, a ruling based on a judge's reading of another's emotions would be immediately appealed and thrown out. Here, it carried the day when the arbitrator decided Morissette had not in fact been raped and explained, "I did not hear the emotion from Ms. Morissette . . . that I would expect to hear from someone describing being sexually assaulted." Morissette's family lost their claim and received a bill from the arbitrator for $3,000 to cover the cost of the venue for the hearing.[28]

Conflicts of interest are inherent problems in privatization arrangements, and arbitration is no exception. Arbitrators make between $300 and $600 per hour. The pressure to please the corporation that selected them and that might hire them again is unavoidable. As part of an investigative series, the *New York Times* reported on a widely known story of an arbitrator who ruled in favor of a plaintiff in a discrimination case and was blacklisted from that point forward on any and all employment cases. Speaking anonymously, nearly forty arbitrators told the *Times* that they felt "beholden" to the corporations that hired them: "Beneath every decision, the arbitrators said, was the threat of losing business." One arbitrator did go on record and pointed out the obvious reason her colleagues might hold plaintiffs in disdain: "Why would an arbitrator cater to a person they will never see again?"[29]

The latest and most comprehensive survey found that workers win only 21 percent of the time in arbitration. Consumers win only 9 percent of the time. Both fare far better in public courts. In a typical year, 6.8 million consumers nationwide get some form of relief from class-action lawsuits, adding up to $440 million, after the lawyers and court costs are paid. In a typical year only sixteen consumers win in arbitration. Their relief totals $86,000.[30]

The game is masterfully rigged from start to finish, but perhaps most disturbing is how readily the conservative majority on the Supreme Court became a partner in this revolutionary project to remake the justice system. The project to kill the class-action lawsuit dates back to the late 1990s and involved lawyers from financial giants like Bank of America, Chase, and Citigroup, who saw the promise in arbitration and wanted a test case. One case that almost made it to the Supreme Court was the brainchild of the future chief justice John Roberts, who was then representing Discover Bank. Roberts argued that the 1925 Federal Arbitration Act, which governed arbitrated settlements between corporations, was much broader than anyone had thought. Applied to consumers, it could be used to force them to give up their right to join a class action.[31]

The Supreme Court declined to hear Roberts's argument, but after he became chief justice, a similar case came before the newly receptive court. In his opinion on *AT&T Mobility vs. Concepcion* in 2011, Justice Antonin Scalia came pretty close to plagiarizing the same argument offered by Roberts when he was a young corporate lawyer crusading to crush the class action. Having handed the power to corporations to strip away our class-action rights as consumers, the court then took up a case that did the same to employees in 2018. In *Epic Systems v. Lewis*, the 5–4 conservative majority ruled that corporations could require employees to waive their rights to class-action lawsuits, again evoking the 1925 Federal Arbitration Act.[32]

But this ruling had to go further because the 1934 National Labor Relations Act plainly stated that employees had the right not only to form unions, but also "to engage in other concerted activities for the purpose of . . . mutual aid or protection." In a ruling as sweeping as it was specious, the conservative majority argued that "other concerted activities" did not include class actions because class actions were not specifically named, because the first part of that paragraph wasn't about suing in court, and because Congress didn't explicitly call out the Arbitration Act.[33]

It takes some very tendentious reasoning to read "other concerted activities" and argue that it doesn't include the one and only recourse most nonunion employees have. It takes a shameless use of smoke and mirrors to fault Congress for not explicitly overturning the Arbitration Act when that act was never intended to apply to contracts between employees and employers. The Supreme Court's ruling essentially blamed Congress for not anticipating and protecting workers against the court's own expansive reading of the Arbitration Act decades later.

But listen to what the conservative side of the Supreme Court is saying: corporations may now brush aside citizens' constitutional rights. It is a return to the legal reasoning of the *right of contract*, which drove Gilded Age inequality, crushed unions, prohibited a minimum wage, stopped states from capping the workweek, and tied the hands of an outraged nation that wanted to stop child labor. It is a reduction of all our rights and freedoms to just one: the right to enter into a contract.

In his opinion for *Epic Systems*, Justice Neil Gorsuch asked, "Should employees and employers be allowed to agree that any disputes between them will be resolved through one-on-one arbitration?" It was a rhetorical question, but so revealing. The nation's workers don't often have the economic freedom to make this a real choice. Corporations don't seek to "allow" employees to enter into arbitration agreements, they *force* it on them by making it a condition of employment. The differential in power could not be more stark, and the unequal outcomes could not be more predictable.[34]

Privatization of public goods often amounts to a transfer of power from democratic government to private corporations. The public has less power when companies performing a public service hide information away as trade secrets. Elected officials lose control over public policy when their governments enter into binding contracts that demand payments if their preferred policy isn't followed. We all have our voices diminished when we support businesses that depend entirely on their ability to lobby governments to their side. We lose control over our very freedom when we give incentives to companies that profit from locking us up or keeping us on probation. Yet powerful people like Justice Gorsuch and conservative intellectuals like Stuart Butler are willing to let this all go in order to preserve the supremacy of the contract.

When the Contract Isn't King

For some, this process of hammering citizens with unbalanced contracts has gone too far. Private probation might be the tipping point. In Arkansas in 2016 two justices—Tommy Fowler and David Boling—ran for seats in the Craighead County, Arkansas, District Court on a promise: they would end the "debtors' prison" system of private probation in the county. Both had been appointed to fill vacant seats by the Republican governor, and had seen the problem from the inside.

Probation is not, Fowler told a reporter, "a money-making arm of the government." And yet, if it is privatized, "that's what's left." Their county had been using The Justice Network (TJN), a private probation company, to handle all misdemeanor probation cases for the county. As with other privatized probation, the probationer paid the company. With TJN, the county signed a contract that contained all manner of opportunities for the company to add additional fees and services. Failure to pay triggered an affidavit filed with the county court, which then invariably forced payment. This went on for twenty years—from 1997 to 2017.[35]

That's when Fowler and Boling brought the scheme to a halt. Insisting that only judges could set punishments, they started "purging" debt if they deemed it excessive and extended an "amnesty" program to start reconsidering TJN probations on a case-by-case basis.

At that point TJN, facing extinction, sued to "enforce their contract rights." The court, TJN claimed, had violated "its civil rights by illegally interfering with the contractual relationship Justice Network had with the probationers." They argued the contract was king because the Contracts Clause of the Constitution prohibits any law that "impairs" the "obligation of contracts." Apparently they believed that their contract with probationers superseded even the power of judges.

The U.S. district court and the Eighth Circuit Court of Appeals dismissed the suit on several grounds, the most important being that, plainly, the judges were doing what judges are supposed to do: "placing a defendant on probation, requiring a defendant to pay a probation fee, discharging a defendant from probation at the court's discretion, suspending the imposition of a defendant's fine, and modifying a defendant's condition of probation." These are public decisions that create conditions on freedoms. They are not decisions to be made with the bottom line in mind.[36]

The case had a good outcome, but the probationers in Craighead County would not have gotten out from under the system without the conscientious intervention of these two judges. The case did not challenge in any fundamental way the ability of a contract to wipe out our rights. And we wonder what the contract-minded U.S. Supreme Court might say about it, if it ever comes to that.

The conservative Supreme Court majority said quite a lot when it came to the arbitration cases. They seem perfectly willing to ignore the vast differences in power that make many of these contracts one-sided affairs, and they seem to believe that the government's main role is to protect the rich from the rest of us. That vision of a society governed by contracts rather than by democratic decisions depends on the unequal access to power that privatization helps create. Privatization, as it turns out, is the perfect tool because it not only limits democracy—it also generates and furthers inequality. The next chapters discuss how.

Part V

EVERY LAST DIME

Shredding the Social Safety Net,
Generating Inequality

ELECTRONIC BENEFITS TRANSFER (EBT) CARDS, WHICH OPERATE LIKE DEB-
it cards, replaced the paper coupons known as food stamps in 2002 and
became the default for public cash assistance. The cards were potentially
a great step forward: they are discrete, convenient, and flexible, and can
protect the user from theft and fraud. They can be used at many ATMs
and grocery stores. But they were introduced in an era that witnessed
both wholesale privatization and the ascent of the financial services
industry. So what should have been a better way to provide public assistance became yet another engine of inequality.

When the federal government switched to EBT it did not merely contract out to financial services companies to handle transactions; it passed
control over the system and its rules and management to some very
powerful players—J.P. Morgan, Xerox, and Fidelity National Information Services, for example. A state typically pays one of these massive
corporations a set price per beneficiary each month. New York went with
J.P. Morgan and paid the bank 95 cents per month for each beneficiary.[1]

And perhaps that's a fair price for an important service. But the cost to
EBT card users does not end there—the banks that run this game know
the value of a well-placed fee. Want to make a balance inquiry at an
ATM? Or to call the customer service line? For EBT holders these calls
or inquiries can cost 25 cents each, and it's withdrawn directly from the
user's account. There's often a fee just for placing the public money in
the beneficiary's account, and then there are fees—as much as $3—for
withdrawing that money as well. In Arizona, a baffling law put a $25 per
day limit on withdrawals, exposing recipients to even more fees along
with the inconvenience of making nearly daily trips to ATMs. These fees
are being charged against monthly benefit packages that can run into the
low hundreds (in 2020 the median TANF monthly benefit package was
$492). To a family trying to stretch their $300 benefit, the impact of these
fees is painfully present.[2]

Some of this, like the Arizona law, is due to lawmakers trying to make
things as hard as possible so public assistance recipients won't get too
comfortable (wouldn't want the safety net to become a hammock, they
grumble). But privatization takes it one step further. Not only do the

poor get punished, but someone with already astronomical riches gets a bit richer.

This is a blatant upward transfer of wealth, pennies at a time, from those living hand-to-mouth to those with the power and reach to turn those pennies into billions of dollars. In our society's widening division between the superrich and struggling working families, privatization actively generates schemes that exist primarily to take money from those who have the least and give it to those who have the most. When the public gives up control over public benefits, those programs become engines of inequality.

Fair and effective public assistance programs are public goods. They include benefits that prevent children from going hungry and a safety net that is available to all of us. They include prevention and intervention programs for veterans, the injured, and those experiencing homelessness. Public benefits include tuition assistance for those struggling to pay for college or job training; we all benefit when those students go on to create wealth, jobs, and innovations. Public benefits include Medicaid, which improves public health and welfare. All these forms of assistance are public goods because they benefit all of us, and because helping those with the least is the right thing to do.

At the same time privatization is shredding the safety net, it is also creating conditions for more people to have to rely on that same net. When a government outsources a service, employees end up with lower wages, fewer benefits (if any), and no union. But the executives of these government contractors almost always make astronomically more than public-sector directors and supervisors. The wealth, comprised of public funds, invariably moves up.

The gap between the victims of privatization and its wealthy beneficiaries couldn't be wider. Yet many of our antipublic politicians are eager to turn private corporations (both for-profit and nonprofit) loose on American families, knowing full well the likely result. And the private sector is likewise eager to be turned loose; there are fortunes to be made in poverty.

13

Teaching Them a Lesson
Privatization Versus the Poor

THE COMPANIES THAT BENEFIT FROM THE PRIVATIZATION OF PUBLIC ASSIS-
tance might be acting simply for their investors' returns, but the politicians who back these schemes are driven by a set of morals. They deny
that public assistance—poverty programs, health care, education, and the
like—is a public good and that poverty is a public problem. They deny
systemic factors like racism or scarce opportunities and say that the cycle
of poverty is a result of personal choices. Such stances informed much
of the 1996 welfare reform, which backed away from direct assistance
and let states divert money from direct relief to programs that promote
marriage and a work ethic. Often these programs are privatized—run by
private companies and nonprofits—and operate on the assumption that
those experiencing poverty just need a better family structure and a better attitude about work. It's all about sending Reagan's "welfare queens"
to finishing school.[1]

Such paternalistic programs made things harder for recipients, but they
are in a way the softer side of the 1996 welfare reform. The other side
consisted of strict time limits and drastically reduced direct payments,
and it was not just about saving money. According to a Giuliani-era New
York City commissioner, the goal was, as previously noted, to provoke
"a crisis in welfare recipients' lives, precipitating such dire prospects
as hunger and homelessness." Only then, presumably, would the needy
wean themselves from public funds. In 2020, no state provided a benefit
that raised a family above 60 percent of the poverty line. No benefits
package could cover rent on a two-bedroom apartment. Accounting for
inflation, thirty-three states provided benefits packages in 2020 that were
20 percent lower than they were in 1996.[2]

The nation's safety net has always been a prime target for those looking to limit the role of the public and diminish our public goods. Attacks
on welfare recipients themselves, often centered on their race and the
false notion that they take more in benefits than whites, are useful ways
to divide us. As a result, we are much less of a cohesive public, less able
to work together on these very problems. And whenever the public is set
aside, private interests step in, ready with the message that their draco-
nian treatment of those experiencing poverty is actually good for them.

Incentivizing the War on the Poor

Encouraged by the near-complete victory of welfare reform, several
states have turned to Medicaid as their next target. The best political
camouflage for defunding is to place it under the guise of fighting fraud,
and the latest incarnation—the HOPE Act—travels this well-worn path.
The HOPE Act professes to be "an Act to Restore Hope, Opportunity
and Prosperity for Everyone," but it offers no new program or innovation
to help the poor and the sick. It merely rewards private corporations for
removing people from public assistance and Medicaid.

This legislation, the brainchild of the Foundation for Government
Accountability, a conservative think tank, has made its way into at least
sixteen statehouses. By late 2020, five states—Tennessee, Arkansas,
Mississippi, Colorado, and Oklahoma—had passed a HOPE Act largely
faithful to the original. At least twenty-eight other states have taken up
parts of the bill. The HOPE Act outsources the laborious task of investigation and enforcement of Medicaid fraud, and then incentivizes these
for-profit companies by tying their payments to how much they reduce
caseloads. The fortunes of these companies utterly depend on how efficiently they deny medical care and public assistance.[3]

The real fraud is perpetrated by providers, like the chain of nursing
homes run by Philip Esformes, who was convicted of fraud involving
$1.3 billion in Medicaid and Medicare claims. He was just a few years
into his twenty-year prison term when President Trump commuted his
sentence. Medicare fraud by recipients is fairly rare, but the investigating
corporations supported by the HOPE Act states don't need to find much

actual fraud when they can rely on late paperwork. A typical feature of these bills is a ten-day deadline to provide personal information to the private contractor upon request; failure to do so is grounds for removal. The eligibility paperwork can be quite involved, and the contractor can be authorized to hammer recipients with reviews four times a year. The more they push people, the greater the chance that someone will slip up. And that incentive—payment tied to reducing the rolls—pretty much guarantees "investigations" on a large scale.[4]

Several states found that they might not actually save money running this program, but supporters are undeterred. "We see this as a moral issue in Tennessee," State Representative Dan Howell insisted. The Foundation for Government Accountability's Terrence Bragdon, an author of the model legislation, claims all his efforts are intended to "give more Americans the life-changing power of work." How does this apply to those who can't work but who are suddenly denied medical care because they missed a ten-day deadline? That's unclear. It is perfectly clear, however, that this is more a moral crusade than a well-considered policy decision.[5]

As such, it is part of a long history in America of putting sanctimonious morality above practicality when it comes to public assistance, and of a reliance on the private sector to instill the necessary morals in the poor. In this ongoing story, privatization has never been incidental.

Let Them Have Charity

In Brooklyn, New York, in 1876, crusading reformers convinced the city supervisors to stop giving relief to poor families and to point them toward private charities instead. This meant more than simply changing who provided the service. The city gave "outdoor relief"—food, coal, and direct payments. The private charities offered a stay in one of their poorhouses. Like the HOPE Act, the poorhouses promised to separate the worthy from the unworthy poor, root out fraud, and instill a work ethic. They also used largely private means, in this case private charities, to do so.

Private charities and nonprofits are an important part of our national safety net. They can also be diverted from serving as a complement to public assistance and become a way to deny the public its vital control over this public good. Sometimes the motivation is moral, sometimes it is greed posing as benevolence, and sometimes it is a bit of both.

The nineteenth-century poorhouses were residential facilities, largely privately run but often supported through a mix of private and public funds, with dual and often conflicting purposes: they were a place to teach values to the laggards, but they were also a place to help the "worthy" poor—those who were unable to work because of injury, old age, or some other reason that was no fault of their own. In practice, this distinction made little difference. All were subject to the same conditions, which were dire. "Common domestic animals are usually more humanely provided for" than poorhouse inmates, claimed a New York Senate commission. Despite the high-minded rhetoric, they were a place where the poor were sent to be punished.[6]

Compared to direct cash assistance, these institutions were not terribly efficient—one analysis found they cost almost four times as much—but since the issue was a moral one, not a pragmatic one, Brooklyn's supervisors decided to eliminate all outdoor relief. The benevolent societies would pick up the slack, separate the worthy from the unworthy, and pack the poorhouses.

The supervisors were committed to this project, which was one of several austerity programs that included cutting nurses' salaries and gutting a program to provide mosquito netting for orphans. Although several supervisors reconsidered when starving citizens surrounded and flooded their homes and offices, begging for food, most of them stood fast in the face of the humanitarian disaster literally on their doorsteps. Before long they declared victory. By weeding out the "frauds," caseloads dropped by 50 percent, and those receiving assistance did so under the moral guidance of the poorhouse.

But at the same time, the number of children in the orphanage shot up dramatically—55 percent by 1880. "Many families were obliged to break up," explained one report, "the parents or parent going to the poorhouse, and the children to the asylums for care, at the expense of the county." The cost of housing an orphan was some forty dollars a month; public assistance of four to eight dollars a month, the report's author claimed, "would have sufficed to keep them together in their own little homes."[7]

The poorhouses were inhumane, expensive, and full of contradictions, and the way they handed power to private interests made them prone to corruption. Often the local business leaders most in favor of doing away with direct relief were the same ones who would profit. In New York State, one early nineteenth-century investigation found that the responsibility for managing a poorhouse typically went not to a public servant but to a local merchant with connections to local farmers. From his commanding position, he could sell one or more poorhouses items from his own inventory at a substantial markup. Even worse, the requirement that inmates work for their room and board invited exploitation of their labor as well, with a private interest being "allowed to profit by all the labor which he could extort from the paupers," according to one critical examination.[8]

Shocking to modern sensibilities, the poorhouses have largely been forgotten, but their values and methods haven't gone anywhere. The HOPE Act similarly focuses on weeding out alleged fraud. Both depend on the idea that those experiencing poverty just need to discover the "life-changing power of work." Both remain blind to the consequences—a flood of children into orphanages or a denial of health care to those who really need it. And, most important here, both depended on private organizations to carry out their mission. This is key. In the conservative, anti-public imagination, only the private sector can fix poverty.

A Gift, Not a Right: The Denial of a Public Good

Remember the poorhouse when you hear today's advocates of slashing and privatizing the social safety net and their imagined history of utterly private poverty relief. In their story, America used to be universally prosperous and work was readily available. When that wasn't enough, the churches and community organizations pitched in (generally during emergencies). George H. W. Bush's "thousand points of light" was an example of this vision. Republican senator Mike Lee echoed the same ideas when he claimed, "From our very Founding, we not only fought a war on poverty—we were winning." And we were winning not with government, but with a "voluntary civil society." Poverty relief was a gift from the heart, not a government handout. When government took over during the New Deal, according to Lee, the war was lost.[9]

No serious historian thinks this conservative trope is true. Poverty programs, especially private ones, have never come close to "winning" and have never adequately addressed the need. The poorhouses never came close, and they were a far cry from the generous, caring visions put forth by Lee and Bush. The idea that there was once a golden age of nongovernmental poverty relief is pure myth, and it is incredibly dangerous.[10]

In 1931 the scope of the economic crisis that would become the Great Depression was already terrifyingly clear, but President Herbert Hoover resisted any relief program that did not "maintain the spirit of charity and mutual self-help through voluntary giving." Any hint of government assistance, and the nation would be "plunged into socialism and collectivism." So he tried to convince the Red Cross to help feed the poor and unemployed. Here he met with a resistance born of the American tendency to equate poverty with immorality. The Red Cross was set up to help only "those whose hunger resulted from a natural disaster" (or a war), and this was a key to their fundraising success; their donors wanted their money to go to only "worthy" causes.[11]

Democrats in Congress attempted to entice the Red Cross into action with $25 million for food relief. Republicans countered with an amendment delaying the appropriation until the Red Cross had a chance to raise $10 million on its own. This would be more faithful to the ideals of volunteerism and charity, but at what cost? By the Red Cross's own estimates, one million people were going hungry. But instead of passing an appropriation to fund relief, the Republican-controlled Congress opened an investigation on preserving the Red Cross's character. Republican House Majority Leader John Tilson asked, "Shall we stab [the Red Cross] to death and make it a cold, lifeless thing by substituting for it a governmental bureau, bound with red tape, administering a Federal dole?"[12]

Millionaire donors made their preferences clear. John D. Rockefeller promised $250,000, but played politics with people's lives by saying he'd take it all back if the Red Cross received *any* public money. Where the money came from was more important than feeding hungry citizens. This was "unaccountable stupidity," according to Democratic senator Thaddeus Caraway of Arkansas. "Everywhere we hear highbrows declaring their opposition to the dole, just as if a charity from the government is any more a dole than a charity through the Red Cross."[13]

Unaccountable stupidity this may be, but Caraway was missing why the Republicans and their business allies were so insistent. When public assistance comes from private sources it is charity; when it comes from the government it is a right. When it comes from wealthy benefactors it is moral and directed at the deserving; when it comes from the government it is corrupt and distributed indiscriminately. Charity preserves the top-to-bottom relationships of patronage; public benefits create side-to-side relationships between citizens. With so much at stake, the government had to be kept out of providing benefits, even if Americans starved.[14]

By 1934, even leaders who had initially opposed the "public dole," like Linton Swift of the Family Welfare Association of America, saw "a general recognition of the primary responsibility of local, state, and national government for the relief of unemployment and similar types of need." Yet still there remained a die-hard group that continued to believe private charity was the only way. And they are still with us today.[15]

The champions of letting private charity displace public benefits sing the same songs today that we heard in 1929–1932. They want the needy to prostrate themselves before wealthy benefactors and moralizing social programs, rather than accept them as neighbors and fellow citizens (and hardened racial attitudes make their job that much easier). They divide us by claiming we are a country of makers versus takers, and they have chipped away at the idea that everyone contributes.

Yes, everyone contributes. The unemployed in the Great Depression had fought a war, paid taxes to feed postwar Europe, and helped, through their labor, to earn fortunes for giant corporations. They had a right to expect that their government might help them in their time of need. Today, minimum-wage workers help create great wealth for executives and investors while making possible conveniences like two-day delivery and low, low prices at big-box stores; yet some leaders deny that these workers deserve help with health insurance. Single moms on TANF raise kids, but somehow aren't lauded for the work they do as parents. People injured at work and stuck on disability are treated as parasites because we somehow forget they were working up to the point where tragedy struck. Everyone contributes.

Erase the notion of makers and takers, and you're left with a set of reciprocal obligations and the realization that public benefits are a public good. As such, they should remain in public control. Removing public control unleashes profiteering, corruption, and ideologically driven inefficiencies—EBT cards that feed fees to massive banks instead of feeding children, private debt collectors that turn bounced checks and missed water bills into virtual debtors' prisons, private investigators incentivized to kick people off Medicaid however they can, or charities that refuse to feed the starving because they suspect some of them may have brought it on themselves.

14

Privatized Medicaid and the Business of Denying Care

As a public, we have largely embraced Medicare. Its beneficiaries are either our parents, our grandparents, or ourselves; broad privatization of this valued and successful program is politically fraught. But Medicaid—medical assistance for the needy—remains an attractive target for conservative politicians, and privatization is often how they take aim.

The 2009 Affordable Care Act, better known as Obamacare, offered states additional funds to expand Medicaid to a wider population by lowering the income threshold for eligibility, effectively giving coverage to more low-wage workers. By November 2020, thirty-six states had implemented the expansion and covered an additional 20 million Americans. Two states had approved the expansion but hadn't yet implemented it, and twelve states stubbornly refused. Senator Orrin Hatch of Utah summed up the rationale for states that left their own citizens uninsured: "You don't help the poor by continually pushing more and more liberal programs through."[1]

The senator's own constituents apparently disagreed; Utah was one of six states that passed Medicaid expansion through ballot initiatives, with the people overcoming the reluctance of their own conservative state and federal lawmakers who wanted all of Obamacare repealed. No ballot initiative to expand Medicaid under the ACA has lost. Americans support this, and are increasingly rejecting the idea that help with health care is a handout for "the poor." In fact, millions have used Medicaid—white, black, brown; adult children of middle-class families; people in rural areas and red states suffering from opioid addiction; and working people who didn't have employer paid health care and weren't paid enough to buy their own. In 2015, 43 percent of Republicans said they or their kids were covered by Medicaid or had been. The figure for Democrats was 40 percent.[2]

Yet the calls to repeal Obamacare have been as loud as ever. In a nod to the growing popularity of the ACA, the calls always came with a promise to replace it with something better. Rarely, however, has the repeal crowd actually provided a plan. The exception has been in places where conservative politicians adopted the long-standing ploy of undercutting a popular service through privatization.

Texas's privatized Medical Transportation Program is illustrative. The federal government requires a transportation program—a way to get people to appointments and treatments when they can't transport themselves—as a condition for receiving Medicaid funds, but Texas chose to grant regional monopolies and pay set rates to contractors that provided rides in a given area. The state could then step back almost entirely and simply write checks. The result, as summed up by the *Houston Chronicle*, was that the program served fewer people, cost more, and got worse: "The number of Medicaid recipients using the program has dropped from 350,000 to 150,000, the number of substantiated complaints has doubled, administrative costs have quadruped and the overall per-ride cost to the public has nearly tripled." Most disturbing was runaway growth in "administrative costs," which include things like executive salaries, from 11 percent of program costs in 2011 before privatization to nearly 48 percent of program costs in 2016. And again, this paragon of free-market efficiency was serving *fewer* patients, not more. "Administrative costs" is little more than privatization-speak for the transformation of taxpayer money into upward-moving wealth.[3]

Iowa (which accepted Medicaid expansion) and Kansas (where the governor vetoed it) utterly privatized and corporatized not only delivery of services but also administration of caseloads, including the power to deny treatments. Such examples represent a large-scale diversion of tax money and public benefits intended for the less fortunate to far-removed corporate interests, further elevating multimillionaires by pushing down the needy through denial of care and services.

Iowa privatized its entire Medicaid system in 2016 and serves as an extreme example of the far-reaching effects of taking a public good out of public hands. First to go was transparency. Open systems are a sign of mutual arrangements between citizens; Iowa's Medicaid privatization signaled from the start that it would not be like that. Bidders who wanted to take over this public service provided two very different versions of their proposals—one to be held in secret by top-level state decision-makers, and a heavily redacted one for public review. The redactions reached the level of the absurd, with one company refusing to release the name of its CEO, another redacting its entire two-page executive summary, and a third, without any apparent irony, blacking out its entire plan for "meaningful engagement" with the public.[4]

From these bids, Iowa ultimately picked four managed care organizations (MCOs)—Amerigroup Iowa, United Healthcare Plan of the River Valley, WellCare of Iowa, and AmeriHealth Caritas Iowa—to manage Medicaid patients, care networks, and the process of denying care. The state became a mere funnel for public money, and the MCOs quickly ended a half century of openness regarding appeals. A citizen could, before privatization, appeal to a state agency if care was denied. In the new system, citizens appealed to the for-profit MCO. In the old system, privacy was protected but appeals were a matter of public record. In the new system, they are trade secrets. Even the person making the appeal might not have access to all the information. One Des Moines resident told a reporter that Amerigroup, one of Iowa's MCOs, filed some seventy-eight exhibits against his wife, who had pancreatic cancer, to support their denial of treatment. He had been allowed to see none of them. These patients and their families are members of the public attempting to access information about a public service; since privatization they have been treated like hostile invaders. The proponents of privatization "seem to have forgotten Medicaid is a publicly funded program . . . accountable to the public," according to the *Register*'s editorial board.[5]

At the same time that MCO per-patient spending on actual care was going down—by as much as 28 percent—administrative costs were on the rise. Administrative costs as a percentage of the entire program shot up by 50 to 200 percent. That was not spending on patients—that was just to administer the program. That was precisely where the much-celebrated free-market efficiencies were supposed to come into play. Instead, these costs swung wildly in the opposite direction while patients saw their care slashed.[6]

"Administrative costs" is often privatization-speak for "executive salaries and perks." So how were the CEOs and executives doing, a lawmaker asked during a hearing in late 2016. The MCOs had been complaining that they weren't being paid enough. Any big raises planned? "We really just don't discuss those things in public settings," said AmeriHealth Caritas's president, Cheryl Harding. If she were a publicly employed administrator of a multibillion-dollar state program there wouldn't even be a question. We'd already know. Instead, in the face of this corporate opacity, we can take a look at the bigger corporate picture. Amerigroup Iowa feeds into Anthem, Inc., a publicly traded company. Anthem's key executives earned $22 million in compensation in 2015, and $37.4 million in 2017. During the same time, United Healthcare execs got a boost of their own, from $43 million in 2015 to $72 million in 2017. Anthem's outgoing CEO went from $13.6 million to $18.5 million, while United Healthcare's CEO saw an even bigger jump, from $11.5 to $17.3 million. Anthem paid $732 million in dividends to shareholders in 2017, while United Healthcare paid $2.8 billion. They claimed that their Iowa operations were hemorrhaging money, but at the same time they were cranking up their administrative costs, cutting per-patient expenditures, and sending their executive salaries further into the stratosphere.[7]

As those salaries rose, care declined. Under the old system, Nathan McDonald had regular at-home visits to help him cope with basic functions that his cerebral palsy prevented him from doing on his own. AmeriHealth cut his visits down to five per week. As the MCO's representative explained during a hearing, his basic hygiene needs weren't worth the cost: "People have bowel movements every day where they don't completely clean themselves, and we don't fuss over [them] too much. . . . You know, I would allow him to be a little dirty for a couple of days."[8]

For these corporate custodians of health care for Iowa's poor and disabled, denied care is profit. So while they will routinely push the limits on how dirty their patients can be or who deserves which treatment, they have also proven to be creative when it comes to tying up their customers in red tape. In April 2017, an administrative law judge pointed out that Amerigroup had waited until the last possible minute before informing a patient about the need to file a trivial piece of paperwork. Amerigroup then claimed the appeal could not move forward because the deadline had passed. The judge was not amused, calling it "a sort of 'gotcha' tactic employed by Amerigroup to avoid determining the underlying dispute on the merits," one that "runs afoul of basic due-process requirements." Iowa's long-term-care ombudsman noticed a "systemic" problem with how the MCOs engaged in appeals processes that took months, even when the deck was clearly stacked against them. After getting scolded by a judge, they would turn around and deny care again after just a few months: "This keeps the member in the appeal process." Summing up Iowa's new profits-before-people Medicaid landscape, the Iowa ombudsman reported that the MCOs' denials and endless appeals were "stubborn and absurd" and made "a mockery of the fair-hearing appeals process."[9]

Medicaid recipients in Iowa were not just being denied medical care; they were no longer citizens deserving of a voice and an appeal. They were now customers of a large corporation. This was a high cost, so what was the trade-off? What did Iowa save by privatizing? The numbers immediately fell into dispute. The governor's promise had been a savings of $232 million for fiscal year 2018. The first accounting of actual savings came out to $47.1 million. This didn't look very good, so the state's Department of Human Services director promised another look and came back with a shiny new number: $141 million in savings. Naturally lawmakers wanted to know how the new estimate of savings came to be nearly triple that of the old. A spokesperson clarified that this was a *cumulative* total of savings since implementation, not an accounting of annual savings. Then, the next day, the same person clarified the clarification. No, it really was annual savings. State Senator Pam Jochum was incredulous: "There is no way for us to verify the information they've provided." The head of an official advisory committee stated that the announcement "answers nothing." But in one respect, this shambolic revisionism was a success. Fighting over the exact number obscured the fact that the savings was not what was promised. And it obscured the fact that as a percentage of overall spending the savings was ridiculously small—somewhere between 0.9 percent and 2 percent, depending on whom you believed.[10]

Before long, AmeriHealth Caritas, which by 2017 had racked up over $1 million in penalties, pulled up stakes. Even after the state gave the three remaining MCOs yet another raise—$103 million more, not the sort of money you find "shaking the couch cushions," quipped one state senator—the massive corporation decided the profit margins in the Hawkeye State weren't what they'd hoped for. It had been the largest of the MCOs in Iowa, with over two hundred thousand patients, but its success in obtaining market share had not translated into sufficient profit margins. AmeriHealth announced its departure from the market on Halloween 2017. By the end of November it was gone, leaving as a parting gift over $14 million in unpaid bills, foisted on much smaller health care providers like locally owned medical supply companies, nonprofits, and the University of Iowa Hospitals and Clinics, which alone was owed some $1 million. Being forced to carry or write off that debt, which should have been paid from public funds received by AmeriHealth, will have a lasting effect on how well these smaller organizations can pay their own employees and provide care to needy patients. It's a particularly sad example of how these experiments can rarely be contained. Privatization failures like this have a way of spreading through the whole system.[11]

Making a profit from the most desperate is difficult, even when the government pays. Those fellow citizens who live on the margins, those in the lowest tenth in terms of income, spend some 35 percent of their pre-tax income on medical care. Those in the top 10 percent of income spend 3.5 percent. But that translates into $2,119 per year for those on the margins and $8,720 for those on the top. These stats speak to the rawness of our inequality; the level of care the top 10 percent enjoys is shockingly out of reach for the bottom 10 percent, who would have to more than quadruple what they spend to match what the upper echelons consider pocket change. Every time a politician hands public health care programs over to private-sector profiteering, it creates a greater burden on those least able to afford it. The obvious result is a group of people who are sicker and poorer, so it's convenient for politicians to do this in the name of the free market, efficiency, and consumerism. It absolves them. But it also gives wealthy corporations a license to radically transfer public funds from the most desperate citizens to their CEOs and shareholders, to push those who are down ever further down while using those pittances to gild the upper reaches of the plutocracy.[12]

15

What's in It for Wall Street

Public Assistance in the Hands of Big Finance

THE SAFETY NET IS FOR ALL OF US. MEDICAID IS THERE IF WE FALL INTO disability or illness. Ambulances are there if we need them. But it's a human tendency to not think about falling, so we are practiced in ignoring the nets below us. This makes them inviting targets for profiteering; the public will often go along, not noticing how the net has frayed. Unless we need its support, we are often too easily dazzled by promises of better quality at a lower cost, all thanks to the magic of the marketplace. We forget that the private sector is increasingly composed not of companies that make things or serve customers, but of financial institutions that raid businesses, acquire and exploit debt, and take advantage of the financial desperation of others.

Twenty-five percent of all active ambulance providers are now privately owned. That's a surprising statistic because for many of these private owners, having a monopoly on such an essential service has not turned out to be the cash cow they thought it would be. Both Transcare and First Med, private ambulance companies that attracted big investors from the world of private equity, failed to live up to the "tremendous growth potential" that brought the investment firms to their doors and fell into bankruptcy. Rural/Metro, the nation's largest private provider of fire and ambulance services, also went into Chapter 11, but emerged with new Wall Street investors and a new way to make emergency services profitable.

EMT service is not free, even when it's provided by a public agency, but local governments are generally restrained about collections. There will be unpaid bills and losses. That's the price of keeping the service universal and available. A private company, on the other hand, sees those unpaid bills as unpanned gold, and sees new billings as potential for growth. They move aggressively and decisively, and when they meet resistance they resort to collections agencies or burdensome lawsuits.

In San Diego, a reporter uncovered multiple cases where Rural/Metro didn't bother with regular billing—the first attempt at contact was from a collection agency. Rural/Metro also enlisted the help of its EMTs, who received training materials tasking them with obtaining signatures that approved massive charges and limited the patient's rights to appeal as the EMTs provided care. "Almost always, if the patient is alert, they will be able to sign," informed a comic-book-style handout. If they can't or won't sign, a family member or a nurse will. "They'll sign—because I won't give up," a jaunty Rural/Metro employee caricature claimed. Indeed, Rural/Metro rarely gave up. The *New York Times* easily found multiple lawsuits by Rural/Metro against its patients, demanding payments anywhere from hundreds of dollars to $59,000. A company like this has legal capacity and practice baked into its corporate structure, and won't hesitate to use it (the same goes for the Iowa MCOs, detailed in the previous chapter, that routinely take their own patients to district court when the administrative court doesn't go their way).[1]

To these savvy investors, public assistance is an opportunity to create revenues. Someone else's debt is their asset. Someone else's suffering is yet another opportunity. These investors are not philanthropists. And the moment they get involved, they fuel inequality by taking money from a public good and transforming it into private wealth.

"Monetizing Prevention" with Social Impact Bonds

Within our fraying web of public assistance, programs of prevention and intervention are perhaps the least maligned, but they are also the most underfunded. In addressing crime, for example, our antigovernment politicians often don't seem bothered in the least at paying for things like prisons and expanded police forces, but adamantly refuse to spend public money on programs to address the root causes. They'll often make an exception, however, if there's a nod to private or free-market solutions, such as when the money is funneled to a private nonprofit or is part of a social impact bond.

Social impact bonds (SIBs) are Wall Street's latest financial innovation. The first thing to know about social impact bonds is that they are not bonds. Bonds are a way for a government to borrow money at low interest rates. Social impact bonds (now often called "pay for success") are a way to entice private investors to fund social-welfare programs with the promise of repayment plus a high rate of return from the public coffers if the program succeeds. The investors lose money if the program fails. Between the government, the private bankroll, and the agency or nonprofit performing the service are organizations that oversee the money and the programming. There's an enormous level of complexity in these SIBs, but this is obscured by a promise of market-driven solutions. The resulting appeal has proven irresistible. Many say they are the future of philanthropy.

Republican and Democratic lawmakers have found the SIB concept to be common ground. Advocacy organizations as ideologically diverse as the Center for American Progress and the American Enterprise Institute have touted the concept as a virtual panacea. Money has flowed in from Bank of America, Merrill Lynch, Goldman Sachs, Northern Trust, and Bain Capital. The key role of the intermediary broker has been taken up by new organizations led by dynamic young disruptors. And in 2018, after gaining bipartisan support, Congress passed the Social Impact Partnerships to Pay for Success Act, which set aside $92 million for social impact bond programs. At least twenty-four states have started exploring or have launched SIB projects; eleven states have their own versions of the federal SIB legislation.[2]

One such program drew broad accolades when it launched in late 2018. Thanks to private capital, raised by the nonprofit SIB specialist Social Finance, 480 military veterans received individualized and intensive job counseling. Acknowledging the challenges faced by vets, a high-ranking Veterans Affairs official told reporters, "We're not just talking about employment but better health outcomes for PTSD sufferers. The hope is to change the trajectory of that veteran's life. . . . We are looking at this as a way to combat suicide." The VA had already piloted the program on its own and found that focusing on permanent placement in a career path, rather than on transitional work and rehabilitation, delivered results. Social Finance's SIB took up this program with a slightly larger group of veterans, and funded it with $5.1 million from BNP Paribas, Northern Trust, the Dakota Foundation, Deutsch Bank, and the Robin Hood Foundation. The program investors stood to collectively make all their money back, plus a bonus of nearly 18 percent, if a critical mass of veterans in the program showed sustained employment and increased earnings.[3]

The accolades that accrued to the program breathlessly described the innovative financing approach, the enthusiastic CEO of Social Finance, and the unavoidable claim of a win-win-win, but failed to ask some very basic questions and failed to note a disturbing moral question at the program's very center. We should, in evaluating such efforts, first ask ourselves why we need to go begging to big banks and offer them ridiculous returns on investment in order to take care of our veterans. Can we really not come up with $5 million to help people who served in our wars? And, since the VA brought it up, can't we come up with $5 million to help prevent our veterans from committing suicide?

Those are just two questions we have to ask. Here is another. The SIB was based on a pilot program, which was developed and undertaken in a public initiative. It had a proven success in a significant trial run. The SIB version is not really an investment risk for those big banks. So the VA effectively took out a *loan*—with an 18 percent premium tacked on—to run a social program. When the SIB craze hit Washington State, one of its state lawmakers, Ross Hunter, asked the key question: "If we have evidence to justify an investment, then why not put aside money for it?" Well, the typical rejoinder (which ignores how Hunter's question is a moral one as well as a fiscal one) is that SIBs are necessary because governments don't have money to put aside.[4]

But the claim that we can't pay for good programs without Wall Street backing is a lie. When governments enter into these programs they are making a promise to pay back the investors. And then they set aside a little more to help the wealthy investors make a tidy profit. (If you enjoy having a bitter taste in your mouth, consider also that tax breaks for wealthy investors are a driving factor behind why governments are so "limited" in their resources.) These investors are not going to settle for spare change, as Representative Hunter pointed out when he challenged an SIB education bill: "As a private investor, what kind of interest rate are you going to ask for? Eleven percent? Nine percent? By contrast, interest rates on revenue bonds can be as low as 4 percent. If early learning is a good idea, I can issue bonds to pay for it."[5]

Turns out Hunter's estimates of SIB investor returns were a little low. Investors are actually making much, much more. In Chicago, Goldman Sachs took up an SIB to expand a proven pre-kindergarten program to six schools. The mayor's office explained that the "CPS [Chicago Public Schools] and its teachers will manage the expanded program in these schools." The program would then expand to "additional schools." Here, Goldman Sachs is taking advantage of a proven program, experienced public employees, and an existing school infrastructure. It faces almost no risk because of a low bar for success and the fact that the public has already shown that pre-K works. Goldman Sachs invested $16.6 million, and it stands to make over $30 million on this deal—and that's money that will be paid by Chicago Public Schools.[6]

Why do this through an SIB? Early childhood schooling is something that has broad political support, a proven track record, and experienced public personnel. And yet our governments act as if they need to get Wall Street's permission to help their own citizens. A group of social services researchers—after detailing how SIBs have failed to deliver on their promises of innovation, cost effectiveness, and efficiency—concluded that they do, however, serve as "an illustration of the cultural supremacy of market principles into all aspects of everyday life, including politics and policy." These market principles include an unshakable faith in the idea that government can't do things—that it must be forced into disciplined spending and decision-making by outside actors from the private sector. And so it makes *perfect* sense for Goldman Sachs, which helped cause the 2008 financial crash through its lack of self-discipline, to instruct the public sector on how to produce results.[7]

What has this market discipline brought the social service sector so far? In the United Kingdom, where the idea was hatched, researchers were unable to find any appreciable savings from the SIB version in nine out of ten programs. In the United States, an evaluation by McKinsey & Company concluded that "SIBs are a more expensive way" to scale up programs. Advocates justify this additional cost by claiming governments won't pay when programs fail, so this extra money is a sort of insurance. But that's not quite right. According to an analysis of an SIB in New York that did fail, "The arrangement required considerable in-kind support from city government leaders and staff." These are real costs. The public was not insulated from paying for failure.[8]

The SIB scam also claims that private-sector mojo will impose increased efficiency and innovation. In the earlier child care and veterans examples, however, the "investment" was in a proven program. Most investors just don't like to take big risks, and so far almost no SIB projects have failed (and even the ones that did fail are touted as successes of the market). Investors have almost always won. Far from encouraging innovation, by introducing profit incentives social impact bonds stifle innovation. Economists have pointed this out, and so did the generally SIB-friendly Government Accountability Office when it noted, "In practice, investors told us they prefer to back programs that already have a rigorous evidence base because these programs have a known likelihood for success." And so too have frontline service providers: "If anything I would say less, there was less flexibility," one social service worker told a researcher. "Because the amount of management structures that are placed on an SIB mean that you have less maneuverability, you have to clear everything with this board to get permission to do anything."[9]

The SIB advocates are in a real bind when they use innovation as a justification. They color their PR and lobbying with the language of private-sector creativity, disruption, and boldness. But they need investors on board too, and this requires them to downplay the very things that got the policymakers and think tanks excited about SIBs in the first place. So while Tracy Palandjian, CEO of Social Finance, told a reporter that she thinks SIBs are best for "test cases," her nonprofit was running a veterans' SIB that *already had a test case.* And in an investor-facing publication, Social Finance's COO, Steve Goldberg, pitched SIBs for the institutional investor, assuring them that the projects would include only "a very select group of social programs that have the strongest irrefutable evidence of effectiveness. . . . If you have rock solid evidence, then a commercial investor can satisfy itself that these are manageable risks." Innovation in social programs has always come from people on the front lines who actually care about the people they are serving. It comes from commitment to service, and from listening to those served. Innovation will never come from those looking to make a safe investment and a high rate of return.[10]

Real innovation requires solid data collection and evaluation, and here again the SIB advocates assume that the private sector will be able to school the public sector into more disciplined behavior. Paying for success means establishing a definition of success and measuring outcomes against that standard. When providers and researchers have this discussion, they are looking for answers. When investors get involved, they are looking for returns on investment. "You're definitely creating incentives that would be considered corruption pressures," the head of the Minnesota Council of Nonprofits, which had participated in SIBs, told a reporter. The same reporter talked to a juvenile justice caseworker in Massachusetts who received, in the reporter's words, "constant phone calls from an investment bank encouraging him/her to have the metrics turn out . . . so that the bank would earn the maximum amount possible."[11]

And sometimes the profit motive gets baked right into the program design. In Utah, Goldman Sachs claimed that it hit a home run with its early childhood program geared toward children who were at risk of needing special education interventions. At the end of the program cycle, 99 percent of children served did not end up requiring special education, and the bank started collecting on each child in that group. To early childhood professionals, that success rate seemed odd. In fact, some of the kids were simply sent to already existing day care centers or to the YMCA. "They seem to have either performed a miracle," one researcher told the *New York Times*, "or these kids weren't in line for special education in the first place." As it turned out, the program determined if kids were at risk by using a screening test that experts said was not designed for that purpose. The Goldman Sachs program quite possibly didn't really start with an at-risk population and didn't really intervene in anything, but the bank got away with it. The first of many payments from the state was delivered on time, and Utah will likely pay much more than if it had financed the project using a traditional bond.[12]

"We're basically trying to monetize prevention," Tracy Palandjian quipped. And those under the spell of SIBs see no ethical problem with a giant bank making oceans of money because a mother didn't take drugs or veteran didn't commit suicide, even if there are cheaper ways to help. We should never lose sight of the fact that every SIB dollar diverted to a bank is a dollar that doesn't go into the public service. It's an upward transfer of public funds. What's more, there's real danger in turning citizens into commodities and seeking validation from Wall Street for our humanitarian efforts, and even SIB advocates have seen some of the holes in their own arguments. Palandjian, in a candid moment that her investors will not appreciate, said that SIBs are the "second best solution" for addressing social issues; government funding is actually the better choice.[13]

The rise of social impact bonds fits a pattern. Throughout our history, private interests have worked to separate the worthy from the unworthy poor and to reinforce the idea that assistance is charity—a benevolence from on high—not a right and a responsibility that we should bear as citizens. Social impact bonds and pay-for-success models are, far from being innovative and disruptive, simply a slightly altered means to the long-standing goal of putting the private sector in charge and sidelining the public while separating citizens from government and from each other.

Privatized Student Loans: America's Inequality Engine

Ronald Reagan's Office of Management and Budget director, David Stockman, helped kick off the great public divestment from higher education in the 1980s. Improving access to higher ed, he said bluntly, "isn't a proper obligation of the taxpayer." Rather, "if people want to go to college bad enough" they should scramble through "the best way they can." For ever-increasing numbers of students, the "best way they can" was really limited to one option—student loans. As Reagan slashed taxes for the nation's top earners, he also slashed spending on higher ed and student aid by 25 percent between 1981 and 1985, even as his own secretary of education, Terrel H. Bell, marveled at how he "could not fathom" the administration's refusal to fund student aid while it gladly funded "subsidies for growing cancer-causing tobacco." But this was just one part of a larger story. States took a knife to higher education as well. In 1975 they funded 58 percent of the total national cost of higher ed. Now it's 37 percent. One study calculated the total loss of public funds to higher education from 1980 to 2016 at $500 billion.[14]

Stockman's denial of taxpayer "obligation" was a denial that higher education is a public good and a legitimate part of public assistance. He and his allies were utterly successful in shifting the costs of higher education onto individuals, primarily affecting those without the means to afford it. In 2020 total student debt stood at $1.6 trillion. When Reagan paid for tax cuts for the wealthy by cutting assistance to higher education it was a direct upward transfer of wealth, one that has had lasting effects on working families and the middle class. In 1977 about one-third of students graduated with student loans. By 2018 it was 65 percent overall, and 75 percent among those graduating from private nonprofit schools. The exception had become the rule. Further amplifying the wealth transfer and intergenerational theft was the fact that banking and finance companies got to take a cut. They had been on the scene since the 1960s, and each new regulation and reform of the student loan system up until 2010 seemed to make it a little easier for them to take a little more.[15]

President Lyndon Johnson insisted that "this nation could never rest while the door to knowledge remained closed to any American," but the Higher Education Act of 1965 opened financial doors to private interests due to an accounting gimmick. Direct loans from the government to students were expenditures; they counted as government spending. Loans made by private banks but *guaranteed* by the government didn't appear at all, unless the borrower defaulted and the government had to pay the bank. For conservatives it was a way to impose a veneer of shrinking government. For banks it was an unbelievable risk-free opportunity, one worth building upon. They have been doing so ever since, at a great social cost.[16]

Their next big windfall came in 1972 with the creation of the Student Loan Marketing Association—Sallie Mae—which took the burden off the banks even further by purchasing student loans from them. It was now possible for private banks to loan money, sell those loans to the quasi-governmental Sallie Mae, and then recycle that money to loan it out again. Profits rose, and as more money magically appeared in the system, the education budget cuts of the Reagan years looked even more viable.[17]

After George H.W. Bush signed a law banning the federal accounting quirks that brought in the banks, his administration made the obvious determination that direct loans from the government would be far cheaper. He even started a pilot program. But by this time the system had taken on a life of its own and had in fact become a powerful special interest. When Clinton tried to expand on Bush's commonsense plan he met with furious Republican opposition. In 1994 the new GOP majority pushed to wipe out Clinton's modest and phased-in conversion to direct loans and bring back the middleman. All this came, once again, wrapped in the language of free markets, efficiencies, and choice. None of these were actually present.[18]

The two sides arrived at a compromise in 1996, one that would upend the higher education landscape and help ruin thousands of lives. The direct loan program was allowed to survive but had to compete with a newly liberated Sallie Mae. Now fully privatized, Sallie Mae was allowed to purchase not just loans but entire companies. It could set up an internal collections shop and handle servicing. It could charge fees. More consequential, it could now originate loans that were guaranteed by the government. Most consequential of all, it could make its very own *private* loans with high interest rates, not backed by the government, and targeted at the same students who were taking out the government-backed loans.[19]

If you wonder whom this might benefit, look to the sudden influx of investment banks and private equity—J.P. Morgan, Citigroup, Chase, Bain Capital—into the formerly staid world of student loans. From their perspective there were only two problems with the new landscape, only two obstacles that stood between making piles of money and making truly monumental piles of money. One, the government was still able to make direct loans, and was now a competitor, and two, it was still possible (although difficult) for a student-loan borrower to discharge her debt through bankruptcy.[20]

The industry racked up millions in lobbying fees to address these issues. The results speak for themselves: a 1997 law gagged the Department of Education—no longer could it advocate for its own loan program or market its services to colleges and universities. While the federal government remained silent, Sallie Mae and others aggressively marketed their loan products to schools. Then the few remaining bankruptcy loopholes were quietly closed. New tough standards, coupled with aggressive legal tactics by the student loan companies, have made the forgiveness of student debt a rare event.[21]

The for-profit student loan industry, now led by Sallie Mae, entered the twenty-first century emboldened by these new laws, empowered by capital investment, and encouraged by the solidly Republican government. The result was an unregulated fleecing of America's youth. The first target was market share. Something had to be done about the government's cheap and convenient direct loans. So student loan companies, according to several investigations, started paying colleges and universities what amounted to kickbacks. Financial loan officers got seats on Sallie Mae advisory boards. The schools received payments and sometimes stock options according to the number of private, nonguaranteed loans they helped guide into private hands. "Egregious," New York governor Andrew Cuomo called it, but this shady practice couldn't compare to another scheme whereby the student loan company would set up call centers for school financial aid offices and staff them with their own salespeople. In a carefully laid trap, a student calling the school with questions about financial aid would be stealthily routed to a student loan call center and given a pitch on the loan company's products. Only after a lawsuit by the state of New York did Sallie Mae require its operators to identify themselves as Sallie Mae employees.[22]

The private loans, not backed by the government, offered high interest rates and strict terms, and they were made to teenagers and to adults embarking on career changes, most often without collateral. They were the very definition of subprime, and they defaulted at a rate of 50 to 92 percent a year between 2000 and 2007, dragging those who took out the loans into a financial undertow at a vulnerable time in their lives. According to documents uncovered in a lawsuit, Sallie Mae was perfectly aware that its customers were woefully underinformed about these predatory loans. Sallie Mae made 165 loans in this category in 2000, but in 2006 it made 43,000. The reason for this increase (26,000 percent), in spite of the high rates of nonpayment, lay in a Sallie Mae strategy spelled out in internal documents. These predatory subprime loans might fail, but they were primarily there to "win school deals" and secure the government-backed loans. Sallie Mae's own documents described them as a "baited hook" for the larger and more lucrative fish—the guaranteed loans that would come once schools came to depend on Sallie Mae money, rather than on direct loans from the government, to cover their mushrooming tuitions.[23]

Finally, perhaps the most unsavory side of this sordid tale is the predatory symbiosis that grew between for-profit colleges and lenders like Sallie Mae. The for-profit colleges served low-income populations, and most of their revenue depended on the free flow of government-backed loans. However, laws were still in place that prohibited them from making more than 90 percent of their income from federal aid and loans. Many for-profits were in danger of crossing this line. Sallie Mae was their savior, because it could help guide students into nonguaranteed subprime loans and keep the for-profit schools under that 90 percent. At least one for-profit, Career Education Corporation, saw such a benefit to Sallie Mae's subprime loans that it agreed to cover 20 percent of the loan giant's losses from 2002 to 2006. Then, it upped the ante to 25 percent.[24]

Those costs had an upside for Career Education, but in real-world terms it meant students were drowning in debt. Those painful stories have been repeated and reported on extensively; they would fill volumes. We all have heard, often from our close friends, about how their lives have become beholden to their monthly payments. They have deferred marriage, children, mortgages, and start-ups indefinitely, possibly for good. The real tragedy behind all of these stories is that the victims were believers in hard work and education as a means to get ahead, but their lives were foreclosed by a quick-and-dirty scam that they didn't even know existed.

In 2010 President Barack Obama succeeded in getting legislation passed that got rid of the costly, inefficient, and ultimately immoral practice of letting banks make loans guaranteed by the government. In doing so, he saved the government an estimated $68.7 billion. Sallie Mae divided itself after the 2008 crash, and the lending operation lives on as Navient; it is fighting several lawsuits and repackaging pre-2010 loans as asset-backed securities that it sells on Wall Street. After Donald Trump's electoral victory, Navient accelerated its lobbying efforts, spending $4.2 million on influence campaigns in Congress in just the first half of 2017.[25]

Student loan companies still haven't gotten their most fervent wish—a return to the wasteful and graft-producing days when the government made no direct loans—but the Trump administration provided ample opportunities for profiteering. FedLoan Servicing is a private corporation that manages government loans. Each active loan in its portfolio earns the company service fees. Therefore, the program that allowed teachers, government employees, and workers at nonprofit charities to have their loans forgiven after years of service and payments meant fewer customers and was a direct threat to FedLoan's bottom line. FedLoan, however, got to decide who qualified for the forgiveness program, and it rejected 99 percent of the applications it received. Education Secretary Betsy DeVos bent over backward to revise regulations in FedLoan's favor, and Trump's Justice Department tried to block a lawsuit by the Massachusetts attorney general over this very issue. Team Trump was persistently loyal. In no case concerning student loans did those in charge of Trump's education policy ever take the side of the student.[26]

Two out of three students have to borrow, and one out of four of those are, on any given day, behind on their payments. Student loan debt surpassed debt owed on autos and credit cards in the wake of the 2008 market crash, and has rocketed skyward ever since. And much of this debt can never be discharged. Unlike auto loans and credit card debt, student loans are supposed to be akin to taking out an investment. They were supposed to lead to future higher earnings. This promise is the only reason the student loan companies and for-profit colleges have been so successful, and it once was largely true. Higher education was supposed to work against inequality and lead to rapid wealth creation, but this promise has, especially since 2008, largely failed.

"People who do have skills haven't been getting wage increases," notes economist Marshall Steinbaum. "Even in sectors like tech and engineering, nobody is getting raises. The only people who do get raises are in the top 1 percent." Steinbaum and like-minded economists question whether the skills gap is really a driver of inequality. Rather, they point to low taxes: "We aren't seeing more job creation because taxes are too low. There are more incentives now within corporations to send money to shareholders and rake in profits, rather than expand operations and give raises to workers." Those low taxes also mean more student loans and less direct support. A Pell Grant used to cover 72 percent of a tuition bill for a needy student. Now it covers on average 34 percent.[27]

So, in essence, we cut funding for higher education and incentivize private student loans so we can give corporations and billionaires tax breaks, which leads to more privatized student debt, which means more money going to big banks and private equity. And those tax breaks disincentivize job creation, so those who borrow earn lower salaries at the same time that a larger share of their incomes goes back to paying their student loans.

This is the inequality engine; it is not a natural result of hard work or good luck on one side and shiftlessness or bad luck on the other. It is a self-perpetuating consequence of neglecting public goods and placing them in private hands.

16

Privatizing Pays Us Less

FOR MANY AMERICANS, THE MOST VISIBLE SAFETY NET IS ONE THAT TIES them directly to employers, who control their health insurance and sometimes their pensions. It is a net that is always in danger of being whisked away, as tens of millions of Americans found out when they lost their jobs in the early months of the 2020 pandemic.

When union membership was the norm in the private sector, in the 1950s and early 1960s, the public decided that public servants would get a stronger version of this frail safety net even before public workers secured the right to collectively bargain. Public-sector jobs, even low-paying ones, came with decent benefits. This was practical—it helped attract and retain workers, and it boosted the economy by giving the middle class a stable core—but it was also the right thing to do. Public servants make all our public goods possible.

Privatization dismantles this corner of the safety net and transforms it into ludicrous executive salaries. Carol Sanders used to make $15 an hour as a cafeteria worker in the New Orleans public school system, where she had twenty-eight years of experience. Then the food service giant Aramark claimed it could improve efficiency and save the district money; what they really had their eyes on were wages and benefits. Aramark won a contract, Carol saw her pay cut to $9 an hour, hours cut in half, and benefits stripped. She went on food stamps to survive. Not long after, Aramark cut her position. A year or so later, Aramark CEO Eric Foss raked in $18 million in compensation.[1]

A New Jersey study on the effects of privatization on people like Carol found her case was not unique. Of all the state's employers, food-service contractors had the highest percentage of employees on Medicaid. So as we privatize and help transform living-wage salaries into starvation-level salaries, and as the cost savings are channeled into CEO bonuses, we are left picking up the tab through taxes for additional Medicaid recipients.[2]

In Chelmsford, Massachusetts, school district custodial jobs went from $19 per hour before privatization to between $8.25 and $8.75 after privatization. In Milwaukee, Wisconsin, housekeepers earned between $14.95 and $15.75 before privatization. After privatization they earned $8.00 per hour with no benefits. In Grand Rapids, Michigan, privatization took nursing assistants from between $15 and $20 per hour down to $8.50 per hour (while the contractor billed the state at $14.99 per hour). And the list goes on.[3]

Through similar privatization arrangements the U.S. federal government has become the largest low-wage employer in the country. A 2013 study estimated that at least two million Americans who work for government contractors earn less than $12 dollars an hour. As the study's authors pointed out, "This is more than the number of low-wage workers at Walmart and McDonald's combined." A follow-up study in 2018 concluded that 4.5 million government contractors were making less than $15 per hour. This included textile workers who make uniforms, health care workers who look after Medicaid patients in nursing homes that thrive on Medicaid dollars, construction workers who complete government-funded projects, and janitorial workers, like Guadalupe Rodriguez, who works in Union Station, a federal property just a few blocks from the U.S. Capitol. "For 19 years I have cleaned this building, yet I only get $8.75 an hour—without any benefits," she told researchers. "I hope the company I work for would offer me health benefits someday."[4]

Guadalupe Rodriguez works for us. She may have a private contractor as a buffer, but we the public have failed to ensure that those who serve us through contractors earn living wages and at least minimal benefits. Privatization allowed the public to turn its back on her and others under the guise of smaller government.[5]

It's not just the low-wage jobs. Privatization devalues trained professionals as well, and it happens even in organizations with nonprofit status and a social justice image to maintain. In 2019 Cesar Chavez Public Charter Schools in Washington, DC, abruptly closed Chavez Prep Middle School, reportedly because it was time to "monetize the asset." The school was not underenrolled or underperforming, compared to the other schools in the Chavez network, but it was unique in that it was the first unionized charter school in DC.[6]

Charter school teachers in DC make about 12 percent less than their peers in traditional public schools. They grapple with high staff turnover rates—26 percent on average in 2017, with about one-fifth of the city's charter schools seeing attrition rates of 60 percent or more and one-tenth at or over 80 percent. Cesar Chavez PCS saw about half its teachers leave in 2016–2017. But the teachers who stayed and unionized didn't demand more money for themselves. The newly organized Chavez employees said that "administrative costs" at their school had soared by 36 percent between 2013 and 2017, while "student-facing services" went up only 2 percent. As noted in previous chapters, the phrase "administrative costs" does a lot of work in privatization contexts. In this case, the teachers alleged, the school pumped $5.3 million into a four-year contract with TenSquare, an outside for-profit consulting company that had a history of delivering questionable results. The teachers wanted more of these "administrative costs" to flow toward actual learning.[7]

Soon after, the Chavez network announced that it was facing a $5 million gap in its budget. What would the great union organizer Cesar Chavez have done? Likely he would not have "monetized" the only "asset" that had an active union. But privatizing organizations, even ones that appropriate the names and images of legendary activists for justice, are never so restrained. Typically the only way they can run a formerly public service while continuing to pay high CEO salaries and millions in consulting fees is to attack their own employees. They cut salaries, kill unions, and create high turnover so their labor force remains less experienced and less able to demand better pay.

Meanwhile, even as the charter system in DC undervalues and underpays charter school teachers, those at the top of the charter school pyramid are earning exceptionally high salaries compared to the leadership of the public school system. Each of the District's 125 charter schools has a mini-chancellor who essentially duplicates the efforts of all the other charter school leaders and who can't take advantage of the economies

	Leader salary	Students	Annual compensation per student
DC Public Schools	$280,000	47,500	$5.89
University of Texas System	$1,500,000	221,337	$6.78
KIPP DC	$257,000	6,300	$40.79
Friendship Public Charter Schools	$355,000	4,200	$84.52
AppleTree Learning Center (preschool–K only)	$231,000	2,000	$115.5

While charter school teachers in Washington, DC, made 12 percent less than their public school counterparts in 2019, administrators often made more even while serving fewer students, and generally make much more when compared on a per-student basis. Included here, for comparison, is the chancellor of the University of Texas system, one of the best-compensated officials in public education. On a per-pupil comparison (last column on the right), DC charter school administrators win hands down.[8]

of scale offered by the traditional school system. Add up all their salaries, typically in the six-figure range, and a clear picture of how charter schools wastefully sap resources starts to come into view.

Privatization, whether of a school or a school's food service, embraces the key ethos of corporate America that lavishes rewards on CEOs by cutting salaries and benefits for others. A high level of turnover is not just acceptable; it is beneficial. Unions must be destroyed, and assets must be monetized. This is not just an attack on those who make our public goods possible—it is a further transformation of our patchwork safety net into upward-flowing wealth.

The Public's Role in Ending Inequality

There's a widespread assumption out there, reinforced by those at the top, that inequality is quite simple. Some earn more, some earn less. Some rise to the top through a combination of luck and hard work; others will never make it. It's a side effect of the market, they say, part of the cost of freedom.

Inequality is not an accident or a side effect or the result of an invisible hand. A significant portion of our inequality is driven forward by deliberate policy decisions that channel wealth from the poorest to the richest. This is insidious and depressing, but it also means the public can stop it.

When we say that inequality can be ended, we do not mean that everyone will be rich or everyone will be middle class. Inequality is not merely about salary; it is about power and access to public goods. In a democracy, these things can be made equal, and dismantling the privatized superstate will get us a long way toward that goal.

If the U.S. government were to enforce a living wage for the people who do its work through contractors, it would have an enormous effect. Local governments and state legislatures across the country have passed ordinances and statutes that require a living wage and paid sick time for millions of workers who serve the public but work for contractors. Some go further and extend those requirements to private companies who receive economic development subsidies or grants of public land. And in a 2021 executive order, Joe Biden fulfilled his promise for a $15 federal minimum wage, one that gave a raise to the federal contractors working at the $10.10 minimum set by an Obama executive order.

If we made it possible for students to go to college without mortgaging their futures and enriching banks, that would have incalculable benefits. If we stopped private businesses and investment banks from monetizing the social safety net, we could spread public goods even further, at less cost.

To get there, we will have to reconfigure the public debate. Right now, with the idea that inequality is just about money and some simply haven't earned it, we are stuck. We look at the less fortunate as largely responsible for their own plights, and ignore the fact that their own governments, which are supposed to protect their rights, have instead given those with means a road map on how to drive the less fortunate further down. We let them put obnoxious fees on EBT cards, buy liens on houses because of overdue bills, incentivize private investigators to kick them off Medicaid, cajole them into subprime student loans, and sue them for private ambulance rides. We talk about their individual responsibility for their own decisions, ignoring the fact that when we privatize public goods we create destructive mechanisms that no amount of individual responsibility can overcome. And we have seen where the profits from such mechanisms go.

Changing the conversation means speaking once again about access to public goods as a right, not as charity. It means recognizing that everyone contributes. In some way, everyone contributes. We are not divided up between makers and takers. We all give something, and we all have a right to public goods, granted by our fellow citizens through a democratic process, in return.

Part VI
THINGS IN COMMON
Privatization and the Erosion of Community

Privatization drives economic inequality, but it also drives a wedge into the very idea of community by creating differences in how we access public spaces—like parks and libraries—and public services such as Social Security and public education. Universal access is the very point of these public goods, but the profit motive and free-market thinking simply cannot abide the idea of treating everyone equally.

Some public state parks, starved for funds, have transformed access into a luxury product. They appeal to a supposedly higher class of customers by offering "glamping"—roughing it with a bit of glamour. Some state parks can charge upward of $250 a night for a pre-pitched tent that comes with air-conditioning, flat-screen TVs, and Wi-Fi, of course. Gourmet meals cooked for you on your campfire and coffee delivered to your tent flap are extra.

Nothing wrong with being pampered, even in the great outdoors, but glampers are competing with campers, and they are paying ten times more. In Moran State Park in Washington, in the San Juan island chain, some of the best sites have been set aside and reserved well in advance by those who can afford it, while those who can't rush to fill what's left. And the state park isn't even getting the lion's share of the profits. It hired a private firm familiar with highbrow tastes to tend to the needs of these new patrons.[1]

This is a familiar pattern to anyone who has watched the decimation of state budgets. States can't (or, more appropriately, won't) pay for something, so they make it fee based. Then private interests come in and promise reduced costs to the government. But they do this by staggering the fees, adding premium services, and creating a tiered system whereby a public good that was once distributed equitably becomes an out-of-reach luxury for the very few.

The privatization of public space has a dark history that remains with us and bursts into the open on a disturbingly regular basis. Video taken at a private pool in 2015, of residents and police officers verbally and physically abusing black teenagers who had been invited to a party in McKinney, Texas, reminds us of where this leads. McKinney has three public pools. None of them are in the wealthier section of town. These wealthier residents strongly prefer to limit access and are willing to pay for pools in their gated communities but have deep hostility to taxes that would pay for anyone else's. Their choices feed an isolation that emphasizes difference. When they see black teenagers at their pool, they feel no empathy or toleration, and instead tell them to go back to their Section Eight housing. They feel justified because it is "their" pool. This can only draw lines, and in 2015 in McKinney they turned out to be racial ones.

Philosopher Bonnie Honig describes how parks, infrastructure, and other "public things," as she calls them, "press us into relations with each other," but she would also like us to dig further. Bringing us together physically is almost the least of it. Public things underpin democracy itself: "Without public things, action in concert is undone and the signs and symbols of democratic life are devitalized. . . . Without such public things, democracy is reduced to procedures, polling, and policing, all necessary, perhaps, but certainly not sufficient." When the people of a democracy have nothing held in common, "there is nothing to occasion the action in concert that is democracy's defining trait."[2] It is not enough that we have parks or places to gather. They have to be public. When segregationists kept black people out of "their" public spaces, it wasn't just about avoiding people they didn't like. They did it to ensure that the excluded others would not become part of their community, to ensure they would remain alien and less than full citizens.

Public space is our most visible and contested element of community, and so is a focus of this section, but many of our examples could have been presented in our chapters on democracy, inequality, or education just as well. These things work together—or they can, given enough public control and inclusion. Social Security, for example, is a function of community. Its universality unites people even as it lessens inequality. Public schools create communities not only of children but also of their parents and even the childless adults nearby. Local libraries inevitably become community hubs, while presidential libraries can, if imbued with enough public control and neutrality, reveal our common history.

Privatization has clear material and systemic effects. It drains public resources and rearranges public institutions. But this section is also about feelings. Privatization affects these as well. Having a nation and living in a community is as much about thoughts and emotions as it is about structures. It involves sensing a common history, conjuring a set of connections, and feeling empathy for strangers. Privatization has a way of undermining all of these by turning us into rival consumers of our public goods, leaving us with a society that's less like the local library and more like Black Friday.

17

Public Places

Parks, Presidents, and Privatization

BEFORE AMERICANS HAD PARKS, THEY GATHERED WHERE THEY COULD. "I have never been long in any one locality, south or north, east or west," wrote the pioneering landscape architect Frederick Law Olmsted in 1870, "without observing a custom of gregarious out-of-door recreation in some miserably imperfect form, usually covered by a wretched pretext of a wholly different purpose, as perhaps, for instance, visiting a grave-yard." Public parks just weren't all that common, so people made do: "Sometimes it is a graveyard, sometimes a beach or wharf, sometimes a certain part of a certain street" but overall, there was in the nation "scarcely a finished park or promenade ground deserving mention."[1]

Parks as we know them did not just happen; they were not bestowed upon us by private industry or the founding fathers. They are one of those public efforts like the creation of waterworks, food safety, a social safety net, and democracy itself, things that would not exist, or would exist only for a fortunate few, if the public had not acted.

While most plans for Central Park modeled themselves after Versailles or some other stately manor, Olmsted and his longtime partner Calvert Vaux looked to evoke nature in the midst of a dense city, and to "induce a sense of freedom and a disposition to ramble." While there was room for some "elegant buildings" in a park, they should be "subservient" to the main idea—that this is a public space: "The idea of the park itself should always be uppermost in the mind of the beholder." Visitors should know that they are in a park, and that the park is theirs.

What's more, Olmsted thought that the park should "produce a certain influence" on its visitors, and that "the character of this influence is a poetic one." While it is also true that Olmsted designed his parks to prove that the public can do great things, to show how a public park is different from an aristocratic garden, and to lessen class strife by bringing people together, they were also designed to provide beauty, a poetic influence. This is something that private recreational spaces typically fail to do. Disneyland can bring joy, but it is not exactly a place of beauty. Stadiums can rally a city around a sporting event, but their structures are far from exerting a poetic influence. America's public parks, designed with the public in mind and designed to emphasize freedom and access, have excelled at creating beauty ever since Olmsted and Vaux set the standard in midtown Manhattan in the 1860s.[2]

A Public Park and a Privatized History

Toward the end of Olmsted's career, he served as landscape architect for the storied 1893 World's Columbian Exposition in Chicago, one of a string of world's fairs. The site, on the South Side of Chicago, had recently become public after a protracted struggle with the Illinois Central Railroad, and in a landmark case the U.S. Supreme Court had ruled that the land was held in public trust: when the people have an overriding interest, the public trust cannot be frittered away. Yet the land itself was not much to look at. Olmsted discovered in the early 1890s a poorly planned and "extremely bleak" park of half-completed piers and "barren sand dunes" left behind by the railroad. He conceived of a great landscape of lagoons and wetlands leading into the exposition, which itself would emphasize water. But Jackson Park would also be separate from the World's Fair, offering a "mysterious poetic effect" in contrast to the fair's grandeur. In keeping with his previous designs, there would be little architecture so that "the idea of the park itself should always be uppermost in the mind of the beholder." As a "public thing," in Honig's sense of the phrase, Jackson Park stands out. It was guaranteed by the doctrine of a public trust, designed by a landscape architect who used parks to promote democracy, and emphasized nature rather than architecture to give visitors a sense of freedom and permission to ramble.[3]

The park's history, the original intent of its designers, and the way it was wrested from the railroad companies all made it an odd choice for the location of the Barack Obama Presidential Center. In a deal cut with the city, the University of Chicago and the Obama Foundation will acquire a lease on nineteen acres of the park for ninety-nine years for a cost of $10. On this land they will build an imposing multistory building. And of course a parking lot. These private entities will have exclusive rights to the parking fees in order to maintain the space, which they will also control. The swift move by the City of Chicago garnered stiff opposition by conservation groups and divided the University of Chicago faculty—two hundred of them signed a letter protesting the plan.[4]

Obama deserves a dedicated museum space. Every president since FDR has one. But even when these museums are public-private partnerships, the public generally has retained control. Here the public, which the Obama Foundation professes to serve, is largely sidelined, although they are encouraged to visit. It all happened without much debate, and it happened in a city that had become almost reflexive in its use of privatization—from its parking-meter debacle to its attempts to fund early childhood education—with much of this guided by Obama allies, including his former chief of staff. The ease with which this group chose the privatization route speaks to how routine it has become to bypass the public option.

So what is lost? Lawyers for the university and the foundation argue that they are not subverting the public, but are giving them a gift. And yet, in this redevelopment of these nineteen acres of Jackson Park, visitors will not have impressed upon them what Olmsted called the idea of the park. They will not be reminded that they are in a public place. They will be reminded that this is now Obama's park.

Something else is being lost here in the reflexive rush to privatize, and while it goes beyond the choice of location, it falls squarely within the way public spaces promote democracy when they "press us into relations with each other" and push us to engage in difficult conversations. Obama will break with tradition by not creating a library. The public records of his presidency will ultimately reside at the National Archives and Records Administration near Washington, DC. Presidents since FDR have had their records held at presidential libraries run by NARA. Obama has chosen to have his foundation's employees, not public archivists and curators, run his "presidential center," which will include exhibits and public documents on loan from NARA.[5]

Something like this has happened before, but its circumstances were exceptional. President Richard Nixon, after his papers were essentially confiscated by Congress, had a foundation run what was supposed to be his library, but which really amounted to a very partisan museum. Ultimately, his foundation wanted the cache (and cash) that comes with being part of the presidential library system, and they worked with NARA to transfer control. The Nixon library's first public, NARA-employed director, Tim Naftali, described what he found there as "a very defensive set of exhibits," including a Watergate narrative that blamed the whole scandal on the Democrats. Contrast that to the publicly controlled FDR library, which openly broaches the issue of Japanese internment, or the Truman library, which leaves open the question of whether dropping the atomic bomb was a mistake. Public curators and archivists can be open about the negative or dicey parts of a president's legacy in a way that those employed by a president's own foundation cannot. Visitors to Obama's center will be seeing Obama's version of Obama's history.[6]

Those publicly run presidential libraries and museums press us into relations with others by forcing us to question our own heroes and listen to those with whom we might disagree. The fact that the information is coming from a public agency gives it the authority of neutrality. As Naftali, when asked about the Obama library, pointed out, "One of the beauties of having the federal government oversee national historical places is that, traditionally, people would believe that the facts they are getting are real." This is, of course, slipping away due to politically motivated attacks on the government and four years of the Trump administration's "alternative facts," but the answer surely is not to do what Obama has done by avoiding the public's role in presenting history and starting uncomfortable conversations.[7]

Obama's foundation and the stories they tell at his presidential center will never have the credibility that comes from public control. Large swaths of the population will dismiss them, and the other swaths will miss out on a chance to engage with opposing ideas and the people doing the dismissing. "I am concerned that we aren't talking to each other as a country," Naftali continued. "That we are reaching a point where we are losing a common baseline of facts." And that is the end result of this erosion of public space, both within buildings where ideas are presented and in the once-public parkland that surrounds them. Conversations stop, empathy shrinks, communities atrophy, and democracy is reduced to mere formalities and enforcement. Obama's contribution to all this may be small compared to how his successor intentionally divided the nation for political gain, but Obama set a precedent. The Trump museum, certain to be privately run as well, will surely take Obama's example into astounding new territory.[8]

The Tragedy of Lake Texoma

A park doesn't have to be deliberately designed by an Olmsted or planned with democracy in mind. If it's public enough, community springs up within and around it. The Lake Texoma State Park sat on a body of water near the border of Texas and Oklahoma that was created by a U.S. Army Corps of Engineers dam in the early 1940s under the Flood Control Act of 1938. It had for generations promised simple pleasures in a beautiful setting. Its campgrounds, cabins, and lodge didn't offer luxury but were accessible to working-class families, who could enjoy a weekend of lakefront living for less than a quarter the cost of a single ticket at Disneyland. Those who have spent time at state and national parks can likely picture the 1950s architecture and practical, rustic campsites. No one goes to such places to be pampered; the main attraction is always the park itself.

But even basic lodgings need upkeep, and the State of Oklahoma had fallen behind. Notoriously averse to public investment, and becoming even more so in the early 2000s, the state quietly started looking to make a sale rather than maintain what it had. A few small hurdles stood in the way: the state had accepted federal grants and promised that it would keep the park in public hands. But future governor Mary Fallin, then a representative in Congress, greased the skids with legislation that she called "one of the last pieces of the puzzle," allowing the wholesale transfer of 750 acres to Pointe Vista Development, LLC, for a mere $14.8 million in 2008.[9]

Pointe Vista, owned by two oil tycoons—Aubrey McClendon, CEO of Chesapeake Energy, and Mark Fischer, CEO and chairman of Chaparral Energy—had a dazzling vision. The old lodge and cabins would be swept away and replaced with a gated community with at least one golf course, a hotel, vacation homes, condos, a spa and gym, private docks, and swank restaurants. It would become an island of affluence in a region of Oklahoma where one in five live below the poverty line. As is so often the case, the developers promised that they and their rich friends would, as they bathed in luxury, provide the longtime residents of the county with jobs, jobs, jobs. There would be tables to wait on, linens to be washed, and minimum-wage salaries there for the taking. All the residents had to do was wait for their saviors to build their vision and sell it to other rich buyers. All they had to give up was access to what had once been their shared land. Oh, also some tax incentives (worth $30 million over twenty-five years) because these oil-rich developers weren't satisfied with the fire-sale bargain they had gotten on the land; they also wanted help with tax avoidance. And infrastructure improvements. And freedom to operate without deadlines. By dangling the promise of jobs, they got all they wanted.[10]

Twelve years later, they had delivered nothing. A local reporter described the eerie quiet of what had once been one of Oklahoma's most popular parks: A "smudge on the earth" where the lodge once stood. A ghost town of empty cabins that the developers had not even bothered to demolish. The developers claimed they hadn't been able to raise enough investment (in fact, they had gone on a buying spree, sucking up private land around the park to extend their domain). The county, unfortunately, had not been so slow to act, and had sunk $400,000 into sewer improvements for a resort that wasn't there. The state had also failed. The law required that a transfer of this land to private hands was permissible only if the state created a new park of equal market value with "reasonably equivalent" amenities and uses. Four years after the sale, officials told a reporter they were "actively working" to create a new public park. Twelve years after the sale, there was still no sign that the law would be followed or that anyone would face consequences for defying it.[11]

The ripples from the loss of Lake Texoma State Park extended outward rapidly. Local business owners suddenly lost all the business that had come from the park's visitors. The stables and the Texoma Land Fun Park, on land transferred to Pointe Vista, were the first to close. Dolores Pitt, the owner of the Creative Corner curio shop, saw a 66 percent decline in sales. The owner of Lighthouse Bait and Tackle lost 30 to 40 percent of his business. The owner of the Bar-B-Q Shack recalled believing in the project: "When they announced this development, I thought we were going to be the next Branson, I really did." She finally called it quits and advertised the sale of her business: "Will sacrifice for $135,000."[12]

"It feels like we've been ripped off," Pitt told a reporter. Another resident felt betrayed by her state: "This should have been brought to a public vote. This belongs to the people." And Stephen Willis, who organized Friends of Lake Texoma State Park to campaign against the privatization, called the situation "the ultimate con job and swindle of the taxpayers." Confronted with this reality by a local reporter, Pointe Vista spokesman Brent Gooden blandly claimed, "We understand and respect their frustration." He then went on to blame a slump in the real estate market.[13]

By 2013 the failures of Pointe Vista were evident enough and the public pressure acute enough to force a reckoning: the state hired lawyers and demanded that the development move ahead or that the land be returned. In 2016 they settled for the right to buy back a fifty-acre portion at $4 million—about four times the $20,000 per acre rate they'd sold it for (if that price had held, the buyback would have cost only $1 million). And then the state promised to remove all restrictions on the rest of the original sale. So Pointe Vista could develop, or not develop, or even subdivide and sell in parcels what had once been one of Oklahoma's most popular state parks.[14]

Did Oklahoma then return those highly valuable fifty acres to the public? No. The state sold the land, along with *another* 11.5 acres of public land, to the Chickasaw Nation for a casino.[15]

"We made a bad deal," reflected State Auditor and Inspector Gary Jones, who has a vote with the Commissioners of the Land Office but wasn't there when the first sale was made. "We made a bad deal without having safeguards built into it." And Bob Anderson of the National Park Service, who was chief of the office that approved the original sale, similarly reflected on the failure to replace the park with one of equal value: "It was supposed to be fast-tracked. . . . I should have known that wouldn't be the case." It's a sad thing, these sorts of regrets. Once you've ground your seed corn, you don't get it back.[16]

The state and the community nearby lost a public thing, something that represented democracy and equality, in addition to economic opportunity—the sort of opportunity that comes to entrepreneurs who know something about cooking or fishing. The Pointe Vista promise of jobs was really an undermining of the economic independence and pride that comes from working in or owning a local business. Even if the project to convert this scrappy public park into a billion-dollar resort had succeeded, the community would have lost something vitally important—actual access to a public space and a sense of belonging. This realization bubbled over as a local reporter spoke to two residents. One pointed out, "They handed this contract to two wealthy white men in Oklahoma City. Low-income people in the area couldn't even afford a room at that four-star hotel." And Lisa Davis put her finger on what the conversion of public space to luxury resort really meant: "I will not be relegated to cleaning the toilets for some place where I used to be able to go in through the front door."[17]

18

School Choice and Resegregation

WHILE WRITING HIS 1950S TREATISE ON SCHOOL CHOICE, THE DANGER OF deepening segregation barely entered the mind of conservative economist Milton Friedman, receiving only a footnote. For some parents, however, the opportunity for segregation has been the main attraction of school choice. In North Carolina in 1956, for example, voters approved the Pearsall Plan, a road map to entrenched segregation and an attack on the public good that allowed districts to close down schools that had been forced to integrate. At the same time, the plan gave vouchers to students who could take them to private institutions that remained fully segregated. Taxpayer dollars, from both black and white citizens, funded this attempt to circumvent the law by proclaiming the primacy of free choice and using public funds to support discriminatory private institutions.[1]

It took fifteen years for the courts, in *Goodwin v. Johnson County Board of Education*, to dismantle this scheme. The ruling reinforced the idea that it was not enough for the school board and the state to stop promoting segregation. It was not enough to simply do away with the rules, set up other rules that were supposedly race neutral, and then look the other way as the policies generated their logical outcomes. Instead, the public officials had an affirmative responsibility to work against segregation. They could not, on the public's dime, offer "choice" that included the decision to avoid integrated schools. Building on this idea, the U.S. Supreme Court ruled in *Swann v. Charlotte-Mecklenburg Board of Education* that busing was an appropriate remedy. It was an incredibly long and painful road, but the combination of local determination and federal intervention over thirty years made the Charlotte-Mecklenburg School District one of the most integrated districts in the country. But that started coming undone in 2001 when a white parent sued over admission policies and won; courts now claimed *Swann* was suddenly irrelevant. Systemic racism apparently was no longer an issue.[2]

So when Betsy DeVos insisted on "school choice" in the form of vouchers and charter schools, it was clear that resegregation would be not far behind. "Choice" sounds full of freedom and promise, and Trump also painted it as a civil rights issue: "We're fighting for school choice, which really is the civil rights of all time in this country [*sic*]." DeVos also wanted choice to be a religious rights issue—while no one would deny the right of a family to send their child to a religious school, DeVos wanted taxpayers to subsidize this choice, even if that meant supporting a school that would not accept transgender children or kids from same-sex marriages. Freedom of choice in this case meant the freedom to discriminate, with the blessing of public funds.[3]

"One size does not fit all," said one charter school leader based in New Orleans. He was reflecting a common mantra of school choice that characterizes public schools as utterly lacking in diverse approaches. He's hoisting up a straw man; no one in traditional public education believes one size fits all. Schools consistently strive to give diverse offerings, and teachers are steeped in strategies for approaching students' unique learning styles. But what he and Betsy DeVos and others really mean is that their schools should be allowed to exclude those who don't fit. "You want to get all the bright kids together," continued this New Orleans advocate, "and boy, magic happens. You know you don't say, 'Well, you know, we're going to have all the dumb kids and a few bright kids and somehow they're all going to get smart.' That doesn't happen and especially with adolescents and children. That just doesn't work." This leader, interviewed by researchers investigating his district, worked in a system that stratified children academically. He worked in the top-tier of New Orleans charter schools, which established admittance requirements. Almost 90 percent of the white children in his city were eligible to attend these Tier 1 schools for "bright kids." Only 23.5 percent of black children were. The rest filtered down to the schools for "dumb kids." We have to keep asking this about school choice and privatized schooling: Who actually gets to choose?[4]

The conservative members of the Supreme Court seem ready to take us back to *Plessy v. Ferguson*, but until that happens, school choice is a useful way to wrap exclusion in the language of freedom and markets. It claims the marketing mantra of the long tail, where products are highly specialized and pitched to increasingly individual tastes, but such specialization carries with it the impulse to either market strongly to a segment of the population or find ways to keep out the undesirables. Or both. Instead of attempting to overcome racism and geography, charter schools often exclusively target minority students with slick marketing campaigns and promises. They zero in on distressed neighborhoods and show no evident interest in diversity. As a result, the overwhelming majority of black students in charter schools (70 percent) go to school each day in a school that is between 90 and 100 percent minority. Forty-three percent of them go to a school that is 99–100 percent minority. This is bracingly different from their peers in traditional public schools. Only a third of these peers are in schools that are essentially all minority. Clearly, if you want to bring back segregation quickly, charters are the way to go.[5]

When so many of these schools are supported by wealthy white donors, who supply start-up and supplemental funding on top of the public funds, it shocks the conscience that they pay so little attention to integration, the single most important domestic moral struggle of the previous century. It is doubly offensive when they frame their efforts as the next frontier in civil rights, as Donald Trump often did as president. And the kicker is that they then use their power, money, and influence to work the system to get public funds to help pay for creating racial isolation.[6]

In Reynolds Lake Oconee, Georgia, wealthy real estate developers, notably the Republican activist and donor Mercer Reynolds III, wanted their gated communities to attract more families. The "cornerstone" of their business plan, according to internal documents, was a school: "We believe if we have a community-based school in this area, the people will move here," the president of the private community told a reporter. But school boards aren't like real estate speculators. They put schools where they are needed, not where developers and investors hope they *might* be needed. So Reynolds Lake Oconee petitioned the school board and then the state for permission to open a charter school with tight preferences for nearby families. Their charter application made their intentions plain: 80 percent of the enrollment would be children from Reynolds properties. The remaining 20 percent of the seats would go primarily to nearby and comparably wealthy and white communities, and 8 percent of the seats would be offered countywide, to a county where 50 percent of children live in poverty.

With a mix of taxpayer and private funding, they built a stunning school. It had a pond. And a "piano lab" with twenty-five pianos. The high school offered seventeen AP classes. The school was 73 percent white. The nearby traditional public school was 68 percent black. While the Lake Oconee Academy charter school grew from an enrollment of eleven students in 2007 to one thousand in 2018, the public school that would have been serving most of the kids from Reynolds's real estate venture saw declining enrollment, from 2,100 to 1,600. This traditional public school, which could never dream of opening a piano lab, has been tightening its budget and reducing staff.

The Lake Oconee Academy made for good business. Pushed forward by well-connected political donors, it filled its role of attracting families and selling them houses. Along the way, it helped feed the same sense of exclusivity and isolation that helps fill gated communities everywhere, but here it used public funds to help drive it forward, and it did so to the detriment of existing public schools that served a much more needy population. And even though on paper it relied on a set of supposedly race-neutral policies and decisions, the predictable outcome was anything but race neutral. This was a clear-cut case of rich whites diverting money from struggling black families in order to further push them to the margins. And they used the ideas of school choice and the free market to justify it.[7]

We should be prepared for more of this. In North Carolina, the site of so much struggle over school integration, history is coming full circle. The far-reaching school district of Charlotte-Mecklenburg includes the city of Charlotte and many of its suburbs. When it was focused on integration, it was one of the most promising settings for pushing us into relations with each other, across lines that were racial as well as economic. But when the public push for a level playing field fell to anti-integration lawsuits, it soon became one of the most starkly divided districts in the nation and the most segregated school district in the state with one of the widest wealth discrepancies. One glimmer of opportunity for integration and access to opportunity came from the fact that the school district drew from several wealthy suburbs. But in 2018, four of them signaled that they felt the glaring separation between their communities and Charlotte didn't go far enough. They wanted their schools to look like their neighborhoods—either black or white—and wanted to use school choice to get there.[8]

The suburb of Mint Hill is 78 percent white. The nearby suburbs of Huntersville and Matthews are 88 and 82 percent white, respectively. But the lakeside community of Cornelius, home of U.S. senator Thom Tillis, is 91 percent white. All of these municipalities are included in the same school district as Charlotte; in this school district as a whole, white children are a distinct minority of 29 percent. The introduction of charter schools and "choice" into this mix has created a new white flight, here and in the rest of the state. When charter schools were just getting started in North Carolina, about 10 percent of them had student populations that were over 90 percent white. By now that figure has doubled. At the same time, statewide traditional public school enrollment has gone from 64 percent white to 53 percent white, while charter school enrollment has gone the other way—to 62 percent white. All this, charter advocates claim, is simply choice and the free market at work. Nothing racist to see here.[9]

In 2018 Huntersville, Matthews, Mint Hill, and Cornelius started a successful and egregious petition to obtain state permission to set up charter schools, and to give admission preferences to their own residents. There was no attempt to hide the intention—this was an effort by these cities to remove themselves from the public school district—but the patina of choice gave it some cover. What's more, they also received permission from the state to channel local property taxes into their municipal charter schools, diverting this funding from the Charlotte-Mecklenburg schools. This move was groundbreaking. The system of pooling money at the state or county level is the only hope of getting anywhere close to equitable funding for schools. Here, four wealthy white localities received permission to focus on their own, to the exclusion of all others. At the same time, their separation would not be absolute. These four towns will continue to receive funding from the Charlotte-Mecklenburg School District, the only real difference being that this district will now be even more pressed for funds.[10]

The town boards in these four enclaves were near unanimous in their support of the plan. Only one dissenting vote arose from these boards, and it came from the only nonwhite member among them. The state legislature voted 64–53, and then overrode a veto attempt by Governor Roy Cooper. The debate was contentious and touched several raw nerves. State Senator Bill Cook was greatly offended at "the implication that we're all a bunch of racists." As is often the case, those offended by this charge take it all too personally. Whether these folks are racist or not is irrelevant. As a former North Carolina teacher of the year explained in an editorial, "It almost doesn't matter, because it's less about individual intentions and more about actual impact. . . . The result of this will ultimately amount to systemic racism. It's about a system, not personalities, that marginalize[s] communities of color."[11]

While these communities may feel as if they've won a battle for local control, all they have done is narrow and limit their own children's opportunities. Their white kids will not grow up to join an all-white workforce; they will not live in an all-white nation. As one white and admittedly privileged graduate of Charlotte-Mecklenburg schools wrote, after reflecting on how diversity enhanced her education, "It is time for middle- and upper-class families to realize that sending their kids to school with students of a different background isn't just OK, it's a privilege worth fighting for. It is time for those same families to no longer be content with opportunity for their kids, but rather seek that same opportunity for every child in Charlotte-Mecklenburg Schools."[12]

Compared to this student's plea, the school choice cliché of "one size does not fit all" seems sadly weak. When held up to the results of school choice, which is still in comparatively early days in the United States, its meaning changes to something downright obscene. Do black kids not "fit" in an expensive school with a piano lab? Or in a 93-percent-white lakeside community?

As the ACLU of Southern California found, there are many ways children can be considered to not "fit," and charter schools have been extremely creative in weeding them out. Their investigation, with the nonprofit Public Advocates, found that 20 percent of California's charter schools had "plainly exclusionary" policies. This is not just distasteful, it is illegal in a state where charters are required to "admit all pupils who wish to attend." But some charters simply defy the law while others find creative ways to skirt it.

Denying enrollment or re-enrollment based on grades was a popular choice for exclusionary California charters. Several charter schools insisted on As and Bs in core subjects and a GPA of 3.0 or higher. This is par for the course at just about any private school, but flies in the face of the requirement for public charters to remain open to anyone. "It looks like this is not the place for you," a school counselor at Orange County School for the Arts told a parent of a child who had struggled academically while tending to serious health issues. "Maybe you should go back to your home school."

One school went so far as to require that parents of English learners enroll in an English language program as well, but intrusion into the lives of parents goes even further. One charter in Santa Cruz County demanded an interview, and parents had to bring two letters of reference and a student writing sample among many other forms and redundant paperwork. Immigrant parents have been extensively asked about their immigration status and told, falsely, that they must bring paperwork like Social Security cards and birth certificates. Other schools demand that parents perform a certain number of volunteer hours (or pay those hours off), and one school insisted that children show up in "protective layers of natural fibers" and have a "media free experience" at home.[13]

All this is a natural outgrowth of school choice. While states like California attempt to keep their charters open to all who wish to attend (and who win a lottery), charter schools themselves operate under an entirely different ethos. For them, "choice" means *they* get to choose what kind of children and families they want in "their" communities. They justify this by claiming that their very special program is not for everyone. That one size does not fit all. And that there are always traditional public schools to serve as a dumping ground for kids who don't fit into their sanctified pedagogy or their idea of a model student.

With all the energy and resources going into choice-driven education reform, it's distressing to see how little attention is paid to those who want to choose integrated schools, especially since we are losing what little ground we gained in the 1960s and '70s. Today, 18 percent of our schools are less than 10 percent white. That's up from 6 percent in 1988. Should we be surprised that racial attitudes are hardening, that white supremacy has become less taboo, and that we had to invent the phrase "living while black"?[14]

It is time to recapture diversity as a public good, and this diversity must go beyond mixing students together. It must also involve a shifting and rebalancing of power toward minority families. This fight goes beyond what some might call political correctness; at stake is our ability to function as a society and as a democracy. There are plenty of moral reasons, and ample empirical evidence of benefits, to prompt us to count diversity as a public good. The effects of school diversity on minority children and those from families struggling economically are clear. They are more likely to receive resources and have access to better teaching at schools that include the middle class. Test scores bear this out. Low-income students at affluent schools are generally two years ahead of their peers at high-poverty schools and are far less likely to drop out of school. Graduates of these schools are two-thirds less likely to fall into poverty as adults.[15]

This alone should force us to consider diversity to be as essential as water, roads, and schools. But we can cast an even wider net. Diversity is also good for all children, in measurable ways. Dealing with diverse surroundings requires adaptation and mental flexibility. When the diversity happens in an educational setting, researchers see evidence of additional cognitive strategies, critical thinking, and an increased ability to shift perspectives. Studies of white students in homogeneous settings show no such increase. When we are in our social comfort zones, our brains get lazy. We might excel at basic tasks, but we never learn to deal with unexpected perspectives and information that requires entirely new thinking.[16]

Finally, and perhaps most surprisingly, exposure to diversity in educational settings has been strongly linked to increased civic engagement, community activism, and participation in democracy. No fewer than twenty-seven scientific studies have borne this out. The part of the brain that learns from difference, apparently, also wants to engage as a member of a community. Reaching out and shifting perspectives, taking on the view of others, and walking in their shoes make us feel more connected, and have us seeking out more of those connections. On the other side, we have strong evidence that those who lack significant direct experience of diversity and have even slightly negative racial attitudes experience a high cognitive cost when faced with diversity. They measurably lose the ability to focus (they become "depleted of executive attentional resources," according to one study) and can feel adrift. In short, harboring racist attitudes is mentally exhausting when you have to deal with diversity in daily life. This can lead only to further isolation, less civic engagement, and a weakened democracy.[17]

We need public things to help press us into relations with others, and we need those others to be diverse. We need those others to be empowered. Both public and charter schools have, in general, failed to put serious effort into diversity, or they've tried to settle for diversity without rebalancing power. But the free market and the pseudo free market of school choice are not geared to be guardians of the public good of diversity. They find it easier to define market segments and chase the long tail, catering to pre-existing tastes and preferences. As consumers, we may appreciate being served in this somewhat more personal way. But education has other purposes; it's not education unless it challenges us and brings us new knowledge and unexpected perspectives. This it can do only if it remains a public thing that serves our needs as citizens.[18]

19
Public Libraries and Apple Pie

IN THE PAGES OF THE *NEW YORK REVIEW OF BOOKS*, AUTHOR SUE HALPERN recalled her time in a "remote mountain town" that was large in area but small in population and had never had a public library. The residents didn't appear to want one at first; a proposal for a really small tax to create one went down in flames, and brought out comments like "libraries are communist." When the town went ahead and created one anyway, with a tiny budget, a makeshift spare room, and three "deputized" staff, they expected they'd need only five hundred library cards, if that, to carry them through the year. They ran out after three weeks. By the end of the year they had 1,500 card-carrying patrons. They started "a book club, a preschool story hour, movie night, and a play-reading group." The library became a community hub where teenagers could use the internet connection to do homework and quilters could trade patterns, and Halpern decided that "the man who had said that libraries were communist had been right. A public library is predicated on an ethos of sharing and egalitarianism. It is nonjudgmental. It stands in stark opposition to the materialism and individualism that otherwise define our culture."[1]

Public libraries have been remarkably resistant, though not immune, to the waves of privatization, even as other public things, including things that are arguably more essential and harder to privatize, have been auctioned off. Some might say that libraries should be the first thing to go: some clearly see them as nonessential, and it would not be hard to see charging a per-use or subscription fee to support them. In our climate of austerity it would make economic sense. It would fit perfectly with the strands in our culture that celebrate materialism and individualism. And yet the idea of introducing even a bit of privatization to public libraries often seems like a bridge too far.

Libraries resist privatization because they are not just about the books. We could easily replace the transactional part of libraries with corporations, but we'd be left with a place where you come in, get your books, pay, and leave. You'd lose the opportunity to get help with homework or trade quilt patterns or meet people who are eager to recommend their favorite reads. And that's just the surface of what libraries do, especially in a time when most other social services have been slashed. Author Deborah Fallows, after crisscrossing the nation, decided that libraries have become "second responders." In Ferguson, Missouri, the library provided refuge during the civil unrest, staying open late and offering classes for kids. Librarians kept their spaces open—without light or heat—in New Jersey and Queens in the aftermath of Hurricane Sandy, even offering story time to kids. Fallows made note of libraries that responded to mass shootings and wildfires, but they were on the front lines even when they were not in the midst of an aftermath. A library in Arizona sponsors a team of nurses to visit patrons; Bend, Oregon, has librarians trained in handling questions about personal finance; some libraries train their staff in how to administer the anti-overdose drug naloxone. And then there's the adult literacy, GED, and English language classes run by libraries, either on their own or through partnerships with nonprofits. Most of this emerges naturally from the dedication of librarians, who are highly educated but rarely well paid. As one library employee told Fallows, "Sometimes librarians are Batman."[2]

One person who would disagree is Frank Pezzanite, co-founder of Library Systems and Services (LS&S), a company that runs privatized libraries. In his view, "a lot of libraries are atrocious." For this, he blames not underfunding, but the librarians themselves. "Their policies are all about job security," he told a reporter. "You can go to a library for 35 years and never have to do anything and then have your retirement." Pezzanite seems to have made it his mission in life to whip these lazy librarians into shape. When his company takes over a library, the librarians who work there—the ones who aren't laid off outright—become his employees, and he has a message for them: "We're not running our company that way. You come to us, you're going to have to work."[3]

LS&S started out as a software company. Now, after doubling in size over the last ten years, it has taken over seventeen library systems in five states and runs over eighty branches. Through this growth, and the backing of the private venture firm Argosy Capital Group, it has become the nation's fifth-largest library system. When LS&S takes over, it receives a set fee from a local government. The corporation gets control over the collection, services, and programs. Most important, it takes over staffing. Librarians at these facilities are no longer public servants; they serve at the pleasure of LS&S. Although it has been building its portfolio since the late 1990s, LS&S has met with little competition; its CEO likes to brag that it boldly goes "where angels fear to tread," namely, into local fights with committed activists who love their libraries and librarians.[4]

LS&S has developed a pitch that promises innovation, economies of scale, and cost savings. In reality, it hollows out everything that makes a local library a public good. The Maryland-based company's leadership swaggers like true Silicon Valley disruptors, but those who know the field don't see it pay much attention to real innovation. The president of the Connecticut Library Association came away from the company's pitch with the comment that "everything that they're talking about is standard practice." An audit of one of its library systems puzzled over the glaring absence of subscription databases and ebook providers, especially given that LS&S, being the fifth-largest library system in America, should be able to get deep volume discounts. The same audit noted, "The absence of a written service plan, staffing plan, technology plan, a contemporary collection development and management plan, and the existence of many dated operational policies, is concerning. Why is this when LS&S has been operating the Library for 10 years?"[5]

Rather than innovate and use its considerable bulk purchasing power to serve local needs, the corporation saves money by narrowing its collection: "They focus on the best sellers and pull the less popular books," explained a librarian during testimony to the Escondido Library Board of Trustees. "This is at odds with what libraries do." An independent investigation of the LS&S-run Jackson County, Oregon, library system found that while the county's Latino population had tripled over a period of twenty-four years, the Spanish-language collection had grown hardly at all. There were no story times in Spanish, the book giveaway for kids included no Spanish titles, and the website was only in English. All this gave the investigators "the overall impression that Spanish speakers are not considered part of the community nor welcome at the Library."[6]

One thing LS&S is good at, however, is devaluing its staff. The company was penalized almost $70,000 for "wage and hour" violations by the Department of Labor in 2017. The company co-founder made clear his contempt for the allegedly lazy librarian doing nothing for thirty-five years, and his company brings this contempt into every contract it secures. The sales pitch made to local governments plays directly to their fiscal anxieties: "Pensions crushed General Motors, and it is crushing the governments in California," Pezzanite claimed. This is a classic example of burdening public servants for leadership failures, and it's deeply wrong. In California's case, governments woefully and knowingly underfunded the pension fund, effectively stealing from their own employees (and it's funny how no one mentions GM's executive salaries and golden parachutes, which remained exorbitant even in the face of failure). Pezzanite's solution is to encourage governments to break promises to these public servants and make them bear the costs by giving up their pensions and/or losing their jobs. The library board of trustees in Prince William County, Maryland, made public the offer it had received and the answers LS&S provided: to achieve the promised savings, 20 percent of staff would be laid off; the rest would have their benefits cut and receive no retirement benefits. The board decided not to privatize, citing as one of their reasons that the offer was "unfair to employees." Another reason was that LS&S "is reluctant to talk with the Library Board in a public setting. We are an open system." The public setting seemed to be one place where LS&S did indeed "fear to tread."[7]

Some governments value their employees; others see them as disposable and as the easiest way to make up a budget shortfall. But what do these savings amount to? By some estimates Escondido, California, was facing a future pension burden of $18 million. The proposal from LS&S would save them $400,000 per year. That savings would catch up with the pension burden in some forty-five years. These privatization solutions to fiscal shortfalls are not comprehensive. They are neither bold nor big, but they do raise big questions about our values. The decision to deprive people who live in the community of their retirement is also a decision to further enrich the private-equity owners of LS&S. While the city saves a pittance, the privatizers cut services to the community and cut benefits to those who provide those services. The more ruthless they are, the more public money they get to take out of the county, and even the state. In Jackson County, the state library report revealed, LS&S spent 28 percent of its contract on "other." No one could tell what this actually referred to. It wasn't librarian salaries, and it wasn't the collection, which were accounted for separately and were determined to be woefully insufficient. Was the county getting a good deal? Hard to tell when there was a gaping hole of who-knows-what in the middle of the balance sheet. The auditors threw up their hands: "The lack of transparency makes it impossible for the Board to determine if it is getting good value for the dollar." But it seemed clear that LS&S was pretty comfortable with the arrangement. It could, to paraphrase the co-founder, keep doing nothing while collecting its fees from the public.[8]

Despite LS&S's strong growth, the strong resistance it has met in several counties and cities appears to have gotten under the skin of Mr. Pezzanite, who seems baffled and frustrated. "There's this American flag, apple pie thing about libraries," he remarked. "Somehow they have been put in the category of a sacred organization." He's absolutely right. Citizens do see them as all-American and utterly sacred. Half of all Americans over the age of sixteen have used a library in the past year. Some of the communities LS&S has approached have participation rates of 74 percent. Mr. Pezzanite should not be surprised at the resistance. When LS&S came to Santa Clarita, California, Jane Hanson, eighty-one years old and a frequent library visitor for fifty years, became an activist for the first time since the Vietnam War and gathered 1,200 signatures over the course of three weekends. "A library is the heart of the community," she explained. "I'm in favor of private enterprise, but I can't feel comfortable with what the city is doing here." Another patron insisted that "public libraries invoke images of our freedom to learn, a cornerstone of our democracy." And a religious leader told the city council of another LS&S target that "a library is a center of a community. Sacred centers belong to the people, should be controlled by the people, for the benefit of the people." Such passion has emerged in each one of LS&S's struggles; in fact, it seems like the only times it wins is when politicians are willing to fly in the face of what the public clearly wants.[9]

In Escondido, California, hundreds of citizens turned out to speak against the LS&S proposal. They waved signs that said, "Librarians are sacred" and "Don't export our tax $$$ out of state." Speakers made arguments such as: "We have a Barnes & Noble in town. I happen to be very fond of that store, but we have one. We don't need our library to be another clone of that." Another objected to LS&S's "Costco approach" to stocking library shelves. In defense of the public librarians, they argued that they are "highly educated civil servants. They live here. They are part of the community." They pleaded: "Do not do this. This proposed contract is a mistake." They begged: "We're paying a private equity firm here $2.4 million a year. It's wrong. Please listen to these citizens."[10]

The library had been serving the community since 1894. It saw 1,400 people every day. It had a collection of two hundred thousand books and no clear indication of what would happen to that collection under privatization. As the city council heard protest after protest, the LS&S representative was largely silent, telling a reporter, "It's an emotional issue and it always will be because libraries are the heart and soul of a community." He then insisted that the company did not do "privatization," only "management services." (This is bunk. When a company controls a public good, in this case employees and the library collection, it is privatization.) The city council, meanwhile, was growing weary of hearing from opposition. "I'm tired of this crap," one council member blurted out, referring to the pleas of his own constituents. None of the citizens in the room spoke in favor of the LS&S plan. And the city council adopted it anyway.[11]

Speaking generally about library privatization, columnist Michael Hiltzik wrote, "If you're looking for a sign that local political leaders are intent on giving up all pretense of working for the public interest, look no further." Yes, stepping away from libraries is a good barometer of public officials' contempt for the public, but we would go further. These are assaults on our communities. They are attempts to undermine our connections to each other, connections that can't be forged at a

Barnes & Noble or a Starbucks. They are efforts to devalue the work and passion of public servants and their role as the glue of our communities. And they are efforts to turn us from citizens into mere consumers. Fortunately, in most places, the public recognizes them as such, and seems willing to fight back. In some ways, LS&S, with its tone-deaf leadership, undisguised greed, and disdain for "sacred" libraries and their staffs, has done us a favor. It reveals how fragile and vulnerable our public things can be and has inspired communities to come together to protect them. Our elected officials, one hopes, will eventually listen.[12]

20

Communities Take Care

How Social Security Defines Us

PUBLIC LIBRARIES, PARKS, AND SCHOOLS ARE MANIFEST EXPRESSIONS OF community and are intensely local, but we can't neglect the public things that make us a national community. Of these is our shared and always-contested history, as captured by public presidential libraries. Such public things connect us to people we will never meet; they create a "we" and create a nation, making it possible for us to define who and what is an American without having to rely on things like race, religion, language, and treacherous blood-and-soil nationalisms. The public has it within its power to define itself, and in the 1930s we added to the definition of *American* when we became a people that takes care of its elders. The idea was audacious when it was proposed, but has become deeply ingrained as part of our national identity. Social Security is by now much bigger than its administration and mechanics. "It's not just a social program," said retired union organizer Winnie Pineo. The ninety-seven-year-old activist had worked to secure the passage of Social Security in the 1930s and was watching George W. Bush attempt to dismantle it. "It's a moral commitment. That's what holds us together. We all give and we all take. We all benefit and we work and do for each other. That's the way a real democracy works."[1]

Among President Franklin D. Roosevelt's New Deal programs, Social Security held an elevated status. It likely would never have been passed without a crisis driving it forward, but unlike many of the work, improvement, and relief programs that passed during the 1930s, Social Security was always intended to outlive the Great Depression and help remake the postcrisis economy. We only have to glance at the conditions of Americans over age sixty-five before and after Social Security to see how it succeeded. In 1930 nearly 60 percent of men over sixty-five were working (despite being excluded from many of the highest-paid industrial jobs); in 2019 about 20 percent continued working or were looking for work after their sixty-fifth birthday (we were doing even better in 1985 when that number was 10 percent). Before Social Security, only about 2 percent of American workers had some sort of retirement plan, almost always provided by an employer and never by right. Despite their high employment rate, Americans over sixty-five were, at a rate of 30 to 50 percent, largely dependent on their children for support and excluded from the highest-paying jobs. What's more, in a culture where the value of people was largely defined by their dependent relationships with their employer and their productivity, Americans over sixty-five were constantly reminded of how they were no longer a part of the national economy. One survey found that nearly a third of American factories wouldn't hire anyone over forty. Most others had informal age limits, and it was rare to find anyone over fifty on an assembly line. Americans aged into permanent exile.[2]

FDR's vision for Social Security was to form a national community and wrap every American into it. "I see no reason why every child, from the day he is born, shouldn't be a member of the social security system," he explained. His program then fell short by excluding farm and domestic workers, who were disproportionately African American. The omission was glaring because universality was key, and a patch arrived with the Social Security Amendments of 1953–1954. The second guiding principle for Social Security was that it had to be *social insurance*—not charity and not an act of beneficence. The reason for this was clear. He wanted the benefits to be a right. "Our American aged do not want charity, but rather old age comforts to which they are *rightfully entitled* by their own thrift and foresight in the form of insurance."[3]

Social Security was one of the more popular of FDR's ideas, but it could not pass without challenges from Republicans in Congress. What's revealing about their most serious challenge, however, was that it was an attempt to privatize Social Security before it even got off the ground. The Clark amendment, developed by an insurance brokerage firm, proposed to allow employers to avoid the program if they offered their own private pensions. Its advocates used the language of free choice and free markets, asking why someone should be forced into a government insurance program if their employer could offer a private one. These critics likely knew the answer. To cover the poorest among us, these insurance programs must be universal. A system that allows those who can afford it to opt out fails to spread risk, leaving the pool to be filled only by those workers and employers who are least secure. What the Clark amendment advocates proposed, in effect, was a social insurance death spiral.[4]

The Clark amendment failed after the small group of experts that the Senate had charged with investigating its viability couldn't find a viable way to structure private insurance. Each attempt to privatize Social Security since then has faced the same daunting challenges; how can one possibly offer viable, sustainable, universal coverage through a market-based system? Whenever the free-market alternatives rise up from the conservative echo chamber, they always forget to mention that investments can lose money. Some investors win, some lose. Stock prices go down. Insurance companies collapse. The privatization boosters seem to either have short memories that magically exclude the last recession or believe that an average rate of return means that everyone will actually get that rate of return. In fact, some retirees will win in a privatized Social Security system, and some will lose spectacularly. On the other hand, there are always stock brokers, money managers, and assorted middlemen in these Social Security privatization schemes. They will always win.

Following the initial struggles over passage of the Social Security Act, there was a broad consensus on the program's value and a bipartisan agreement to keep it viable. The think tanks and many government advisers had long led the charge toward privatization, but those who had to answer to the nation's voters typically lagged behind. This changed after George W. Bush won his second term. "I've earned capital. Political capital. And I intend to spend it," he said just days after his reelection. His timing and rhetoric acknowledged that what he was going to attempt was wildly unpopular. During the campaign he and his surrogates had insisted that Social Security was off limits. But in private he promised campaign contributors that he would "come out strong" in favor of "privatizing Social Security." When these comments leaked, his campaign called the quotes "made up" and part of a "false, base-less attack." Then, two days after his election victory, he revealed that "reforming Social Security will be a priority of my Administration." He knew it was an unpopular position that could have stood between him and the White House, so during the campaign he had kept silent.[5]

His advisers and conservative strategists knew the plan was unpopular, and much of their reform efforts went not toward developing robust and effective policy proposals, but toward honing their rhetoric and creating distrust in the Social Security system. Nancy Altman, who'd served as an assistant to Alan Greenspan when he was a Reagan appointee to a Social Security reform committee, remarked that the "Guide to Social Security Reform," issued by the GOP congressional leadership, "resem-bled a playbook for a football team rather than a serious policy analy-sis for necessary reforms of a complicated statute." The guide focused instead on how to talk to constituents panicked about entering retirement in poverty. Use "helpful messaging techniques" that had "already been tested in the field," the handbook advised. Use "personalization," not "privatization," for example. Always emphasize personal ownership, and always downplay the corporate takeover.[6]

This was an attempt to turn us from citizens who support the uplift of all into consumers concerned only with our individual returns, and the public saw through it. One engineer who worked for a defense contractor got a lot of attention when he went public with his own analysis show-ing that in his case, private investment would have netted him $5,873 less than Social Security. The reason was simple: he started working when the Dow was high and retired when it was relatively low. His hypo-thetical privatized retirement account was subject to timing and pure chance—just like any investment. And besides, Social Security is not just a saving program, it is also an insurance program. It benefits those who fall out of the workforce due to disability and it protects those who might outlive their retirement savings.[7]

The experts, even those who generally supported the Bush administra-tion, agreed. Economist Olivia Mitchell, who was a member of Bush's Commission to Strengthen Social Security, was one of a team that pub-lished a paper showing that the promises made by the fanciful think

tanks and conservative reformers were "misleading." Once you take risk
and transition costs (a huge factor that's always ignored by privatization advocates) into account, the supposed gains evaporate. "A popular argument suggests that if Social Security were privatized, everyone
could earn higher returns," she and her team wrote. "We show that this
is false." Goldman Sachs published "Seven Myths About Social Security Reform," warning potential investors that after adjusting for risk
and transition costs, "the difference in returns between personal saving
accounts and the current system disappears. There is no free lunch available via privatization."[8]

The crisis was not there; the supposed savings were not there. It is
fair, then, to ask what was and is really motivating the Social Security demolition team—especially since they consider the destruction of
Social Security, in the words of George W. Bush's director of strategic
initiatives, to be "one of the most important conservative undertakings
of modern times." Certainly plain and simple greed was in play; imagine
the windfall to stockbrokers' commissions if Wall Street came to manage
the retirement accounts of every single American. But the profit motive
alone doesn't explain the sheer amount of passion and persistence behind
the struggle to undermine social insurance, or why it would become such
a lodestar for conservatives. It is not just the fact that it is a government
program that draws conservative ire—there is also the fact that people
have very strong positive feelings about it. In the minds of those steeped
in the paranoid ramblings of Friedrich Hayek, these positive feelings can
only pave the road to serfdom. But this can be inverted, the critics claim,
and these warm feelings can be directed instead toward capitalism. Libertarian scholar Peter J. Ferrara quite honestly explained the overriding motivation for why Social Security had to be privatized—it would
transform potentially revolutionary forces into docile capitalists: "With
minorities and other workers all owning a share of the nation's business
and industry, they would more vigorously support open market policies
that promote prosperity for everyone."[9]

This and similar statements deserve a chuckle, but they also reveal
quite a bit about their authors. Support for social insurance programs isn't
incompatible with support for open markets, even among "minorities and

other workers." We are still a capitalist society, even with Social Security increasingly embedded in our national ideal. In fact, it's likely that Social Security has gone a long way toward *saving* capitalism by honing down its sharpest edges. And it should be clear by now that it's possible to believe in capitalism and also believe that our elders and those unable to work should not suffer because of it. We have proven repeatedly willing to support such an ideal each and every pay period with a significant tax contribution, knowing that we all pay. And knowing that we all benefit.

The original opponents of the New Deal, much like today's opponents of any new public program, claimed Social Security would transform us into slaves and animals. Representative Daniel Reed, Republican from New York, insisted that "the lash of the dictator will be felt and 25 million free Americans will for the first time submit themselves to a finger print test." Herbert Hoover disdained the very idea of economic security: "We can find it in our jails. The slaves had it. Our people are not ready to be turned into a national zoo, our citizens classified, labeled and directed by a form of self approved keepers." And Representative John Taber, another Republican from New York, insisted that Social Security was "insidiously designed" to "enslave workers."[10] None of these things happened. Instead of devolving into dictatorship, slavery, a prison, or a zoo, this effort became a very different form of collectivism. It became a community based on a set of values, one made up of individuals willing to make small sacrifices that benefit ourselves and our neighbors.[11]

In small ways, like public parks, and in large ways, like social insurance, pressing us into relations with each other creates a different kind of collective than the one feared by the political right. If those public things can remain open and accessible, they provide the foundation not for enslavement or totalitarianism but for democratic action. Those much-feared authoritarian collectives are in fact much more likely to arise from the process of exclusion. We saw this in our own country under Jim Crow, when access to public things was limited and those limits were upheld through often brutal force. Privatization of public things by definition creates exclusion. It limits discussion, as the private Obama Presidential Center is prone to do. It limits participation, as the transformation of public parks into luxury hotels has done. It reinforces racial divisions, as charter schools often do. It reduces community participation to mere transactions, as the privatization of libraries does. And it creates winners and losers, as Social Security privatization would do. None of this is in any way conducive to community, free thought, or democracy. None of these are possible if we live our lives only as consumers and avoid being pressed into relations with our fellow citizens. Republicans and conservatives often scoff at the notion, typically attributed to Barney Frank, that "government is simply the name we give to the things we choose to do together," but Social Security illustrates how true this can be.[12]

Part VII

PRIVATIZATION DOESN'T
WANT YOU TO KNOW

The Corruption of Public Education

AFTER A SERIES OF FRUSTRATING ENCOUNTERS WITH SELF-STYLED EDUCA-tion reformers from the private sector who told them to run their schools "like a business," Jacob Remes and Gerry Canavan, both experienced educators, took to Twitter with a response. Run schools like a sandwich, they insisted (#runitlikeasandwich). Because that makes just about as much sense.[1]

It's easy to become frustrated to the point of absurdity when faced with neoliberal education reformers who give no quarter to the notion that maybe market rules don't apply to every single aspect of human activity. They insist that if there is competition, innovation will spring forth and the best will win. Others will imitate the winner, and the new innovation will spread. These reformers insist on applying this principle to schools, universities, and public research, revealing a vast blind spot in their worldview. In these contexts, "running it like a business" only stifles innovation, limits education, and restricts access to the benefits of both.

Sometimes market-style competition will generate something we haven't seen before. Sometimes it generates ideas. But the vast major-ity of human discovery, innovation, and education has been the result of processes that are wholly incompatible with the competition for profits. The most efficient way to generate knowledge is to share new ideas; the best way to generate profit is to prevent others from learning and selling your new ideas. Truly new innovations arise before it's clear how they will be used; the profit motive seeks only innovations that have clear use cases and a path to market. Educators not only share existing knowledge and know-how, they freely give away their best practices to colleagues, even those at other schools; when profit-making services have something new, they keep it to themselves.

Budget cuts and extreme free-market ideologies have crippled our ability to create knowledge and spread education. Privatization of K–12 schools has hampered the innovation that comes from sharing ideas and techniques; charter schools were supposed to be laboratories of innova-tion, but many of them instead embraced a model of zero-sum competi-tion. Drastic cuts to higher education funding have created a void that's been filled by wealthy donors with ideological motivations and for-profit colleges that have focused on market share rather than education. Science has had to contend with profit-motivated paywalls, extended patents, and attempts to own and monopolize public research. What's worse is that the public is paying for it. Our guaranteed student loans support the for-profit college industry. Our public research dollars give for-profit academic publishers something to publish. Our research grants provide the basis of knowledge for patented drugs and vaccines. The corporations that excel in turning knowledge and education into revenues are some of the most profitable in the world, with margins that rival or exceed those of big tech and big oil. The reason they can be so profitable is simple: the public is covering much of their research, development, and overhead.

People enjoy competition. People like making money. People also will do things that economists often can't fit into their models: We learn for the sake of knowing. We give for the sake of sharing. We want to see human progress, not just economic progress. So we build research institutes, schools, universities, libraries, and public agencies dedicated to gathering and creating knowledge. We set these up deliberately and distinctly from the marketplace because they work better that way. But now billionaires are telling us that we are doing it all wrong. We should be running it like a sandwich.

21

School Choice and Competition

When Creative Destruction Is Just Destruction

THE NOTION THAT MARKETPLACE COMPETITION IS A MERITOCRACY THAT efficiently separates the good from the bad and in the process generates innovation and knowledge is these days rarely argued; it is simply assumed. Policymakers have followed these assumptions into the rapid and haphazard development of charter schools and school choice. Again, the assumption is that competition will spawn innovation. Families will flock to success and what works, forsaking what does not. To hear Donald Trump's education secretary Betsy DeVos tell it, "We are the beneficiaries of start-ups, ventures, and innovation in every other area of life, but we don't have that in education because it's a closed system, a closed industry, a closed market. It's a monopoly, a dead end."[1]

It is well past time to push back against this notion. The winners in private industry do not always get where they got through brilliant innovations that benefit or please the consumer. Often they just find a better way to work the system or lock out competition. That's often the easiest way to succeed, rather than doing the hard work of innovation and creation. That's just a hard truth of the free market. And that's why we should keep our schools out of it.

Strangling Innovation with the Free-Market Siphon

In Washington, DC, almost half of all children are in charter schools. The experiment has gone on for over twenty years. Yet one of the most successful sets of innovations came not from a disruptive charter school, but from an experiment within a traditional public school. It is still referred to as School-within-School (SWS) even after moving out and standing up on its own as one of DC's traditional public schools in 2013. Since then, it has been in demand. In 2019, over nine hundred families entered a lottery for twenty-five seats. One of the authors of this book was lucky enough to send his kids to SWS.

The school eschews teaching to the standardized tests, but its test scores are among the best in the city. Ninety-three percent of its fifth graders tested as highly proficient in English language arts in 2019—better than any other traditional or charter DC school. Its innovations involve combining academics with arts integration and social-emotional learning, but one of the key innovations has been team teaching, whereby a math specialist and an English language arts specialist share responsibilities for two classrooms. Team teaching has been an astounding success and is in effect for most of the upper grades, but not in fifth.

Why not in fifth? Because although this public school is a school of choice for at least nine hundred families interested in entering the lower grades, the number of children returning for fifth grade at SWS is typically less than half of the fourth-grade class. Families who were lucky enough to get into one of the best elementary schools in the district spurn that school's fifth grade. And it's not simply because better-quality programs are luring them away.

The reason is because the charter school competition works the system. It's because the DC charter schools with middle and high school programs are competing for those kids and the per-student funding that follows them. The charters have figured out that they need to lock in kids at a younger age than their competitors. So they established programs not for grades 9–12, or for the DC middle school standard of grades 6–8, but for grades 5–12.

So if you are a parent who is trying to decide between a traditional public 6–8 grade middle school and a charter middle school/high school, you play the citywide lottery to get a spot for fifth grade, not sixth. If you get that spot, you better take it. The system dictates this decision by placing incredible pressure on the parents. If you wait a year, you may miss your chance—especially since the odds get longer after fifth grade. So even if you think your ten-year-old kid isn't ready to walk the halls with high schoolers, even if you like your elementary school and want to stay for fifth grade, the grade 5–12 charters have structured their programs to convince you that if your kid wins a seat for fifth grade in one of their programs you have to grab it.

It is not the case that the more innovative fifth-grade program wins. Nor does the program with the best test scores win—no charter school outperformed SWS in 2019 on percentage of fifth graders scoring as highly proficient in math and English language arts. Only one charter school outperformed SWS in fifth-grade math *basic* proficiency in 2019, by a few percentage points. What wins is a cynical play to parental anxieties and the mathematical fact of diminishing odds. What wins is not the better fifth grade program but the grab for market share. SWS experiences this drop-off from fourth to fifth grade every year, as do all DC public elementary schools, but not all experience this as acutely as some. The much-loved and successful Brent Elementary School on Capitol Hill has seen fifth-grade classes 70 percent smaller than expected.[2]

The system that was supposed to reward success and spark innovation instead stifles them both. Team teaching at SWS cannot continue into fifth grade because half of the per-pupil funding for that grade reluctantly walks out the door, every year. This means it can't afford another fifth-grade teacher. Instead, the system largely rewards schools that are not as successful at that grade level, that pay their teachers less, and that have no solid pedagogy behind the decision to start their high school programs in fifth grade. In fact, what few studies have been done on this issue suggest that middle school and high school is not an ideal place for fifth graders (study or no study, just about any parent could tell you the same thing).[3]

Some of these schools have won praise from families and do well, overall, by their students. When they do innovate and succeed, we should pay attention. But many of their marketplace victories aren't decided based on who was the most innovative. Sometimes the winner is simply better able to game the system or is more ruthless in the grab for market share. Competition doesn't guarantee that schools will be driven to innovate. Sometimes they will just be driven to win.

Locking Down the Laboratory

When it comes to education, knowledge, and innovation, competition and market approaches are not the best grease for the wheels that generate new ideas and inspire teachers. "There appears to be less innovation than originally anticipated," was the conclusion of a report by the IBM Center for the Business of Government that surveyed charter school curricula. There also appeared to be little use of evidence-based practices and also little credible collection of data. Instead, what the study found was a resurrection of old practices. There were the hyperacademic schools that used high-stakes testing to pressure kids into higher performance (or into leaving the school), there were the schools that demanded longer days, and then there were the hyperdisciplinary schools that meted out harsh punishments for a broad range of trivial infractions, tightly policing student dress, movement, and speech. And, of course, many schools adopted all three of these "innovations." This is about what you'd expect from a competitive environment that revolves around test scores. And it has little to do with reaching those kids who are really struggling and really need innovative approaches.[4]

Charter schools were supposed to be "incubators of innovation," according to Barack Obama, and "laboratories of innovation," according to Greg Richmond, president and CEO of the National Association of Charter School Authorizers. Richmond, and many others before him, asserts that spurring innovation was the prime driver behind the creation of charter schools. He claims that the much-admired and deeply liberal Albert Shanker, a past president of the American Federation of Teachers, invented the charter school idea expressly for the purpose of spawning innovation through competition. This is a pernicious myth. Shanker's vision for an innovative school bears almost no resemblance to charter schools as we have them today. And innovation through market-style competition seems to have never crossed his mind.[5]

Shanker dreamed of small experimental schools, "schools within schools," that were part of the school district but featured "a way for a teaching team to govern itself." They had to be organized so teachers "would no longer be isolated in the classroom throughout their professional lives, but would have the time to be available to share ideas and talk to and with each other." And they had to be open: "The school would announce in advance to the community what it is that it's trying to achieve and announce how it's going to test it." Teachers had to be prepared to announce failures as well as successes. Shanker's proposal shared far more with the scientific model than with the marketplace model, and it's jarring to compare his vision to current charter school practice. It's not simply that the apple fell quite far from the tree; it came from a different tree altogether.[6]

Instead of sharing successes and failures, a surprising number of charter schools tend to lock down the laboratory. The Jubilee Academic Center Inc. charter school's 2014 employee handbook requires all teachers to sign a nondisclosure agreement and makes sure they understand that they will face legal action if they reveal Jubilee's "trade secrets." What are these trade secrets? They included but were not limited to "curriculum systems, instructional programs, curriculum solutions . . . new materials research, pending projects and proposals, proprietary production processes, research and development strategies, technological data, and technological prototypes." The Texas school may be a laboratory for innovation, but it's one ready to sue its own employees if they dare to share their discoveries outside of the lab.[7]

Chavez Schools in DC similarly defended "academic policies and strategies" as "trade secrets." The Bright Stars charter school in Los Angeles locks down "techniques and concepts" as well as "lesson plans, teaching materials, educational strategies and all know-how and show-how whether or not protected by patent, copyright, or trade secret law." Both threatened teachers with legal action.[8]

It's worth noting that sharing successful lessons is, for most teachers, second nature. When they have something that inspired a classroom, when they find something that *works*, they want to tell the world. The idea that they must hide their ideas from "competitors" is completely alien to them. But in the corporate world, keeping secrets is key to success. It's just as reflexive as the teacher's impulse to share. When schools are run like businesses, we should expect secrecy to trump the sharing of knowledge and know-how, and we should not be surprised when this is taken to extremes. When the Arizona-based BASIS schools wanted to expand into Texas, they formed BTX Schools, Inc. and submitted a 393-page application. State charter officials saw the whole thing, but the publicly available version had seventy-two pages totally redacted, completely obscuring BASIS's answers to prompts like "Discuss the educational innovations that will distinguish this school from other schools." A quarter of the application's pages had at least some redactions. The nine-page section on "Educational Program" was redacted in its entirety, as were the sections "Measurable Student Goals," "Professional Development Opportunities for Teachers," and even "Extracurricular Activities." Also obscured from public scrutiny: "Bylaws of BTX Schools, Inc."—all twelve pages.[9]

Locking down your ideas naturally leads to locking down your employees. Silicon Valley executives and engineers quickly got used to noncompete contracts; they were a way to prevent ideas from walking out the door. Now charter schools are adopting this innovation. Journalists have described charter school contracts that prohibit teachers from taking employment at another school, public or charter, despite the fact that many of these teachers are on one-year terms and have no job security. In Ohio, Summit Academy Schools brought punishing lawsuits against fifty of their former teachers in just three years, all because they found better jobs. The Covenant Keepers Charter School in Little Rock, Arkansas, which had been placed on state probation in 2012 for finances and received an "academic distress" designation in 2014, held its teachers under threat of $100,000 for damages, "plus court costs, litigation expenses, and actual and reasonable attorneys' fees" if they dared disclose trade secrets or went to work "in competition" with Covenant Keepers.[10]

Teachers at the Ozark Montessori Academy faced noncompete clauses extending two years from the time they quit and covering "any area in which Employer plans to solicit or conduct business." On top of that, they were banned from sharing "trade secrets" with "competitors." The school defended its choices to Rachel Cohen of the *American Prospect*: "We pay for our teachers' Montessori training, and since that's such a big expense for us, we wanted in [the contract] that we're not going to pay for a teacher's training and then they go quit and work for someone else." The widely used Montessori approach, incidentally, wasn't invented at this school; it was developed in Italy in the 1890s.[11]

For a solution to the so-called government monopoly on education, charters often act a lot like monopolies and engage in quite a bit of anti-competitive behavior. They don't seem to want to compete for the best talent, preferring instead to strong-arm their teachers into noncompetes. They don't seem terribly interested in a marketplace of ideas, preferring instead to limit the spread of techniques and innovations through nondis-closures. They certainly seem adept at creating complex corporate struc-tures, aggressive marketing campaigns, and pipelines for new pupils, but it's hard to see how these improve the overall system or how they benefit actual students.

Albert Shanker's idea for school reform started where teachers already were, and recognized that they were driven by something stronger than competition: "Consider six or seven or twelve teachers in a school who say, 'We've got an idea. We've got a way of doing something very differ-ent. We've got a way of reaching the kids that are now not being reached by what the school is doing.'" From there he proposed teacher- and student-centered laboratories based on democratic governance. Giving teachers the freedom to experiment doesn't mean they have to be subject-ed to the free market. In fact, that free market may offer some semblance of consumer choice, but in far too many other ways it tightly restricts the real freedoms that allow education and knowledge to thrive.[12]

22

Higher Education

Who Fills the Void?

AFTER WORLD WAR II, AMERICANS MADE HIGHER EDUCATION A PUBLIC good. The war had shown the value of publicly funded research; the Cold War made continued funding imperative. The standard discriminatory rules still applied; women and minorities were largely left out, but making higher education a public affair meant they couldn't be kept out forever. A broad consensus developed around the idea that higher education should be as accessible and affordable as possible. In Minnesota, for example, the 1963 state legislature determined that no citizen of the state should live more than thirty-five miles from a public higher education campus. Today, because of that commitment, 63 percent of Minnesotans have attended at least some college. By the 1960s, most politicians in state governments had come to assume that running a university system was one of the state's most central functions, and they knew that not only was this the right thing to do, but it also paid dividends. Minnesota sees $13 generated in the state economy as a direct result of every dollar it spends on the University of Minnesota.[1]

Altogether, in a typical year, American public research universities are the driving force behind some thirteen thousand patent applications, five hundred start-up companies, and three thousand licenses. They have changed the course of our lives with everything from antibiotics to touchscreens. American life would not be anything like it is today if we had not made this decades-long public investment.[2]

Those decades were something without parallel, and future generations may look back on them as an aberration. The university system's unambiguous successes and unwavering economic benefits have not spared them from deep funding cuts driven in part by misplaced budget priorities and in part by ideological blinders. We saw in 2019 the governor of Alaska pushing for a devastating 41 percent cut to the University of Alaska's budget. This came on the heels of a sustained attack on the University of Wisconsin system by Governor Scott Walker, who had insisted on a 13 percent cut in one year. Such cuts are extremely popular among Republican governors, but no state is immune. State funding of public research universities fell, on average, 34 percent across all states between 2006 and 2016. Community colleges, widely acclaimed as a source of workforce development, were forced to shift away from public funding—from 64 percent of their budgets to 52 percent—and they cranked up tuition as a result. In 2019, for the first time, students in a majority of states paid more in tuition than the public paid in overall funding.[3]

This retreat from public higher education means fewer citizens with college degrees and less research. But the retreat has had, and will continue to have, much wider-ranging consequences. The universities won't simply die; they are too valuable. Instead, private interests will take control of this public good, either to make a profit or to use the power of higher education to advance an ideology. This is already taking place. Cutting public support of higher education will only create more opportunities for the privatization of knowledge. Our late twentieth-century public investment in higher education transformed American society by broadening our middle class and creating an engine of innovation. Our retreat from higher education will also be transformative, but we might not like the results.

Filling the Void: They Have Money, We Don't

"We've made more progress in the last five years than I had in the last fifty," Charles Koch bragged during a meeting of donors to his network of education-focused philanthropies. "We can change the trajectory of the country." The depth of his commitment can be measured by the $100 million the Charles Koch Institute gave to colleges and universities in 2018. The intent can be surmised from the writings of his board members and the strings secretly attached to his giving.[4]

Changing the trajectory of the country is not just an applause line. The Charles Koch Institute plans to do this. Richard Fink, the institute's executive vice president and a member of Koch Industries' board of directors, made this plain in an article for *Philanthropy*. "The Structure of Social Change" outlined how the institute would give money and apply pressure to universities (which will generate conservative ideas), think tanks (which turn those ideas into policies), and activist groups (which push for implementation of those policies). His slender essay does an awkward dance with Hayek's theory of production to give his ideas some libertarian bona fides, but his plan depends on rigid, not-so-libertarian, top-down control. Each of the institutions has to be purposefully steered in order to work in concert with the others. The network's power was in being "fully integrated," to use the words of another Koch employee in his pitch to supporters, "so it's not just work at the universities with the students, but it's also building state-based capabilities and election capabilities and integrating this talent pipeline. . . . No one else has this infrastructure."[5]

The Koch Institute's march through institutions starts with the universities. They provide the "raw materials" in the form of ideas and indoctrinated students. But to be "fully integrated," they have to be tightly managed. The current environment makes this easier: many of the tax breaks that built the fortunes of the Kochs and their supporters have also left universities desperate enough to accept strings on "charitable" giving—strings that run directly counter to the academic freedom at the core of the university mission.

At Florida State University, one of the Koch network's targets, the donors didn't get everything they wanted—the university shied away from the most outrageous demands after they became public—but what they asked for, and what many at FSU were ready to give them, is revealing. The millions of dollars offered *had* to fund an antigovernment, libertarian curriculum. The Koch network would be at the table when faculty hiring decisions were made. The network's hand-picked conservative, Bruce Benson, would remain chair of the economics department.

Benson seems to have known that this was a shady proposal when he tried to sway his department to accept the gift with all its strings. "There are no free lunches. Everything comes with costs." And, "We cannot expect them to be willing to give us free rein to hire anyone we might want." Benson's lament perfectly captures the fatalism that has infected higher education. It was not all that long ago—Benson himself probably remembers—when gifts didn't come with strings and universities could *always* expect to have the freedom to hire exactly who they wanted. Another example of that depressing resignation to the power of wealth also comes from FSU. "I know you hate them," the chair of a university project told a colleague who was skeptical about a Koch-backed gift. But they had to accept, she continued, because one fact was plain: "They have money. We don't."[6]

The Koch network has been even more generous at Virginia's George Mason University, once a no-nonsense public commuter school in the DC suburbs. Its $10 million donation convinced the law school to rename itself after Antonin Scalia, and no one doubts the right-wing bias of the campus's Koch-funded Mercatus Center, which bills itself as "the world's premier university source for market-oriented ideas." But unbeknownst to most of the university, the billionaire brothers also got a say in who the public university brought on board to teach and do research. For nearly eight years, the university gave them a voice in faculty hiring through arrangements that GMU president Angel Cabrera admitted "fall short of the standards of academic independence I expect any gift to meet." And the Koch network was not alone. Leaders of the conservative Federalist Society showed up as representatives of an anonymous philanthropist, there to remind the university that payments on the donor's $20 million gift could be stopped at any moment. The society thereby gained a voice in hiring decisions and at least one graduate student admission. After these clandestine arrangements were made public through Freedom of Information Act requests, the donors insisted that they had been there only to make suggestions, not give final approval. But as FSU had learned, they have money, and we don't. Their suggestions are always more than mere suggestions.[7]

"How are we going to undo this mess?" asked a GMU professor after the release of a tranche of documents revealing the extent of private influence at his public university. "How are we going to move forward and rebuild our reputation as a reputable institution?" There is a simple reason universities value their independence; any appearance of outside influence calls into question their research and the knowledge they impart. And for public universities, there is another reason: they exist to serve the public, not the ideologies of a particular segment of the public, no matter how much money they have.[8]

This seemed to matter little to Charles Koch: "I'm not doing anything I'm ashamed of." He explained that his funding was all in the service of convincing people that "more of this government control" is not going to make society more fair or change people's lives. Yet he seemed more interested in winning the ideological war through subversion and influence than by winning in the marketplace of ideas. His vision, which involves using his wealth and power to integrate the university into his own policy and activism efforts, is one that inevitably corrupts the pursuit of knowledge. He may not realize how most serious researchers look askance at the products of the Mercatus Center, how every one of its papers and reports is tainted by his influence. Likely he does not care, because his own network is the center's primary consumer. An op-ed by the Koch-backed advocacy group Americans for Prosperity reported on a recent Mercatus study with some revealing praise: "Yet another study has confirmed what we already knew—states with lower taxes do better. . . . Economic freedom works, and bigger government means bigger trouble." It appears that Mercatus is doing its job—confirming what Charles Koch already knows—and is performing this task as if its future funding depends on it.[9]

All this is made possible by the fact that the private funders have money and the universities don't. When we took public funds out of higher education (in large part to give massive tax breaks to people like Charles Koch), we gave away higher ed's independence. When we force our educational institutions into austerity and send them begging, we don't just get less knowledge, education, and research. We force them to give up the very values that made them a precious and effective public good.

Filling the Void: The For-Profit College "Cesspool of Corruption"

"I'm not sending anyone to jail yet," Judge Sallie Kim said from the bench in October 2019. She was looking at lawyers from the U.S. Department of Education as she spoke. "But it's good to know I have that ability." The department had, Kim ruled, failed to follow her instructions and had continued to attempt to collect student loan payments from students who had been defrauded by for-profit colleges. Judge Kim was "astounded" that some 16,000 students had learned, incorrectly, from the department that they had payments due and that some 1,808 had suffered seizure of tax refunds and wages: "At best it is gross negligence, at worst it's an intentional flouting of my order."[10]

An intentional flouting would not be out of character. Secretary of Education Betsy DeVos had made it clear what she thought of an Obama-era settlement that granted loan forgiveness to victims of predatory for-profit colleges. She called the forgiveness program "free money" and claimed, incorrectly, that all a student had to do to get some was "raise his or her hands." Her department rewrote the rules, making it harder for victims to qualify and giving them less time to apply. The department slow-walked the 160,000 applications for loan forgiveness that it had received. Two years after a settlement that required the refunds the department had processed ten applications (*ten*—not a typo).[11]

This was just one facet of an unctuous triad involving DeVos, President Donald Trump (the former owner of a fake "university"), and the for-profit higher education sector. These schools had prospered in the 2000s and 2010s due to a combination of deregulation, student loan privatization, and the public retreat from higher education funding. As cash-strapped community colleges started cutting courses, the for-profit colleges professed to fill the void. Free-market absolutists rejoiced. They had long wanted public and nonprofit private colleges and universities to conduct themselves more like businesses. Now, with for-profits on the rise while public funding was on the decline, their theories could be proven.

But instead of competition bringing out the best in these enterprises, instead of the market delivering a better product at a lower price, we got higher tuition, a vastly inferior product, thousands of broken dreams buried under mountains of debt, lawsuits against fraudulent schools, and flagrant conflicts of interest that one former undersecretary of education called "a giant cesspool of corruption." The experiment failed in a spectacular fashion, but its champions will not let it go. When Department of Education officials had to choose between serving defrauded students and the for-profit colleges, they chose the latter—even to the point of skirting the law, even to the point of having a judge remind them that she can start jailing people at any time.[12]

Why such commitment? The blundering failures of for-profit higher ed are there for everyone to see. They are not cheaper than public or even private nonprofit options; many have tuition price tags twice as high as what you'd find in the Ivy League, and five to six times more than what you'd find at a community college. Despite the high price, they are not offering highly resourced instruction. Spending on students can be as low as $700 per year. Graduation rates are typically lower than the traditional options, but the borrowing rate is much higher—96 percent of for-profit graduates carry student loans when they collect their diplomas, and they typically have twice as much debt as their counterparts in the traditional system. For-profit grads in 2013 defaulted on their loans at a rate of 21.8 percent, while the figure for traditional grads was 13.7 percent. And while associate degrees from public and nonprofit institutions have been shown to boost salaries by up to 50 percent, economists have not been able to find any marked difference in salary between those with a for-profit degree and those with a high school diploma. In other words, the for-profit degree, on average, is a waste of both time and money.[13]

So why would Trump's Department of Education go to the mat for for-profits? Certainly it has a lot to do with who was whispering in Secretary DeVos's ear; a surprising number of her advisers came from the for-profit college world, and she put them in charge of overseeing (what else?) for-profit colleges. But this explanation isn't enough. For those driven by rigid free-market ideology, and DeVos is certainly one of them, education is the biggest prize and for-profit colleges are in the vanguard of the transformation of education from public to private.

Their efforts will inevitably fail to produce better education. The consumer benefits of the free market simply will not accrue to students in a for-profit educational system, for very specific reasons. Some commentators have evoked the economists' concept of "adverse selection" and suggested that this for-profit education market fails simply because the seller (the school) and the buyer (the student) have asymmetric information. The school knows more about the quality of the product than the student and hides the truth from her. A market where such deception is pervasive (like the market for used cars) fails to improve quality because those who offer quality products can't distinguish themselves from those who offer lemons, and can't get the prices that they deserve. So they give up on quality, which in this situation is less profitable. In the for-profit college market this makes a lot of sense. Shortly after a round of deregulation in the early '00s, the Department of Education's inspector general testified that of all his fraud cases, 74 percent were directed at for-profits. This points to a systemic effort to hide product information from students, and we should expect in a situation like this to see low-quality products not just survive, but thrive.[14]

The Obama administration tried to fix this by forcing transparency on the for-profits and punishing cases of fraud. The money owed to students that so irked Judge Kim was an outcome of this policy. But Obama and his advisers were far too optimistic, and failed to see another fundamental problem with for-profit education. It's not just that the buyers don't have enough information. The fact is that the schools aren't even *trying* to provide students with the product they actually want. The for-profits make money by selling seats in a classroom. Although students want that seat, their ultimate goal is knowledge and a degree. But the for-profit colleges don't make money from imparting knowledge or from granting degrees. They make money, to put it bluntly, by putting asses in classes. And the fact is they can make a boatload of money that way.

Publicly traded for-profit schools have wowed investors with profit margins of upward of 20 percent. Their CEOs can expect compensation in the range of $5 million to $7 million. One CEO had a particularly good year in 2011, raking in $13 million as head of the scandal-plagued EDMC during a time of layoffs, school closures, and stranded students. These are amazing outcomes for such consistently low-quality institutions, but perhaps less amazing if we think about them differently. David Halperin, who spent years investigating this sector, talked to an insider executive who'd grown disillusioned, and Halperin found himself disabused of some of his own fundamental assumptions. "The biggest misconception about for-profits is that they are schools," his source told him. But they are not schools: "They are call centers that happen to have a school built around it." The goal is selling those seats. Getting students in the door. Getting them to take out massive loans. Everything else, including ethics, is less than secondary.[15]

One program director revealed how they kept online students enrolled even if they'd disappeared from virtual sessions. Management told him that dropping students was a business decision. EDMC faced claims that it paid recruiters for signing up students—essentially paying a commission—which was against federal rules. Whistleblowers claimed that EDMC encouraged students to falsify financial aid forms (a "pervasive" practice, according to one insider) and guided military veterans into excessive loans. Corinthian, the second-largest chain of for-profit schools, also allegedly encouraged fraud by students, pocketing $1.4 billion in federal financial aid each year. Several colleges were confronted by students who said they'd been told their credits were transferable, when they were not. And Corinthian faced investigation by the Consumer Financial Protection Bureau, which alleged students had been steered into private loans that then paid kickbacks to Corinthian.[16]

As bad as the fraud is, as bad as it is to have self-dealing oversight by those implicated in fraud, the problem with for-profits isn't just when they break the law. The worst of what they do is perfectly legal, and it's baked into what they are. It is what they inevitably have to do as profit-seeking institutions. They sell, no matter what. They find people who want an education and they sell them a seat in a classroom. They are primarily call centers, not schools. In testimony before a House committee, a former EDMC employee described a "systemic problem" embodied in the fact that EMDC employed nine people to handle career placement and 1,600 people to do recruiting. Recruiters at the top of their game made three times a typical career services employee's salary. "I believe these facts speak volumes as to where the real priorities lie within these companies," the former employee argued.[17]

For-profit colleges have honed their sales pitches and narrowed their target audience. A training slide entered into evidence in California encouraged salespeople to target prospective students who had "low self-esteem" and "few base hits." The best prospects were "isolated" and "impatient." They have "few people in life who care about them." One former recruiter admitted, "We would use hope and fear to drive our results." Several former salespeople claimed they would regularly call a potential recruit up to six times a day: "We'd just slam them with phone calls, with emails." There was money in all their targets' anguish and sense of failure: "Create a sense of urgency. Push their hot button. Don't let the student off the phone. Dial, dial, dial," commanded one director of admissions. At another training center, salespeople were told to "dig deep" into the pain and loneliness of the prospective students and "convince them that a college degree is going to solve all their problems." Another former recruiter admitted, "We were really focusing on recruiting the bottom-of-the-barrel-type students, the ones that rarely had the means." They were the target because the prize was ultimately not them and the goal was not to improve their lives. The prize was the loans they could take out if they enrolled. "Essentially, if you have a heartbeat and you can sign your name, you qualify for Stafford loans," admitted a former recruiter. Said another, "It pains me to think of the lives that I helped derail with massive amounts of student debt."[18]

As this widespread fraud became evident, an array of lawsuits followed. EDMC agreed to forgive loans to eighty thousand former students and settled with the U.S. Department of Justice in 2015. DeVry faced a lawsuit that ended with the chain refunding students to the tune of $49 million, part of a $100 million settlement with the Federal Trade Commission, which argued that the company "deceptively" claimed a 90 percent employment rate in the student's chosen field within six months of graduation, and falsely stated that graduates made 15 percent more than "the graduates of all other colleges or universities." Corinthian

Colleges, the second-largest for-profit chain, came under such a threatening lawsuit that it declared bankruptcy in 2015, leaving thousands of students hanging in the balance, with no diploma to show for their loans and no guarantee that their credits would transfer. A judge ultimately ordered restitution and penalties of $1.1 billion.[19]

As they struggled to obtain the student loan money which had once flowed so freely, for-profit colleges looked toward a bleak and uncertain future in the waning years of the Obama administration. They could not have, at that time, dreamed of a more complete reversal of fortune than what Donald J. Trump delivered. After the 2016 election DeVry's stock bounced back, rising 43 percent, while its competitors Grand Canyon and Strayer University each saw stock prices rise 37 percent. Even before Trump's inauguration, industry insiders joined "beachhead" teams that advised the incoming secretary of education on hiring and policy changes. DeVos clearly signaled her intent to turn the tables for the for-profits during her confirmation hearing. When Senator Elizabeth Warren asked her if she planned to enforce Obama's gainful employment rule, she simply said, "We will certainly review that rule and see that it is actually achieving what the intentions are." Warren noted that "swindlers and crooks are out there doing backflips when they hear an answer like this."[20]

Within months, DeVos had stopped the department from taking on new fraud cases against for-profit colleges, stopped processing the backlog of 65,000 applications from students seeking forgiveness under an Obama rule, moved to gut the gainful employment rule that forced these colleges to prove their graduates actually got what they'd been promised, delayed a rule that would let students have their day in court by banning forced arbitration agreements, and disbanded an interagency, intergovernmental task force that rooted out fraud. She hired Robert S. Eitel as her "special assistant." Eitel had a long history with for-profits that had been forced into settlement with students who claimed fraud, including a stint at Career Education Corporation's political action committee (CEC paid $10.25 million to get out of a lawsuit over inflated placement rates), and one at Bridgeport, which settled with the Consumer Financial Protection Bureau. As her pick for the Student Aid Enforcement Unit, DeVos tapped Julian Schmoke Jr., who had been dean at DeVry, which had just recently paid $100 million to settle claims of misleading students. When the Obama administration's Department of Education founded the Student Aid Enforcement Unit, it mentioned the DeVry case as part of the reason this new enforcement tool was necessary. Now the unit was in the hands of a leader of one of its former targets. In the words of a student and education advocate, "The for-profit college industry appears to have gotten everything they lobbied for and more."[21]

DeVos's department restored accreditation to some three hundred institutions that had lost it, allowing those schools to once again tap federal funds. But in at least one case they didn't even bother with a shady accreditation. In 2018, $10.7 million in federal loans and grants went to two schools managed by Dream Center Education Holdings, even though, according to documents unearthed by the House Committee on Education and Labor, department officials knew full well that they were not eligible. Further, according to the committee chair, "high-ranking Department officials knew that Dream Center misrepresented this key information, failed to immediately act, and instead worked to secure *retroactive accreditation* for the unaccredited Dream Center [institutions]." This goes way beyond feeding deregulatory desires; this sort of pandering verges on the extralegal.[22]

It appears that laws and rules have been bent and broken to help satisfy the demands of the for-profit college industry. A judge, frustration discernible in her voice, threatened department officials with jail. And yet, all of the Department of Education's actions in this area seem geared toward funneling more and more federal money into these failing institutions while burdening students with more and more debt. A free-market experiment that should have been abandoned long ago got a second life because a cabinet secretary and her insider advisers made herculean efforts to keep it going.

None of these efforts will produce quality education. It's simple: for-profit colleges are interested in filling seats, while students are interested in getting an education. It's simple, but Betsy DeVos clearly did not understand. Senator Patty Murray asked her, in a hearing, if she thought that "fundamentally different types of corporate control structures—governance by owners versus governance by trustees—results in different decisions and behaviors by for-profit institutions compared to nonprofit and public schools?" Secretary DeVos's reflexive answer consisted of one syllable: "No." This is what she truly believes: the profit motive serves the public good. She has often been criticized for not understanding education, but it's also likely that she simply does not understand business. The decisions by for-profit schools—hiring 1,600 recruiters and nine career counselors, targeting "bottom-of-the-barrel" prospects—make perfect sense from the shareholders' perspective. They would be pleased to see their college operating as a call center with a school attached. They are not charged, as trustees of a nonprofit school are, with protecting the integrity of the institution and providing students with an education.[23]

DeVos can't be dismissed just because she's out of office. She was a powerful player in education before she was a cabinet secretary, and she has the money to continue her campaign. And although no one should spend too much time inside her head, it's important to understand why she's so incredibly committed to for-profit higher ed. Likely she needs to hold on to the idea that the market will save us once we've eliminated all federal education support (aside from the life-crushing student loan program, which for-profits need to survive). You'd need such an outlook to justify the cuts we've made. So far, such cuts have succeeded in driving about 10 percent of the student population to for-profits. A good start, from the perspective of DeVos and her colleagues.

But these for-profits, in their heyday, sucked up more than 25 percent of all federal student assistance. That amounts to $33 billion per year. Not only did we not get our money's worth, but we could easily have done it more cheaply. Some estimates claim we could serve all the students in the for-profits' clutches for a mere $15 billion per year if we focused on direct support to the community colleges and career-oriented four-year colleges that the for-profits are trying to displace. In fact, it was not so long ago that we were doing just that, and for-profit colleges were a rarity. When we chose to defund public higher education, we allowed these so-called schools to arise, thrive, and warp the public good into something unrecognizable. We let politicians and billionaires lead us away from our public higher education system, one of our nation's greatest achievements, and the vultures swooped in.[24]

Part VIII

"THE CASH JUST POURS OUT"

The Privatization of Public Science
and Research

WHEN JONAS SALK ANNOUNCED THE POLIO VACCINE IN 1955, EDWARD R. Murrow asked the triumphant scientist during a television interview who owned the patent. His answer was incredulous: "There is no patent. Could you patent the sun?" The vaccine was for people, owned by the people, and developed to end suffering, not to make a fortune. Enforcing intellectual property rights at such a time was absurd.[1]

We are living in a very different world. Wall Street depends more than ever on extraction of profit from intellectual property. In early 2021 the CEO of Pfizer celebrated his company's development of a COVID-19 vaccine and the good it would do, and then slammed those who suggested that pharmaceutical companies should avoid profiteering from a global pandemic: "You need to be very fanatic and radical to say something like that right now." The private sector saved us all, he continued: "Who is finding the solution? The private sector found the solution for diagnostics, and the private sector found the solution for therapeutics. . . . So how can you say something like that? Doesn't make sense."[2]

Salk recognized how the public had contributed to his research through public funding, public education, and one of the largest volunteer clinical trials ever undertaken. He also recognized that corporate profits should not be an obstacle to ending public suffering. In 2020 Pfizer got a $1.95 billion contract for its vaccine, still in development, from the federal government. Moderna, the second company to receive approval for a COVID-19 vaccine, took almost $1 billion from the government for research and development. Both companies relied on a broad base of public research on coronaviruses and genetics that was done well before COVID-19 hit. Most likely their profit margins will be between 60 and 80 percent because public money, not their own investment, paid for much of what they needed to complete the research and bring the vaccines to market.[3]

But what is more surprising is how the public approach wasn't even considered. We have become so quick to associate innovation with competition and the free market that we gave no credence to the idea that a public effort might have been just as effective. Our polio effort didn't depend on the profit motive, and we didn't try to fund competing space programs for our 1960s moon shot. But today our pharma CEOs are telling us that only the private sector can ensure innovation, and that resisting the profit motive doesn't make sense.

They have it backward. What doesn't make sense is for the public to fund research, give up control of the knowledge that results, and then pay again for the products that private companies eke out of it. What doesn't make sense is for all of this to be happening in plain sight and for us to continue to believe that the private sector is the only place where innovation happens. What *does* make sense, however, is why the private sector is so interested in public-sector research. When the public pays and private companies don't have to, the profits are astounding.

Some will say that's a fair trade-off and we should not begrudge those profits, inflated as they may be. But even if we put the dollar figures aside, we have to recognize that those profits mean something. They mean that the public has lost control of publicly developed knowledge that could be put to use solving problems and saving lives.

23

Academic Publishing

How to Pay for Knowledge Three Times Over

WHEN ELSEVIER, THE PUBLISHING COLOSSUS, WAS IN THE PROCESS OF BUY-
ing academic journal publisher Pergamon, Elsevier CEO Pierre Vinken
bragged to a colleague that "the cash just pours out" of these seldom-
read academic journals and "you wouldn't believe how wonderful it is."
When Pergamon was starting out, it had to assemble editorial boards,
take academics to nice dinners, and sell subscriptions to libraries. But
in his business, Vinken explained, you don't have to do that for very
long. In academic publishing, authors generally do not get paid by the
publishers for their work. Editorial review is primarily done by other
academics who volunteer their time to perform peer review. Journal editors are typically employed by a university and get time carved out of
their research and teaching schedule to serve as head of a journal. All of
this expensive and irreplaceable labor would have to be compensated in
a nonacademic setting, but in this curious ecosystem it's all done (and
done at an extremely high level of quality) at no cost to the publisher.
That's why, Vinken told his colleague, "You have no idea how profitable
these journals are once you stop doing anything."[1]

That profitability is unmatched by just about any other industry. In
2010, 35.7 percent of Elsevier's revenues were pure profit. That year it
outpaced ExxonMobil, which had a profit margin of 28.1 percent, and
had higher margins than Apple, Google, and Amazon. In 2018, Elsevier
cleared 36 percent profit on revenues of $3.3 billion. Academic journals
have an incredibly narrow readership—they are comprised of articles
written by specialists for specialists—but they are more than twice as
profitable as the most popular magazines, which clear 12 to 15 percent after they have paid their writers and editors. For-profit academic

publishers are publishing journals on molecular biology and theoretical mathematics, but they may as well be printing money.[2]

While these publishers aren't paying for most of the labor, that labor is not free. Someone pays the scientist or researcher. Someone pays for their laboratories and equipment. The editorial volunteers are employed in an academic setting that expects participation in peer review and provides time for it. So in the vast majority of cases, it is we the public who pay. Even if the labor comes through a private university, it is often supported through public research funding and, indirectly but no less certainly, through public student tuition grants and federally guaranteed student loans.

Having obtained this free labor, the academic publisher needs to sell it, and the problem here is that the audience for its esoteric material is very small. However, as academic publishers discovered, university libraries, in order to be relevant, generally *have* to provide the journals their professors demand. They don't have a choice. That makes the subscription price elastic beyond belief: one exceptionally obscure mathematics journal, *Tetrahedron*, went for $40,000 a year. What's more, academic publishers have taken a page from the cable TV companies and typically force university libraries to buy bundles. The University of Virginia paid $1.8 million to Elsevier in 2018, up from $1.7 million the year before. The University of California system paid $45 million a year for journal subscriptions, $11 million of which went to Elsevier. UVA also gave $672,000 to Springer for close to four thousand journals, a relative bargain. Its data revealed that no one ever consulted 1,400 of them. Like your cable TV bundle, you have to pay for Animal Planet even if you only ever watch HGTV.[3]

And if UVA or the UC system paid to buy these journal subscriptions, what that really means is that you and I paid for them, just like we paid for the labor that went into them. We, the public, support these institutions' research libraries when we fund the institutions themselves. So we pay for-profit academic publishers as they sell us the results of research that we paid for, which was reviewed by an editorial process that we also paid for. "Bizarre" was how Deutsche Bank, no enemy of capitalism or profiteering, described this "triple pay" system whereby "the state funds most research, pays the salaries of most of those checking the quality of research, and then buys most of the published product." Despite the poor economics and optics of this arrangement, it has persisted largely undisturbed since the 1950s, even as prices have skyrocketed: libraries increased their spending on recurring materials by 521 percent between 1986 and 2014.[4]

The public started funding research in a big way during the Cold War but neglected to put funding and planning into the process of dissemination. Policymakers and scientists had faith that their system of peer review and publication, which largely happened through scholarly societies, would be enough. We didn't anticipate how the volume of papers would overwhelm the small-scale journal operations run by the scholarly societies, or how anyone would work out a way to make money from them. A small number of astute publishers, often with very few connections to the academy or the scientific community, saw an opportunity in the vast amounts of funding pouring into the universities. Among these was Robert Maxwell, a former intelligence officer with a gift for languages, who built a vast publishing network based largely on personal connections. His Pergamon publishing outfit was the result of a multiyear hustle, a pitch to top scientists that promised better distribution for their articles at no cost to them. He appeared to lift the burden from scholarly societies and shake the dust off their musty journals. All the while he was expanding, he was concentrating the journal-publishing industry into fewer and fewer hands, and the sale of Pergamon to Elsevier was a logical step. Maxwell had little interest in science or the academy. His overwhelming drive was "to become a millionaire," he told a friend. And once he succeeded, he joined the ranks of the new Conservative Party power brokers in the United Kingdom who worked to privatize every public good that postwar Britain had funded. This from a multimillionaire who had made his fortune almost entirely from public funds spent on his pricey journals.[5]

Elsevier's acquisitions gave it control over 18 percent of the world's research papers, which it publishes through some three thousand journals. Its holdings include *Cell* and the *Lancet*, which convey unmatched prestige to researchers who manage to have papers accepted by them, and which research libraries believe they cannot do without. Elsevier doesn't quite have a monopoly, but it is close. Just five companies in 2013 controlled 53 percent of the research papers published, up from 20 percent in the early 1970s.[6]

We are told that free markets drive prices down through competition, so we get better products for less money. But the abandonment of research dissemination to for-profit publishers has had nothing close to this effect. The quality of the product is determined solely by nonmarket forces, namely the research and peer review that the journals get for free. Prices have only gone up. The profit motive and the free market have added no value to this process; instead, they have only helped distort how research gets done.

Researchers build on the work of other researchers, but according to the Research Information Network, 60 percent of those surveyed said that the lack of access to others' work, due to expensive subscriptions, hindered their own investigations. Specifically, 40 percent ran up against problems accessing the papers they needed at least once a week. Sixty-six percent hit problematic paywalls at least once a month. In the internet age this should not be happening, but the market has driven competing journals into silos, each with its own set of paywall restrictions. Few libraries have the resources needed to maintain subscriptions with all of them, but that has not translated into more-rational pricing and wider access. Instead, it has narrowed the field in which innovation can happen. Only the best-resourced researchers can get access to everything they need. Those working at a tier below the best-funded institutions have to work around restrictions. Those in developing countries are almost completely locked out of the conversation.[7]

Meanwhile, the profit motive also affects what kind of research gets done. In order to sell journals, companies want big discoveries. They want to see headlines. They are scarcely interested in the yeoman's work of science—the verification of other studies or studies that failed to prove a hypothesis—and yet this work is critical to advancing knowledge. If the null results are never published, researchers will repeatedly follow fruitless paths, simply because they don't know it's been tried before. And lack of information about verification studies means the knowledge we do have is resting on shaky ground. All this research is still going on, to some extent, but it's apparently not the business of for-profit journals to spread the word. The results of about half of all clinical trials in the United States, for example, never make it into publication. That creates duplication, waste, and inevitably real danger for consumers.

If all human activity is ultimately shaped by material self-interest and competition, as acolytes of the free market would have us believe, then the reaction of researchers upon learning of the staggering profits being made from their work would be to demand their share of the pie. Instead, the reaction has largely been an increased demand to tear down the pay-walls. We are seeing a growing realization that the interests of knowledge and for-profit publishing are incompatible. And the more practical realization is that the current model is unsustainable. The University of California dropped all its Elsevier subscriptions—worth $11 million a year—because the price was absurd, the bundles were inflexible, and it was wrong for UC to pay for research created within the UC system. The standoff ended with Elsevier agreeing to publish UC-generated research without paywalls, and UC agreeing to pay for publication. The agreement, touted as a victory by UC, still has a lot of public money—$13 million per year—going to a for-profit publisher, only now it's paying to keep publicly funded research open to the public. The publishers, sitting on piles of public money, are not going to simply abandon their perch.[8]

The Fair Access to Science and Technology Research (FASTR) Act would mandate that publicly funded research become freely available after a short embargo period. The bill has bipartisan co-sponsors in both the House and the Senate, and has been introduced in 2014, 2015, and 2017. So far it has only made it out of committee—and that committee vote was unanimous. The bill's previous incarnation, the Federal Research Public Access Act, failed to gain traction in 2006, 2010, and 2012. There is no overt and concentrated opposition to the measure in Congress, so far, but neither is there public pressure to move it forward. The current system may be just functional enough to prevent it from collapsing in on itself. Or the topic may be too arcane. Even if this is so, the values behind the move toward public access to research are easy to understand. We have been moving in the direction of openness and sharing for centuries, hindered at first only by the physical materials that contain our knowledge and the space through which they had to travel. It was only recently that the narrow interests of profit-centered publishing got in the way as well. But this odd moment overlapped with another development. "For all of human history before the digital age, writing has been rivalrous," Peter Suber reflects in his book on open-access publishing. Even if no one wanted to make a profit, the media—paper or stone—meant that only a few could have it at any given time. "Despite its revolutionary impact, writing was hobbled from birth by this tragic limitation. We could only record nonrivalrous knowledge in a rivalrous form."[9]

Now, Suber concludes, we have no reason to let this situation persist: "If we all have the right equipment, then we can all have copies of the same digital text without excluding one another." The digital revolution we have all experienced should have gone much further, but those massive profit margins got in the way, and they forced upon us gaping inequalities where there should be none. Suber notes that while Harvard subscribed to nearly one hundred thousand journals in 2008, the Indian Institute of Science had ten thousand subscriptions, and a number of major African universities had zero. We have needlessly allowed market players to embed themselves in a process that is inherently nonrivalrous. Not only did the market fail to bring down prices and improve quality, but it also allowed private interests to lock down a public good, restrain knowledge, and promote inequality on a global scale.[10]

24

They Even Want to Own the Weather

THE PUBLIC INVESTMENT IN RESEARCH UNIVERSITIES DURING THE COLD War ran parallel to its investment in meteorology, but while the U.S. government framed much of its science and technology funding in terms of competition with the Soviets, studying the weather was grounds for cooperation. President John F. Kennedy, for example, proposed to "explore promptly all possible areas of cooperation with the Soviet Union and other nations 'to invoke the wonders of science instead of its terrors,'" and a "weather prediction program" was a major part of this. While the World Meteorological Organization predated Kennedy's announcement, the effort to collect data through satellites, balloons, and sensors expanded rapidly with an influx of public funding and now includes 193 nations and territories, all bound by an agreement to provide "essential data" on "a free and unrestricted basis." Each day, global observations add up to twenty terabytes of data, which is processed by a supercomputer running 77 trillion calculations per second. It's an incredible, worldwide, concerted, and ongoing effort that has no parallel. It's also one that has had dramatic results.[1]

"When I started in the 1970s," recalled Dr. Louis Uccellini, the National Oceanic and Atmospheric Administration's (NOAA's) assistant administrator for weather services, "the idea of predicting extreme events was almost forbidden. How can you see a storm before the storm can be seen?" But he recalled how in 1993 the National Weather Service took the radical step of predicting a major storm. The predictions were borne out; the storm shut down the East Coast and killed dozens of people, but without the predictions it would have been much worse: "This time, states declared an emergency before the first flake of snow. It was just amazing for us to watch. We sat there wrapping our heads around what we'd done." When Uccellini started his career, an accurate six-day forecast was unthinkable. Today, we take the NWS six-day forecast for granted, and it's as accurate as the two-day forecast was in the 1970s. Today, cities can confidently brace for major storms days in advance. When Hurricane Andrew hit Miami-Dade County in 1992, the first warning came twenty-four hours before landfall. Today, we can expect an accurate warning five days out. Everything about meteorology, from data collection to modeling to forecasting, has improved exponentially. Uccellini confidently calls the revolution in weather forecasting "one of the major intellectual achievements of the twentieth century." Dr. John Zillman, director of the Australian Bureau of Meteorology, called the worldwide system "one of the world's most widely used and highly valued public goods."[2]

It had to be public. No private corporation would be able to enlist the help of nearly two hundred other nations and convince them to give up their data for free. No private corporation would sustain a project with such uncertain outcomes for decades, hoping that eventually the mass of data and the power of computing would grow to a point where the weather forecast would pay dividends. Today the National Weather Service's data and forecasts can be freely used by any commercial enterprise—agriculture, shipping, fishing, air transportation, and even commercial weather services. The worldwide system of weather services has an annual worth to its users of $100 billion; it costs a mere $10 billion to maintain. The NWS itself has a budget of only $1.17 billion.[3]

In the 1990s, at about the same time that forecasting got consistently good, private interests and free-market absolutists started insisting that the NWS and related agencies were "competing" with private enterprise. As they had with schools and trash collection and myriad other public services, they accused the government of running a "monopoly" that prevented private business from entering the sector. Barry Myers, head of AccuWeather, led the charge. In his mind, the government has no business making forecasts. Perhaps in a life-threatening emergency government had a role, but even here, he claimed, "The National Weather Service does not need to have the final say on warnings." According to Myers, the prosaic daily forecasts were products to be sold, and "the customer and the private sector should be able to sort that out." His bottom line took things to extremes: "The government should get out of the forecasting business."[4]

Myers found plenty of sympathy for his position among the Republicans who took over Congress in 1994. Michigan's Republican representative, Dick Chrysler, carped about how we were needlessly spending on the NWS. Why waste this taxpayer money when we could all just tune in to the Weather Channel? Music to Myers's ears, no doubt, but Chrysler was speaking from a place of profound ignorance. Both the Weather Channel and Myers's AccuWeather are utterly dependent on the National Weather Service for their underlying data and much of their forecasts. The commercial services may produce slightly different forecasts and slick graphics, but these rely completely on data gathered by NWS, NOAA, and the WMO. In other words, they rely completely on data that the American taxpayer has already paid for. In essence, Myers and his allies want the public to pay for data collection through taxes, agree to stop the publication of that data by the government in a useful form, then pay AccuWeather to access that data through their platforms (this bears a strong resemblance to the arrangement academic publishers have gotten away with since the 1950s).[5]

Myers has repeatedly accused the NWS of not playing fair. Testifying before Congress, he claimed that his situation was just like "the Post Office and Federal Express, except that it would be like the Post Office offering to carry every letter without postage." Like Federal Express, his whole business model is based on promoting the idea that his service is superior, but he has had a hard time proving this because overall it is simply not true. Instead, ever since the 1990s, he has campaigned against the National Weather Service. As a reward for his extraordinary efforts to hamstring a stellar federal agency in favor of a mediocre private business, President Donald Trump nominated him to be head of the National Weather Service in 2017, a position from which he could give AccuWeather everything it wanted. Trump's move was as ridiculous and audacious as Myers's constant whining about how unfair the government is when it provides citizens with information they paid for. But it was also a perfect capstone to Myers's thirty-year campaign against the public good.[6]

In the late 1990s and early 2000s, AccuWeather executives flooded the campaign coffers of Senator Rick Santorum, and Myers soon got an audience with the senator to complain about how unfair NWS was

to him when it gave away its forecasts for free. Soon a Senate committee was considering a Santorum-sponsored bill to "clarify the duties and
responsibilities" of NWS and NOAA. The 2005 bill banned the agencies from "providing a product or service" that "could be provided by
the private sector" unless it involved an emergency or if the secretary
of commerce determined the private sector was "unwilling or unable to
provide such a product." After vocal opposition by Senator Bill Nelson of
Florida, a state that knows the value of good weather predictions, the bill
died in committee. Next came Representative Jim Bridensteine's 2011
attempt to prevent NOAA from developing any new product or program
without first checking with Congress to make sure there wasn't a chance
that a for-profit business might want to use NOAA data to make a profit
from the idea. He tried again in 2016. Then he was tapped by Trump to
lead NASA.[7]

Myers didn't get his legislation, and withdrew himself from the nomi-
nation to lead NWS after the Senate dragged its feet for two years. But
he then wrangled an appointment to an NWS advisory board and pushed
forward a rule barring NWS employees from creating any kind of mobile
app. It happened soon after the 2011 Joplin tornado, a monster storm that
killed 158 people in Missouri. NWS employees had proposed a smartphone app to better deliver warnings to the public. Myers was apparently
"very helpful in drafting" a rule to kill the proposal, according to an
NWS policy director. Or as an NWS employee put it, "Barry Myers is
the reason we don't have the app." NWS employees, through their union,
pointed out that the rule prevented them from completing a core part of
their mission: communicating with the public. And their union lawyer
pointed out that they simply wanted to save lives. But this ultimately took
a backseat to Myers's insistence that his AccuWeather apps shouldn't
face "unfair" competition. Myers then expanded his crusade by arguing
that NWS shouldn't even be permitted to communicate through social
media.[8]

The year 2017 saw more weather-related damage than any previous
year on record. The year 2018 saw the Trump administration propose
deep cuts to the National Weather Service. The service was already
understaffed by 57 percent, and cuts called for the permanent elimina-
tion of 355 jobs. Of those, 248 were essential forecasting jobs (the func-

tion that the private weather services want to take over—they're okay with keeping the data collection going). The cuts would mean $2.2 million out of the weather balloon data collection program and $12.5 million from the observation stations. It spelled the end for the Vortex-SE tornado research program. "Literally, this is risking all of our lives to save a few million dollars," noted Dan Sobien, president of the NWS Employees Organization. When Congress defied Trump and specifically appropriated money for NWS hiring, the administration failed to follow through, causing lawmakers to charge that they were trying to get their cuts through defiance. Trump's war on the weather service continued into 2019 as he again tried to appoint Myers as its director and railed against the agency for clarifying that Hurricane Dorian would not in fact impact Alabama after the president claimed it would. The infamous attempt by the president to save face with a Sharpie soon followed.[9]

Two issues lie at the heart of the argument of those trying to dismantle the National Weather Service. First is the odd assertion that it's appropriate for a private company to force citizens to pay for weather data that they've already paid for through taxes. This is a hard sell, but privatization's disciples use the second issue to wave away the first. They claim, once again, that competition will spur innovation and lead to better forecasting at a lower cost; that the government is stopping this from happening by doing forecasting for free. So far in this book we've seen how the free market has stifled innovation in the charter school movement, delivered higher prices and lower quality in for-profit higher education, and created astronomical pricing in academic publishing. It's much the same for weather forecasting. The nation's favorite statistician, Nate Silver, a self-described "big fan of free-market competition," puts it simply: "Competition makes forecasts worse."[10]

In Silver's analysis, the three biggest players, AccuWeather, the Weather Channel, and the NWS, are all "pretty good" in terms of accuracy— when they keep things close to conventional methods and honor the fact that accuracy diminishes with the length of the forecast. An eight-day forecast, or maybe ten days at the outside, is about the limit of what most models can predict, and the NWS website limits itself to a one-week time frame. That's good science and good sense, and NWS can stick to that because it's not competing with anyone. But the Weather Channel, trying to draw viewers and clicks, pushes things out to fifteen days, well beyond the point where any existing models are useful. And AccuWeather attempts to win against all other services by offering an essentially meaningless ninety-day forecast.

Serious weather professionals hate this. Meteorologist Jason Samenow at the *Washington Post*, for instance, noted that "AccuWeather is putting out a product that has no demonstrated value, and they've never proven otherwise." Cliff Mass, professor of atmospheric science at the University of Washington, plainly stated that "these forecasts have no value at all." The problem is inherent in the amount of data we have and the fact that the weather two weeks from now depends on the weather one week from now. While we might get pretty close to predicting the weather one week from now, any error will be compounded if we stretch it out to two weeks, and so on. "This kind of thing should be condemned," insisted Dan Satterfield, a meteorologist who writes for the American Geophysical Union, "and if you have an AccuWeather app on your smartphone, my advice is to stand up for science and replace it."[11]

But AccuWeather didn't do this in the name of science. It did it to win against the Weather Channel and to gain additional clients for its high-end enterprise services. It did it for the revenue. So in this case, competition delivered to the market a nearly fraudulent product.

As bad as this willful misrepresentation is, the accuracy of even the short-term forecast faces distortion by commercial pressures. By way of explaining why "competition makes forecasting worse," Nate Silver lays out the concept of "wet bias," a tendency to overestimate the likelihood of rain. It's easy to see why commercial weather reports are willing to sacrifice accuracy on the altar of presentation: viewers are less likely to forgive getting caught in a rainstorm and more likely to forget the times they needlessly packed an umbrella. So the weathermen fudge. "The further you get from the government's original data," Silver writes, "and the more consumer-facing the forecasts, the worse this bias becomes."[12]

No matter what Barry Myers says, the government should not get out of the forecasting "business." The free market has fully demonstrated that it will warp forecasting to meet the perceived needs of its customers. It will prompt companies to go well beyond accepted science to entice consumers. But beyond the science and the models and the impressive data sets, there's another reason we have to keep our weather service strong and strongly public. The NWS's mission includes saving lives. The business model of corporations like AccuWeather includes saving lives of paying customers only.

Boasting about AccuWeather's pinpoint forecasting service, Joel Myers, founder and former CEO of AccuWeather and brother to Barry, told a reporter from CNBC how the company had saved Union Pacific Railroad from major losses with a tornado alert. "Two trains stopped two miles apart, they watched the tornado go between them." Amazing. And it was all possible because Union Pacific was a paying customer. But then he continued: "Unfortunately it went into a town that didn't have our service and a couple dozen people were killed. But the railroad did not lose anything."[13]

The immorality of this business model, which involves denying people life-saving information unless they pay for it, is ghastly. But it gets worse. The NWS did issue a warning in this case. People did take shelter. But Barry Myers and AccuWeather are actively seeking to limit how much the NWS can interact with the public, and are using campaign donations and lobbyists to do it. Recall that the NWS does not have a life-saving warning app because Myers didn't like it. It represents competition. And this was the man President Trump wanted to put in charge of our National Weather Service.[14]

Contrast the values and character of this man and his brother, based on how they run their business, with what Nate Silver saw when he visited the NWS in Maryland. "The meteorologists I met in Camp Springs were patriotic people." And they were excited about their role, "rarely missing an opportunity to remind me about the importance that weather forecasting plays in keeping the nation's farms, small businesses, airlines, energy sector, military, public services, golf courses, picnic lunches, and schoolchildren up and running." Contrast these values and that passion with those of the Myers brothers. Now, who do we want to be responsible for this public good?[15]

25

Drug Prices and the Pirates of the Patent System

IF WE VALUE DISCOVERY AND INNOVATION, IF WE BELIEVE THAT EACH NEW discovery is "a service rendered to society," as Immanuel Kant argued, then we should value open knowledge and its broad dissemination. But we also value those who made the discoveries, and we know that many of our geniuses deserve to be paid. Our Constitution captured these sometimes competing needs by giving Congress the "power . . . to promote the progress of science and useful arts by securing for limited times to authors and inventors the exclusive right to their respective writings and discoveries." We should take note of the intent. It was not to protect individual property rights; it was explicitly for the purpose of promoting progress. Whenever our patent system, a delicate balancing act between public and individual needs, becomes distorted by private interests, we should err on the side of promoting progress.

Economist Mariana Mazzucato has a powerful insight into how our thinking about patents might return to this original understanding. The patent system, she argues, should be understood not as a defense of "intellectual property 'rights' in the sense of something that is universal and immutable, but as a contract or deal based on a set of policy choices." The owner of that patent is making a deal. He gets a government-protected monopoly for a limited amount of time. But to get this benefit, he must show his hand, and accept the fact that his invention will ultimately be incorporated into the body of open knowledge as a public good.[1]

Over time, unfortunately, the balance has moved to the private side of the transaction. We have begun to assume that the whole purpose was always to protect property rights rather than the public good. "The current dominance of the narrative of entrepreneurs as wealth creators has," Mazzucato notes, "shifted the balance of the patent system away from an emphasis on the diffusion of knowledge towards private reward." The patent system now does more to inhibit the expansion of knowledge than it does to promote it. Patent trolls thrive in an environment where it's easy to get a patent covering vague "discoveries." Repeated budget cuts to the U.S. Patent Office mean there are fewer reviewers with less expertise in charge of making decisions on an even larger, and growing, number of applications. Faced with a long backlog and a loosening of regulations, they are forced to approve even questionable applications while hoping that the courts can figure it out down the line (this of course just amounts to shifting the costs).

What's more, we allowed private businesses, after extensive lobbying, to rewrite patent law and redefine the boundaries of what can be roped off and placed in the private domain. The Bayh-Dole Act of 1980 effectively allowed patents not just on products but also on ideas and discoveries that might lead to a useful purpose. While the definition of what could be patented was changing, so too were business expectations regarding how long a patent monopoly can stay in place, and the brand-name pharmaceutical companies led the way. In the early 1980s the big pharmaceutical companies lobbied hard for changes to the Hatch-Waxman Act of 1984, which was supposed to encourage generic drugs. According to a patent lawyer who represented the generic pharmaceutical industry, "it did not take brand-name manufacturers very long to realize that it was more profitable to find ways to improperly delay generic competition on older medicines than to invent new medicines." And so, even though the law was supposed to level the playing field, "for decades, brand-name manufacturers have gamed the provisions of Hatch-Waxman to delay competition."[2]

The result has been higher prices and less innovation, except when it comes to delaying generic versions of a drug from coming to market. Big pharma has developed tactics like authorized generics, pay for delay, product hopping, and citizen petitions. In 2017 Amgen attempted to evade U.S. patent law by housing its patent for the dry-eye treatment Restasis with the Saint Regis Mohawk tribe, an attempt the courts shot down.[3]

But no tactic for extending a monopoly is perhaps more pervasive than "evergreening" patents. Hatch-Waxman opened the door, ever so slightly, to patent renewals, and the pharmaceutical companies kicked it wide open. A typical scheme involves making small changes to a drug, its manufacturing process, or its delivery system and using that opportunity to apply for a new patent. Just the application triggers federal protections, so they file lots of applications. The scale of the effort by name-brand pharma to keep popular drugs evergreen is staggering. One study found that each of the top twelve name-brand drugs in the United States have, on average, 125 patent applications associated with them. This strategy amounts to an average of thirty-eight years of applied-for patent protection—almost twice what the law allows. The most popular name-brand drug in the United States, the arthritis treatment Humira, is surrounded by a thicket of 247 patent applications representing a corporate plan for thirty-nine years without competition from a generic. Since 2002, the cost of Humira has risen by 144 percent.[4]

But that price increase is relatively modest. We've also seen the high-profile example of Daraprim, which Turing Pharmaceuticals raised from $13.50 to $750 a tablet in 2015. Or Sovaldi, used to treat hepatitis C, which debuted at $84,000 for a full twelve- to twenty-four week treatment. Overall, we've seen drug prices triple over the last ten years. Most industry analysts see at least another doubling in the next ten years. Everyone knows this is a problem. One out of four people with diabetes is rationing their insulin doses—taking less than the required amount so more doses will be available—because they can't afford this life-sustaining drug. Hospitals are making expensive drugs less accessible. When the University of Utah hospital system saw its annual cost for Isoproterenol, a heart medication that can help stabilize patients in shock or after a heart attack, go from $300,000 to $1.9 million (or from $440 to $2,700 a dose), it took drastic measures. According to Erin Fox, the system's director of drug information, "We were forced to remove isoproterenol from our 100 emergency crash carts. Instead, we stocked our pharmacy backup boxes, located on each floor of our hospitals, to have the vital drug on hand if needed. We had to minimize costs without impacting patient care." Our fellow citizens are taking trips to Canada and Mexico for drugs, or taking risks with dodgy online suppliers. We all know this is wrong. We have been slower to come to the realization that it doesn't have to be this way.[5]

The lack of action on drug prices is rooted in the argument that if we regulate or control prices we will kill innovation. The argument assumes that the free market is the main driver of innovative drugs. This is false. A long history of partnerships between the public and drug manufacturers shows how false this is. The pharmaceutical industry would likely not exist if it weren't for the stream of public funding—nearly $900 billion—that started flowing in the 1930s. Even after the industry received government protections during the 1980s that were supposed to lead to more innovation, the public kept chipping in. Between 2010 and 2016 every single one of the 210 drugs approved by the FDA had received an assist from the National Institutes of Health through a total of $100 billion in funding for research projects. Those 210 drugs were the result of some 118,000 NIH Research Project Grants, which shows how complex and involved drug development can be. Like some of our highest achievements, they can be realized only through extensive support and vast resources. Seldom does a single private company have the resources to go it alone.[6]

Sovaldi, the hepatitis C drug that costs $1,000 a dose, and its later incarnation Harvoni, are derived from a compound discovered under NIH- and Veterans Administration–funded research. The public provided some $300 million toward this research, and the drug company Gilead did the follow-up research, making an important but smaller contribution to bring the drugs to market. The real breakthrough was in the discovery of the compound, and it's this kind of research that's often too risky for private investors to get behind. But once the groundwork is there, companies and investors start to line up. In this case, given how these drugs could be priced, it was a no-brainer for investors. Gilead made $45 billion in revenue in the first three years. It's hard to imagine how it could have spent more than the public's $300 million on research. One thing we do know about big pharma, however, is that they spend more on marketing than they do on R&D.[7]

The big drug companies have become "financialized" and have a huge role in the Wall Street ecosystem. They are significant lures for private-equity and hedge funds that have no real interest in biotechnology but have lots of interest in lots of money. Martin "Pharma Bro" Shkreli was a poster boy for this phenomenon, before he was sent to prison. He and his ilk see a winning formula in pharmaceuticals, and it's not unlike the one harnessed by the academic publishers and AccuWeather. First, find useful and important knowledge funded by the public. Take it, for free. Then get the government to protect you so you can "innovate." Pump money into marketing and draw investors. Set an absurdly high price knowing that people will pay because the public has protected you through patents. Rest assured that the profits you make won't have to be sacrificed to R&D because the public is already working hard on the next big innovation. That means you can reward your investors.

Big pharma rides this formula toward profit margins of 15–20 percent, and then turns to tell their customers that high drug prices, and all the suffering these prices produce, are just the cost of innovation. Meanwhile, 74 percent of the patents they file are just variations on a theme—an old drug with either a new delivery system, different dosage, or slightly altered manufacturing process. The real innovation still comes from the public: nearly 75 percent of all new "priority rating" compounds, the most radical new drugs, originate in NIH-funded research.[8]

The public has not abandoned research and innovation; private drug firms have. And they have become infected with a particular Wall Street virus, one that prioritizes money made from interest, rents, patents, market manipulation, and extraction over money made from actually creating things. The public, having already paid once for the research that gives us our most important treatments, has every right to lay claim to the knowledge behind these products as public goods. What's more, the very legislation that contributed to the current problem contains key solutions that have been largely ignored. The Bayh-Dole Act from 1980 tried to balance the loss of public control over publicly funded research by permitting price caps on important products. This provision has never been used. Not once.[9]

If we are realistic about how innovation happens, if we look at the facts of how important inventions arise through a combination of public research and private follow-through, we could do away with the view that the common good must be sacrificed to immutable property rights. The public contributed to these useful inventions; the public gets a say in how they can be accessed. Long before our current era of religious-level fervor for the free market, we granted the public the right to use patents. Under current law, the government has the right to create or have created generic versions of drugs in order to serve a public need. The government must also pay a "reasonable and entire compensation" to the patent holder. The amount can be negotiated or challenged in court, but the right of the people to access patented public goods cannot be denied. This right exists. It's codified in U.S. law. But our current slavish devotion to private profits ensures that its use is exceedingly rare.[10]

There have been a few exceptions. The military asserted government patent use for night-vision goggles and lead-free bullets. The Treasury has adopted patented software without permission. The patent holders received royalties, they made a lot of money, the free market did not collapse, and we didn't slide into socialism. If we can do this for soldiers and accountants, we can do it for fellow citizens who pay taxes that go toward pharmaceutical research. In fact, it might not even come to that, if we simply assert the leverage that government patent use conveys. During the 2001 anthrax scare, Tommy Thompson, the secretary of health and human services, tried to create an emergency stockpile of Bayer's Cipro, the only effective anti-anthrax drug. Bayer first pushed back on requests to ramp up production; then it quoted an unconscionable price. Secretary Thompson's moves to assert the right to a government patent use, however, got the company's attention. The public obtained the supply it needed at half the regular price.[11]

Can we expect to see such forceful moves again? Today's Republican Party seems to have sprinted in the other direction. President Trump's rhetoric on lowering drug prices rang hollow after he appointed no fewer than sixteen drug-industry insiders to top health-related administration positions. Even after losing his HHS secretary, Tom Price, to a scandal arising from his coziness to the health industry, Trump doubled down on his romance with big pharma by replacing Price with the president of Eli Lilly, Alex Azar. At the time, Azar's company was suffering PR blowback from its steep hike in insulin prices and a lawsuit claiming it engaged in price fixing. Perhaps sensing that his new secretary had no interest in affordable drugs, Trump opted for his favored policy option—

the shameless lie. "Drug prices are coming down, first time in 51 years because of my administration," he said in 2019, despite recent reports that the prices of 4,412 name-brand drugs had gone up in the year prior. Only forty-six drugs saw prices go down.[12]

Still, the need to lie tells us something. We all know, on a gut level, that the current situation is wrong. But it is exponentially more wrong when we realize that we have been paying for the research and that the drug profiteers are taking advantage of a patent system designed to benefit the public. And even that wrongness is compounded again by the fact that our politicians have long had the tools to fix this problem but have refused to act.

That lack of political will goes back to our ingrained belief that innovation arises only from competition and lightly regulated corporations. This belief has brought us secretive charter schools, a defunding of public higher education, an absurdly inefficient system for publishing research, attacks on the National Weather Service, and unconscionable drug pricing. When it comes to the creation of knowledge and real innovation, it's the public that has the resources and willingness to take risks, and it has the added benefit of being able to work toward a solution that benefits all, not merely a solution that enriches a few. Such solutions, as with drug pricing, are at hand. But first, as we said at the beginning of this book, we have to change the conversation.

Part IX

BECOMING PRO-PUBLIC

THIS BOOK IS ABOUT POWER—POWER OVER THE THINGS THAT MATTER TO all of us, that we need, that are essential for health, life, economic security, and our ability to participate in our democracy. But even though these are very real needs, our politics has been dominated by the theory that public power over such things is dangerous, that only the free market can guarantee freedom.

This book is also about what happens when we subscribe to that theory. As political scientist Corey Robin argues, we must "change the argument from abstractions of the free market to the very real power of the businessman." As this book has shown, the power of businesses, when given control over a public good, is immense. Corporations entrusted with public goods have effectively been given the power to lock people up, force them into a parallel justice system, deny them life-saving treatments, place vital information behind paywalls, divert money from poverty programs to wealthy investors, tie the hands of governments, and undermine our constitutional rights. Giving power over public goods to the free market does not dilute power; instead, it concentrates power in private hands and makes it unaccountable.[1]

But the central lesson shouldn't be simply that private corporations have too much power and control over public goods. And the central point shouldn't be simply that we've starved government of revenue, acquiesced to wholesale deregulation, and agreed to wild experiments that privatized our public goods. All of these small decisions transferred real power to real businesspeople. The most important lesson of this book is that, because we gave private interests that power, *we can take it back*.

If we take back control of our public goods—if we reject what political philosopher Michael Sandel calls "a market society"—we will gain an incredible opportunity to build instead a society based on public values and a commitment to ensuring that public goods are available to all. And as we increase access to public goods, we strengthen our ties to each other. We're all better off when we limit privatization and market competition over things that we all need—things including public health, key infrastructure, water, education, and democracy itself.

A society in which the public is in control is not one that completely eliminates the free market and the role of private companies in creating products and services we need; a pro-public society is merely one that ensures that the market does not capture power over public goods. A democratic, pro-public society is one in which the public decides, through deliberation, discussion, and debate, what stays in public control and what ought to be left to the rivalries of the free market. These are pragmatic decisions—some things, for example, simply have to be done at the scale of government—but they are also based on values. Our public decisions show what we care about.

Our definition of *public good* boils down to a few simple ideas. Public goods are things we all benefit from even if we don't personally use them, such as education, public transportation, the safety net, and the justice system. They are the things that are essential for life, including water and clean air. They are things that can make such broad and fundamental improvements to our quality of life that no one should be excluded, such as electricity and, increasingly, broadband internet service. They are the things that recognize our interconnectedness and interdependence and make us a healthier, fairer, more compassionate, and more democratic nation.

The Road Ahead

In one of the first acts of his presidency, Joe Biden signed an executive order phasing out the use of federal private prisons. But he didn't immediately cancel existing contracts. Contracts tie our hands. A contract signed by one administration is a way to force the next administration to continue a policy—or at least make it harder to undo. Likewise, President Biden was also unable to end the use of private immigrant detention centers. He simply couldn't. The federal government has grown utterly dependent on private companies for immigrant detention, and has had a hand in creating legislative requirements and profit incentives to fill them with detainees. Should detention be privatized? Should border crossers even be locked up? These important questions get pushed aside because privatized immigrant detention is now locked in as part of the landscape.

So, while the public mood is turning against privatization, it will be tough to root out, especially at a time when state and local governments are coping with the economic devastation caused by COVID while maintaining a long list of budget-busting tax cuts. Andrew Vitelli, a reporter for Inframation News, quotes a transportation investor who said, "There is going to be a fundamental shift on the other side of Covid-19 that is going to arise from the decimated state of state and local government finances." Historically, this scenario has led to more privatization because it is simply easier than creating a responsible budget that's fully funded. But the decision to privatize or maintain public control should not be dictated by expediency, circumstances, or opportunism. These important decisions should be made based on what we value and what we understand to be public goods.[2]

Taking It Back: Six Steps to Regaining Public Control over Public Goods

A different vision of society and citizenship, rooted in public values, is the way forward. But vision alone isn't enough. We need a shared commitment to public values and a movement that can embed those values into systems of laws, policies, institutions, governing practices, and decision-making at all levels of government. And we must continually respond to, refine, and improve those systems.

1) Define the Public: It's All of Us

We all contribute, we all benefit. When we make decisions about public goods, we must always strive to make sure no one is excluded. We cannot segment our public into winners and losers, the way the market segments us. We cannot exclude members of the public from the democratic process of conversation, deliberation, and decision-making as we determine what should be a counted as a public good.

We must avoid exclusions not just because it is right, but because we are fundamentally interconnected. Even though modern life has made it easy to pretend we are independent from each other—thanks to targeted marketing; gated communities; smartphones; and ideological, racial, and economic segregation—our interdependence has only increased, thanks to globalization, limited resources, environmental impacts, and integrated economies. Our choices affect others; that makes us responsible to others, just as they are to us.

Privatization got a huge boost from racism. When African Americans won voting rights, access to segregated spaces, and public benefits, a racist core of the American public reacted by vilifying public goods. These goods became viewed, inaccurately, as things that white people gave to black people, and this racist segment of the public simultaneously denied that they themselves were also beneficiaries of public goods. We will only become a real public if we all share in not only public goods, but the power over them. That means we will have to confront racism as it pertains to everything public: underfunded schools, water systems laced with lead, limited access to higher education, restrictions to home ownership, and lack of access to health care. All of these have antipublic thinking and racist structures at their very center.

Privatization also got a huge boost from consumerism. Mass production and mass marketing efficiently fulfill our desires for life's non-essentials, and we make the mistaken assumption that they can do the same for basic public goods. Democratic and Republican political leaders exploit this by treating us as mere customers of public services rather than as citizens. As historian Lizabeth Cohen wrote in her groundbreaking book *A Consumers' Republic*, "the market relationship" became "the template for citizens' connection to government." Bill Clinton's Reinventing Government initiative, for example, sought to provide a "customer service contract with the American people." This framework needs to change.[3]

We can't let private interests sell us public goods as consumers, because the free market can't avoid creating exclusions. School choice quickly devolves into segregation. Public parks and highways are divided into general versus premium services. In the midst of a national health crisis, ventilators go to the highest bidder.

If we want public goods for ourselves, we must be willing to be part of a public that includes all. This means fighting for everyone's right to have power over public goods as hard as we would fight for ourselves.

2) Let the Public Decide

In a democracy, the public, not the market, gets to determine what counts as a public good. When citizens in several towns and cities in Colorado overcame state-level roadblocks and corporate opposition to public broadband, they defined a public good. When voters in five states approved ballot initiatives that expanded Medicaid—something their own state governments had refused to do—they defined and embraced a set of values that counts health care as a public good. When cities chose to recognize that public transportation doesn't require treating riders as consumers, they defined a "right to the city" and created new economic opportunities.

These are not the acts of a top-down authoritarian regime. These are examples of citizens of a capitalist democracy taking control of public goods. A pro-public society will recognize that such actions need an ongoing public dialogue and a space for public deliberation. Ideally, facts and values will drive these conversations, not an appeal to "the market" or an insistence that government can't do things. The conversation shouldn't be about the proper size of government or whether it is intruding on someone else's profits, but whether the policy under discussion involves a public good and therefore whether the public needs to gain or maintain control.

We need to take these discussions out of the chambers of political insiders and corporate boards, and proactively create mechanisms and processes that let the public decide. Sometimes that means making those decisions at the ballot box and other times in legislatures, but in all cases it recognizes that technological, demographic, economic, and cultural shifts—or crises such as COVID—can drive new conversations about what should be public goods.

3) Pay for Things We Value

The pro-privatization argument often begins and ends with the promise that the public doesn't have to pay—that we can enjoy things we need and value without paying for them. This is simply not true. We will always pay; whether we pay through taxes or fees, whether we pay now or pay later, we must collectively bear the costs of the things we want. The supposed private-sector efficiency that's often promised to bring savings typically disappears in inflated executive salaries and "administrative costs," and the profit motive proves irresistible once companies realize they can insert contract riders guaranteeing public revenue even when times are bad. The public always pays.

We do, however, have choices about whether we will pay as citizens or as consumers. As citizens, our concern should be with making sure that public goods are equally available to all. This means paying for things we value through our taxes, and it means that our tax system should be progressive enough to avoid being painful, and widespread enough so that everyone does their part. We have to keep reminding our political leaders that paying taxes is not punishment; it is part of the responsibility of being a citizen. It follows that certain reforms to our tax system are in order, beginning with the idea that we should no longer tax income earned through investment at a lower rate than income from actual work. It also follows that astronomically high incomes should be taxed at a higher rate, as a way of asking those who have benefited most from the country to contribute the most back.

We should be concerned not merely with how we pay for public goods, but also with *when* we pay. When we invest early, we reap social, economic, and other benefits. Avoid visits to the dentist, lose teeth later. Don't fix the roof leak now, pay for a new roof later. Invest more in education now, spend less on prisons later. Prepare for the next pandemic with a few billion now, and maybe we won't be forced to lose trillions because we had to shut down the economy. It's common sense.

In 2011 the state emergency manager in Flint, Michigan, was faced with a $25 million budget deficit. He followed the austerity playbook and ended the practice of piping water from Detroit, using instead the less expensive water from the nearby polluted Flint River. The improperly treated water leached lead from the city's aging pipes and poisoned the city's residents. As a result, Michigan taxpayers received a bill for $600 million resulting from a legal settlement brought on behalf of the people of Flint, some of whose children will never recover from lead poisoning. Austerity can be very, very expensive, and can carry immeasurably high human costs as well.[4]

As citizens, we look after each other, and we pay our bills. We can be smart about taxes and control government spending without cutting the revenues we need so as to meet our basic needs and avoid leaving our fellow citizens stranded. But we should always pay for public goods. In fact, there's no one else who can.

4) Don't Let the Free Market Limit Freedom

Privatization is, in part, designed to close the door on public alternatives and programs and to eliminate public "competition" with the private sector. The design has had a great deal of success. Wholesale outsourcing, coupled with austerity policies, results in a hollowed-out government limited by the contracts it has signed and regulations that limit its scope.

Politicians who trumpet pro-market policies are often actually doing the bidding of corporations and end up limiting competition. They create a version of crony capitalism and replace what they fancifully call a state monopoly with an actual monopoly.

Commercial weather interests successfully created roadblocks so the National Weather Service couldn't create its own public weather app. Private health insurers blocked public health insurance options. The American Bankers Association and other financial trade groups have blocked postal banking. And the so-called Free File Alliance has limited the IRS's ability to offer online tax filing.

Such companies make a profit from being middlemen, and the fact that the public could easily replace them should make us question their value. If we really believe that the free market generates efficiencies, perhaps we should stop propping up companies that force us into inefficiencies by standing between us and a public good. What's more, there's an enormous amount of pent-up creativity in the public sector, all of it targeted at improving services to the public. But we can tap this creativity only if we stop shooing public servants away from their own good ideas in order to protect some fairly unimaginative corporations.

5) Create and Enforce Pro-Public Standards and Rules

Once we've decided what we consider public goods and establish basic standards, they become real only after we create procedures, rules, and rigorous enforcement that anticipate risk, allow us to monitor progress, and make sure that every person's voice is heard. Securing public control over public goods is the hard grunt work of governing, but it is absolutely essential.

Government agencies across the country purchase $2 trillion in goods or services every year—everything from fighter jets to janitorial services to COVID vaccines. Local, state, and federal government agencies adopt rules and standards for every aspect of our economy (and many of those rules, such as clean air and auto safety regulations, actually drive innovation). Setting minimum standards and establishing rules and regulations to protect public goods clearly falls within this governmental role.

Public decisions about public goods must remain fully in public hands. This means banning contract clauses that create obstacles for democratic decision-making and giving public goals precedence. We must avoid any arrangement that creates profit incentives that run counter to the public interest. Private prisons, for instance, profit from high crime rates. Private incinerators profit from low recycling rates. Public values aren't just the template for policies and regulations; they should permeate every contract the public enters.

Public decisions should strengthen and expand access to essential public goods—not weaken and exclude. That means identifying and evaluating potential long-term impacts and risks—positive and negative—when policy or spending decisions are made. For example, will an infrastructure agreement lead to more greenhouse gas emissions or less? Will the jobs created by a major procurement increase or decrease economic inequality? Will there be greater or fewer opportunities for citizens to have a voice in their communities? Are people of color not just included in the policy but also empowered to guide its implementation?

Public information must remain fully public. Any private corporation that accepts public money must also accept public scrutiny, and can't hide behind the concept of "trade secrets." Government transparency is essential for public accountability looking backward but also, and, perhaps more important, for decision-making looking forward. We need access to documents such as contracts, financial documents, and communications between policymakers and outside vendors. But we also need what Ethan Porter, a political scientist at George Washington University, calls "operational transparency" that isn't focused only on costs or specific metrics, but also on how public action and spending accomplish larger public goals.[5]

6) Surface the State: The Public Needs to See It

"Oddly," journalist Michael Tomasky wrote, "no one on the liberal side really defends government much." That may be changing, but not decisively or quickly enough to counter the ongoing attacks from the other side. And those attacks have consequences. As William J. Burns, president of the Carnegie Endowment, explained in the *Atlantic*, "If our political leaders continue to belittle public service, hollow out government institutions, and put patriotic Americans in the crosshairs of our culture wars, bureaucratic drift and dysfunction will become a self-fulfilling prophecy, and the gap between citizens and the state will only grow." His diagnosis and prescription are absolutely correct; the attacks need to stop. January 6, 2021, showed us all where they lead.[6]

We must all become more aware of what our government accomplishes. As *New York Times* columnist David Leonhardt reports, "The best way to improve the image of government is not through soaring speeches by politicians. It's through a version of the old journalism cliché: Show, don't tell."[7]

The results of public action are all around us yet almost entirely invisible. Cornell political scientist Suzanne Mettler argues that what she calls the "submerged state" is a central obstacle to building support for public action. According to Mettler, citizens' lack of knowledge of government's activities and successes will do "nothing to restore confidence in government, the awareness of the role government plays in their lives, or their engagement in the political process." She concludes that when people are "unaware that it is government that aids them, they embrace anti-government attitudes. Stateless governance does not beget citizens, it breeds cynicism and alienation."[8]

To turn the tide we need to "surface the state" that surrounds us. Most people don't realize, for instance, how decades of public investment in science and R&D have fueled American innovation in the products we all use in our daily lives. Political scientist Christopher Newfield argues, "A more effective mode through which government agencies could reconnect with the public is by telling accurate stories of the trail" from the lab bench to the things we find on our nightstand—in other words "from bench to bedside." Failure to do so, he concludes, suppresses "public interest as well as public financial support."[9]

While the preceding recommendations are presented as distinct steps, they aren't a menu of choices or a checklist to work through. They represent a way to govern for the common good—always. When they become standard practice and are carried out well, we can replace a vicious cycle of decline with a virtuous cycle of solidarity and common purpose.

Throughout this book we have pointed to the incentive structures baked into contracts and public-private partnerships that allow profit-seeking to drive and control public goods and services. Those incentives lead to exclusion, segregation, stratification, exploitation, and poverty.

We wrote this book to say that there's another way, that we can replace those incentives with ones that connect us to each other. We can choose to craft policies and make public investments that acknowledge and reinforce our linked fates and knock down structures of exclusion, segregation, and stratification. That's the right starting point for a pro-public future.

Acknowledgments

A BOOK OF THIS BREADTH NECESSARILY COMES FROM THE MINDS, IDEAS, and knowledge of many. First and foremost, Shar Habibi, Jeremy Mohler, Bob Lawson, Clare Crawford, and Lee Cokorinos, the stellar team at In the Public Interest, laid the foundation with incredibly high-quality research and analysis. Their extraordinary skills in communicating complex ideas powerfully to the general public and their deep commitment to the common good give the work special meaning and far-reaching impact. Paul Booth, a longtime labor leader, mentor, and supporter of this work, was instrumental in fostering our deep respect for and insight into the value and importance of public service. We lost him far too soon and we need him more than ever.

Sanjiv Rao during his time at the Ford Foundation and after has been an invaluable intellectual partner who has helped sharpen the thinking and ideas represented in this book. The enthusiasm for the project by leadership and staff at The New Press made the book better and more accessible, and will certainly add to its impact. We couldn't have done it without the support, encouragement, and skillful editing of Diane Wachtell, Rachel Vega-DeCesario, Kameel Mir, and Emily Albarillo. We are particularly grateful to literary agent Susan Rabiner. She offered extremely helpful guidance and advice at the crucial early stage of this project before we had secured a publisher. We owe her a dinner.

Two foundations, the Fine Fund and the Cloud Mountain Foundation, provided essential financial and moral support that helped make the book possible.

Finally, the authors would also like to acknowledge the largely unsung investigative journalists at both large and local outlets who help hold governments and privatizing corporations accountable. Much of this book is possible only because of their dedication to finding what their subjects would prefer to keep hidden.

Notes

1. Public Goods for the Common Good

1. "Remarks by President Trump, Vice President Pence, and Members of the Coronavirus Task Force in Press Conference," White House, March 13, 2020, https://www .whitehouse.gov/briefings-statements/remarks-president-trump-vice-president-pence -members-coronavirus-task-force-press-conference-3.

2. Chris Dolmetsch and Malathi Nayak, "Amazon, Walmart, Ebay Pushed by States to Stop Gougers," *Fortune*, March 23, 2020; Louise Matsakis, "Google Will Make a Coronavirus Site—but Not like Trump Said," *Wired*, March 15, 2020; Thom Hartmann, "Privatization May Be Killing Us: Mystery of Why the Trump Administration Still Hasn't Sent Out Promised Million CV Tests, as Delay Is Facilitating Transmission of the Virus by Undetected Carriers," *Buzzflash*, March 12, 2020; Linette Lopez, "If America Is Going to Survive the Coronavirus, the GOP Is Going to Have to Give Up on a 40-Year Crusade," *Business Insider*, April 10, 2020.

3. Timothy R. Homan, "Trump Faces Mounting Pressure to Unleash Defense Production Act," *Hill*, March 24, 2020; Peter Nicholas, "There Are No Libertarians in an Epidemic," *Atlantic*, March 10, 2020.

4. "Remarks by President Trump, Vice President Pence, and Members of the Coronavirus Task Force in Press Conference"; Stephanie M. Lee and Dan Vergano, "The Federal Government Is Planning to Order 5-Minute Coronavirus Tests—but Not Nearly Enough for Everyone Who Needs One," *BuzzFeed News*, April 4, 2020; Rob Stein, "Coronavirus Testing Backlogs Continue as Laboratories Struggle to Keep Up with Demand," *NPR*, April 3, 2020.

5. Eliza Relman, "Andrew Cuomo Says States Are Outbidding Each Other and Raising Prices for Critical Coronavirus Medical Supplies," *Business Insider*, March 23, 2020; Rachana Pradhan, "Why the Hunt for Ventilators Was a Mess—and Why It's Not Over," *Daily Beast*, June 14, 2020; Katherine Eban, "'That's Their Problem': How Jared Kushner Let the Markets Decide America's COVID-19 Fate," *Vanity Fair*, September 17, 2020; Katherine Eban, "'We Think the Markets Will Sort It Out': Could White House Action on COVID Testing Have Saved the American School Year?," *Vanity Fair*, December 16, 2020.

6. Pradhan, "Why the Hunt for Ventilators Was a Mess."

7. Homan, "Trump Faces Mounting Pressure to Unleash Defense Production Act"; Relman, "Andrew Cuomo Says States Are Outbidding Each Other"; Lee Fang, "Banks Pressure Health Care Firms to Raise Prices on Critical Drugs, Medical Supplies for Coronavirus," *Intercept*, March 19, 2020.

8. Pradhan, "Why the Hunt for Ventilators Was a Mess."

9. Paul C. Light, "The True Size of Government," Issue paper (The Volcker Alliance, October 4, 2017), https://www.volckeralliance.org/publications/true-size-government.

10. In the Public Interest, "Out of Control: The Coast-to-Coast Failures of Outsourcing Public Services to For-Profit Corporations" (Washington, DC, December 2013); Daniel Vock, "Indiana Governor Mitch Daniels' Toll Road Lease Will Have Major Impact on His Legacy and the State," *Stateline*, June 19, 2012, http://www.pewtrusts.org/en/research-and

-analysis/blogs/stateline/2012/06/19/indiana-highway-building-ramps-up-as-daniels-term -winds-down; Ellen Dannin, "Infrastructure Privatization Contracts and Their Effect on Governance," Penn State Legal Studies Research Paper No. 19-2009, July 10, 2009, http://dx.doi.org/10.2139/ssrn.1432606; Mike Ludwig, "When Outsourcing Public Services to Private Companies Goes Wrong," *Truthout*, December 11, 2013; Justin Prichard, "Fewer of Tomorrow's Freeways Will Be Free," *Florida Times-Union*, June 26, 2015; Dave Johnson, "5 Ways Privatization Is Fleecing American Taxpayers," *Salon*, May 20, 2014; Ryan Holeywell, "Public-Private Partnerships Are Popular, but Are They Practical?," *Governing*, November 2013; Jeffrey Leib, "Toll Firm Objects to Work on W. 160th," *Denver Post*, July 23, 2008.

11. B.J. Lutz, "IG Says City Lost Nearly 4 Billion Quarters," *NBC Chicago*, July 22, 2009; Samuel Kling, "That Parking Meter Deal Is Still Haunting Chicago. Here's One Fix Lightfoot Can Make," *Chicago Tribune*, April 4, 2019; Office of the Inspector General, City of Chicago, "Description of the City's Reserved Powers under the Parking Meter Concession" (Chicago, October 2012), https://igchicago.org/wp-content/uploads/2012/10/Description-of-Citys-Reserved-Powers-under-the-Parking-Meter-Concession.pdf; Office of the Inspector General, City of Chicago, "Report of Inspector General's Findings and Recommendations: An Analysis of the Lease of the City's Parking Meters" (Chicago, June 2, 2009), https://igchicago.org/wp-content/uploads/2011/03/Parking-Meter-Report.pdf.

12. Carl Takei, "Is the Private Prison Industry Still Too Big to Fail?," *Democracy: A Journal of Ideas*, August 31, 2016; Madison Pauly, "A Brief History of America's Corporate-Run Prison Industry," *Mother Jones*, August 2016; Shane Bauer, "Private Prisons Are Shrouded in Secrecy. I Took a Job as a Guard to Get Inside—Then Things Got Crazy," *Mother Jones*, August 2016; Erik Larson, "Captive Company," *Inc*, June 1, 1988.

13. Bauer, "Private Prisons Are Shrouded in Secrecy."

14. Ibid.; Eric Schlosser, "The Prison-Industrial Complex," *Atlantic*, December 1998.

15. Kay Whitlock, "Community Corrections: Profiteering, Corruption and Widening the Net," *Truthout*, November 20, 2014.

16. Michael J. Sandel, "Citizens or Consumers?," *Song of a Citizen*, accessed September 7, 2020, http://www.songofacitizen.com/songofacitizen.com/Michael_S.html; Sherrilyn Ifill, "A Matter of Democratic Survival," *Poverty and Race*, March 1, 2018, https://prrac.org/a-matter-of-democratic-survival.

17. Ifill, "A Matter of Democratic Survival"; Robert Reich, "America Has No Real Public Health System—Coronavirus Has a Clear Run," *Guardian*, March 15, 2020; David Armiak, "ALEC Leading Right-Wing Campaign to Reopen the Economy Despite COVID-19," *PR Watch*, April 30, 2020.

18. Alex Kotch, "Devos-Funded Group Organizes Protest Against Michigan Governor's Stay-at-Home Order," *PR Watch*, April 17, 2020.

2. The Roots and Reasons of Privatization: A Very Brief History

1. Donald Cohen, "The History of Privatization: How an Ideological and Political Attack on Government Became a Corporate Grab for Gold," *Talking Points Memo*, June 9, 2016; Paul C. Light, "The True Size of Government," Issue paper (The Volcker Alliance, October 4, 2017), https://www.volckeralliance.org/publications/true-size-government.

2. Milton Friedman, "The Role of Government in Education," in *Economics and the Public Interest*, ed. Robert A. Solo (New Brunswick, NJ: Rutgers University Press, 1955).

3. Milton Friedman, "The Social Responsibility of Business Is to Increase Its Profits," *New York Times Magazine*, September 13, 1970; Friedman, "The Role of Government in Education."

4. Friedman, "The Role of Government in Education"; Leo Casey, "When Privatization Means Segregation: Setting the Record Straight on School Vouchers," *Dissent*, August 9, 2017.

5. Chris Ford, Stephenie Johnson, and Lisette Partelow, "The Racist Origins of Private School Vouchers" (Washington, DC: Center for American Progress, July 12, 2017).

6. Cohen, "The History of Privatization"; E.S. Savas, "Getting on Top of the Problem," *New York Times*, August 6, 1975.

7. Nancy MacLean, *Democracy in Chains: The Deep History of the Radical Right's Stealth Plan for America* (New York: Viking, 2017), 144.

8. Cohen, "The History of Privatization"; Peg Masterson, "Should the State Divest?," *Milwaukee Sentinel*, October 14, 1986; MacLean, *Democracy in Chains*, 144.

9. Cohen, "The History of Privatization"; Jeffrey R. Henig, "Privatization in the United States: Theory and Practice," *Political Science Quarterly* 104, no. 4 (1989): 649–70, https://doi.org/10.2307/2151103.

10. Cohen, "The History of Privatization"; Robert Poole Jr., "Municipal Services: The Privatization Option" (Washington, DC: Heritage Foundation, January 11, 1983).

11. Cohen, "The History of Privatization"; Bud Newman, "Key Word of New Budget: 'Privatization,'" United Press International, January 26, 1986, https://www.upi.com/Archives/1986/01/26/Key-word-of-new-budget-Privatization/6143507099600.

12. Ronald Reagan, "Statement on the President's Commission on Privatization," Speech, September 3, 1987, https://www.reaganlibrary.gov/research/speeches/090387a.

13. Cohen, "The History of Privatization"; Reason Foundation, "Transforming Government Through Privatization: Reflections from Pioneers in Government Reform" (Washington, DC, 2006); Ronald Utt, "Improving Government Performance Through Competitive Contracting" (Washington, DC: Heritage Foundation, June 25, 2001); Stuart M. Butler and Kim R. Holmes, eds., *Mandate for Leadership IV: Turning Ideas into Actions* (Washington, DC: Heritage Foundation, 1997).

14. Pat Beall, "Big Business, Legislators Pushed for Stiff Sentences," *Palm Beach Post*, October 27, 2013; Madison Pauly, "A Brief History of America's Corporate-Run Prison Industry," *Mother Jones*, August 2016; Scott Keyes, "How Scott Walker Built a Career Sending Wisconsin Inmates to Private Prisons," *Nation*, February 26, 2015; American Civil Liberties Union, "Banking on Bondage" (New York, November 2011); Ed Pilkington, "Scott Walker, First ALEC President? Long Ties to Controversial Lobby Raise Concern," *Guardian*, July 22, 2015.

15. American Civil Liberties Union, "Banking on Bondage."

16. Keyes, "How Scott Walker Built a Career Sending Wisconsin Inmates to Private Prisons"; Pilkington, "Scott Walker, First ALEC President?"; Jason Stein, "At ALEC Meeting in California, Walker Touts Wisconsin Laws," *Milwaukee-Wisconsin Journal Sentinel*, July 23, 2015.

17. U.S. General Accounting Office, "Welfare Reform: Federal Oversight of State and Local Contracting Can Be Strengthened" (Washington, DC, June 2002), https://www.gao.gov/assets/240/234841.pdf.

18. Dave Lesher, "Privatization Emerges as a New Welfare Option," *Los Angeles Times*, January 27, 1997; Wendy Bach, "Welfare Reform, Privatization, and Power: Reconfiguring

Administrative Law Structures from the Ground Up," CUNY Academic Works (CUNY School of Law, 2009), h9p://academicworks.cuny.edu/cl_pubs/204; Andrew Flowers, "Most Welfare Dollars Don't Go Directly to Poor People Anymore," *FiveThirtyEight*, August 25, 2016; Monica Potts, "The American Social Safety Net Does Not Exist," *Nation*, October 13, 2016.

19. Bach, "Welfare Reform, Privatization, and Power"; Eric Lipton, "Rejecting Favoritism Claim, Court Upholds a City Welfare Contract," *New York Times*, October 25, 2000.

20. Bach, "Welfare Reform, Privatization, and Power."

21. Ibid.

22. Ibid.; New York City Bar Committee on Social Welfare Law, "Welfare Reform in New York City: The Measure of Success" (New York, August 2001), http://nycbar.org/member-and-career-services/committees/reports-listing/reports/detail/welfare-reform-in-new-york-city-the-measure-of-success.

23. Jeremy Kuzmarov, "'Distancing Acts': Private Mercenaries and the War on Terror in American Foreign Policy," *Asia-Pacific Journal* 12, no. 52 (December 21, 2014), https://apjjf.org/2014/12/52/Jeremy-Kuzmarov/4241.html; Kathy Gilsinan, "How Mercenaries Are Changing Warfare," *Atlantic*, March 25, 2015; Spencer S. Hsu and Victoria St. Martin, "Four Blackwater Guards Sentenced in Iraq Shootings of 31 Unarmed Civilians," *Washington Post*, April 13, 2015; Jason Peckenpaugh, "Army Contractors Earn Higher Salaries, Study Finds," *Government Executive*, July 26, 2001; Sean McFate, "America's Addiction to Mercenaries," *Atlantic*, August 12, 2016; James Risen, "Use of Iraq Contractors Costs Billions, Report Says," *New York Times*, August 11, 2008; Michael Boyle, "How the US Public Was Defrauded by the Hidden Cost of the Iraq War," *Guardian*, March 11, 2013.

24. Kate Lao Shaffner, "Pa. Cities Consider Leasing Out Water System to Balance Budget," *Keystone Crossroads*, October 23, 2014; Gary Suhadolnik and Jacqueline Thomas, "Pitfalls of Leasing Turnpike," *Cleveland Plain Dealer*, October 29, 2011.

25. Kate Zernike, "Betsy DeVos, Trump's Education Pick, Has Steered Money from Public Schools," *New York Times*, November 23, 2016; Julie Bosman, "Public Schools? To Kansas Conservatives, They're 'Government Schools,'" *New York Times*, July 9, 2016.

26. Forrest Knox, "Public Schools' Biggest Mistake," *Cowley Courier Traveler*, February 4, 2015, http://www.ctnewsonline.com/opinion/columns/article_0b587715-e565-5b0b-aa9e-724132b150b4.html.

27. Justine McDaniel, "Education Secretary Betsy DeVos Personally Funding 'Opportunity Scholarship' for Philly Girl Cited by President Trump," *Philadelphia Inquirer*, February 5, 2020; Madeleine Carlisle, "Trump Gave a Scholarship to a 4th Grader 'Trapped' in a 'Failing' Public Education at the State of the Union. She Reportedly Attends a Top Charter School," *Time*, February 8, 2020; Daniel Politi, "State of the Union Scholarship Recipient Already Attends Top Charter School," *Slate*, February 8, 2020; Jonathan Chait, "Trump and DeVos Propose to Eliminate Federal Charter School Funds," *New York*, February 10, 2020.

28. David Dayen, "Trump's Transition Team Is Stacked with Privatization Enthusiasts," *Nation*, December 28, 2016.

29. Chait, "Trump and DeVos Propose to Eliminate Federal Charter School Funds"; Nat Malkus, Richard V. Reeves, and Nathan Joo, "The Costs, Opportunities, and Limitations of the Expansion of 529 Education Savings Accounts" (Washington, DC: Brookings Institution, April 12, 2018).

30. Kevin Carey, "New Kind of Student Loan Gains Major Support. Is There a Downside?," *New York Times*, December 16, 2019; Malcolm Harris, "What's Scarier Than Student Loans? Welcome to the World of Subprime Children," *New York Times*, May 11, 2019.

31. Monsy Alvarado, Ashley Balcerzak, et al., "'These People Are Profitable': Under Trump, Private Prisons Are Cashing In on ICE Detainees," *USA Today*, December 20, 2019.

32. Eric Lipton and Lisa Friedman, "E.P.A. Contractor Has Spent Past Year Scouring the Agency for Anti-Trump Officials," *New York Times*, December 15, 2017; Aram Roston, "Trump Campaign Cochair Was Part of Team Pushing to Privatize Spy Operations to Evade 'Deep State,'" *BuzzFeed News*, January 3, 2018.

33. Amy Goldstein and Lena H. Sun, "Hospital Officials, Experts Say New Federal Rules for Covid-19 Reporting Will Add Burdens During Pandemic," *Washington Post*, July 15, 2020; Lenny Bernstein, Josh Dawsey, and Yasmeen Abutaleb, "Growing Friction Between White House, CDC Hobbles Pandemic Response," *Washington Post*, May 15, 2020; Adriel Bettelheim, "Trump's Covid-19 Data Reporting Switch Draws Outcry from Health Groups," *Politico*, July 15, 2020; Sheryl Gay Stolberg, "Firm Helping Run U.S. Coronavirus Database Refuses Senators' Questions," *New York Times*, August 14, 2020.

3. Privatizing Public Health Makes Us Sick:
An Epidemic of Market Failures

1. Katherine Eban, "'That's Their Problem': How Jared Kushner Let the Markets Decide America's COVID-19 Fate," *Vanity Fair*, September 17, 2020; "Remarks by President Trump, Vice President Pence, and Members of the Coronavirus Task Force in Press Conference," White House, March 13, 2020, https://www.whitehouse.gov/briefings-statements/remarks-president-trump-vice-president-pence-members-coronavirus-task-force-press-conference-3.

2. James C. Capretta, "On Public Health and Private Incentives," American Enterprise Institute, May 15, 2020, https://www.aei.org/articles/on-public-health-and-private-incentives; Michael Brendan Dougherty, "We Need More Libertarianism Too," *National Review*, April 7, 2020; Austill Stuart, "In Early Stages of Coronavirus Fight, the Private Sector Was Ready to Help, But the Federal Government Didn't Let It," Reason Foundation, March 23, 2020.

3. Kent Babb, "As Thousands of Athletes Get Coronavirus Tests, Nurses Wonder: What About Us?," *Washington Post*, December 3, 2020.

4. Sarah Kliff and Margot Sanger-Katz, "Bottleneck for U.S. Coronavirus Response: The Fax Machine," *New York Times*, July 13, 2020.

5. Sarah Kliff, "Most Coronavirus Tests Cost About $100. Why Did One Cost $2,315?," *New York Times*, June 16, 2020.

6. Dana Milbank, "When You Drown the Government in the Bathtub, People Die," *Washington Post*, April 10, 2020.

7. Julie Bosman and Richard Fausset, "The Coronavirus Swamps Local Health Departments, Already Crippled by Cuts," *New York Times*, March 14, 2020; Milbank, "When You Drown the Government in the Bathtub, People Die."

8. Robert Reich, "America Has No Real Public Health System—Coronavirus Has a Clear Run," *Guardian*, March 15, 2020.

9. Pierre Lemieux, "Public Health Officials Far Too Often Ignore the Costs and Trade-Offs Involved in Policy Decisions," Reason Foundation, April 7, 2020.

10. Julie Bosman, "Health Officials Had to Face a Pandemic. Then Came the Death Threats," *New York Times*, June 22, 2020 (emphasis on "our" added).

11. "Federal Officials Allowed Distribution of COVID-19 Antibody Tests After They Knew Many Were Flawed," *60 Minutes* (CBS, June 28, 2020).

12. "Remarks by President Trump, Vice President Pence, and Members of the Coronavirus Task Force in Press Conference."

13. J. David McSwane and Ryan Gabrielson, "The Trump Administration Paid Millions for Test Tubes—and Got Unusable Mini Soda Bottles," *ProPublica*, June 18, 2020.

14. Rob Stein, "Supplies Sent to Labs by Trump Administration to Boost Testing Are Not Always Helpful," *All Things Considered* (NPR, June 22, 2020); McSwane and Gabrielson, "The Trump Administration Paid Millions for Test Tubes—and Got Unusable Mini Soda Bottles."

15. Stein, "Supplies Sent to Labs by Trump Administration to Boost Testing Are Not Always Helpful."

16. Lorine Swainston Goodwin, *The Pure Food, Drink, and Drug Crusaders, 1879–1914* (Jefferson, NC: McFarland, 1999).

17. D.J. Wagstaff, "Public Health and Food Safety: A Historical Association," *Public Health Reports* 101, no. 6 (December 1986).

18. Hearing before the House Committee on Agriculture, June 6, 1906; Ruth deforest Lamb, *American Chamber of Horrors: The Truth About Food and Drugs* (New York: Farrar & Rinehart, 1936); Written testimony to Senate Committee on Commerce hearings, December 7 and 8, 1933.

19. Stephanie Armour, "Food Sickens Millions as Company-Paid Checks Find It Safe," *Bloomberg*, October 11, 2012; Marian Wang, "FDA's Findings on Salmonella-Linked Egg Farms: Mice, Maggots, Manure," *ProPublica*, August 31, 2010; Michael Moss and Andrew Martin, "Food Problems Elude Private Inspectors," *New York Times*, March 5, 2009.

20. Armour, "Food Sickens Millions as Company-Paid Checks Find It Safe."

21. "Top Chicken Brands Now Inspected by Own Employees," *Food and Water Watch*, May 25, 2016, https://www.foodandwaterwatch.org/news/top-chicken-brands-now-inspected-own-employees; Jill Richardson, "The USDA's Reckless Plan," *OtherWords*, September 11, 2013, https://otherwords.org/usdas-reckless-plan.

22. "Top Chicken Brands Now Inspected by Own Employees"; Rod Leonard, "The USDA Plan for Deregulating and Privatizing Meat and Poultry Inspection: A Short History," Institute for Agriculture and Trade Policy, December 5, 2013, https://www.iatp.org/documents/the-usda-plan-for-deregulating-and-privatizing-meat-and-poultry-inspection-a-short-history; J. David Cox Sr., "Why It's Time to Dump the 'Filthy Chicken Rule,'" *Huffington Post*, April 23, 2014.

23. "Food Safety Group: Privatizing Poultry Inspections Result in Contaminated Food," *Industrial Safety & Hygiene News*, October 15, 2015; "Inspectors Warn Against USDA's High-Speed Hog Inspection Program," Food Integrity Campaign, January 30, 2015.

24. Leonard, "The USDA Plan for Deregulating and Privatizing Meat and Poultry Inspection."

4. "They Just Have to Pay": Privatizing the Public's Water Supply

1. Erwin Wagenhofer, *We Feed the World*, documentary (Allegro Film, 2005); Aaron Miguel Cantú, "Private Water Industry Says Water Bills 'Have to Go Up,'" *Truthout*, May 14, 2015.

2. Dan Bacher, "Activists 'Shut Down' Nestlé Water Bottling Plant in Sacramento,"

Alternet, April 1, 2015; "Majority Against Nestle California Water Bottling," *Forbes*, May 11, 2015.

3. James Salzman, "Thirst: A Short History of Drinking Water," Duke Law School Legal Studies (Durham, NC: Duke University, December 2005).

4. Committee on Privatization of Water Services in the United States, National Research Council, *Privatization of Water Services in the United States: An Assessment of Issues and Experience* (Washington, DC: National Academies Press, n.d.); Gerald J. Kaufmann Jr., "The Delaware River Revival: Four Centuries of Historic Water Quality Change from Henry Hudson to Benjamin Franklin to JFK," *Pennsylvania History: A Journal of Mid-Atlantic Studies* 77, no. 4 (Autumn 2010): 432–65, https://doi.org/10.5325/pennhistory.77.4.0432; Salzman, "Thirst."

5. Elbert J. Taylor, "The Beginnings of Philadelphia's Water Supply," *Journal of the American Water Works Association* 42, no. 7 (July 1950): 633–44; Niva Kramek and Lydia Loh, "The History of Philadelphia's Water Supply and Sanitation System" (Philadelphia: Philadelphia Global Water Initiative, June 2007).

6. Salzman, "Thirst."

7. Martin V. Melosi, *Precious Commodity: Providing Water for America's Cities*, History of the Urban Environment (Pittsburgh, PA: University of Pittsburgh Press, 2011).

8. American Society of Civil Engineers, "Infrastructure Report Card: Drinking Water" (Reston, VA, 2017), https://www.infrastructurereportcard.org.

9. Ibid.

10. Rachel Dovey, "4 Things to Know Before Your Water Is Privatized," *Next City*, January 7, 2015.

11. Darryl Fears and Brady Dennis, "One City's Solution to Drinking Water Contamination? Get Rid of Every Lead Pipe," *Washington Post*, May 10, 2016.

12. Katrina vanden Heuvel, "The Poisoning of Flint," *Washington Post*, January 19, 2016; Merrit Kennedy, "Lead-Laced Water in Flint: A Step-By-Step Look at the Makings of a Crisis," *NPR*, April 20, 2016.

13. Alan Greenblat, "State Budget Fallout: 'A Hurricane That Hits All Over the Country,'" *Governing*, April 9, 2020; Rachel A. Davis, "Bankruptcy and Privatization Will Not Lead Us to Recovery," *Hill*, May 14, 2020; Tony Romm, "Over 700 Cash-Strapped Cities Halt Plans to Repair Roads, Water Systems or Make Other Key Investments," *Washington Post*, June 23, 2020.

14. Robert Kuttner, "Privatizing Our Public Water Supply," *American Prospect*, July 7, 2020; Action Center on Race and the Economy, et al. to John Barrasso and Tom Carper, "Oppose Voluntary Water Partnership for Distressed Communities Act," Letter, May 16, 2018; Food and Water Action, et al. to Mitch McConnell et al., "Opposition to the Voluntary Water Partnership for Distressed Communities Act," Letter, May 16, 2018, https://www.foodandwaterwatch.org/sites/default/files/opposition_to_the_voluntary_water_partnerships_for_distressed_communities_act.pdf; Tammy Duckworth, Mike Braun, and Dianne Feinstein, "Voluntary Water Partnership for Distressed Communities Act, S. 2596" (2019), https://www.congress.gov/bill/116th-congress/senate-bill/2596/text; "New Report Shows U.S. Water Systems Dangerously Behind on Capital Improvements," *Truth from the Tap*, January 27, 2020, https://truthfromthetap.com/new-report-shows-u-s-water-systems-dangerously-behind-on-capital-improvements.

15. Lindsay Abrams, "Water Is the New Oil: How Corporations Took Over a Basic Human Right," *Salon*, October 5, 2014; Julian Brookes, "Why Water Is the New Oil,"

Rolling Stone, July 7, 2011; Shaffner, "Pa. Cities Consider Leasing Out Water System to Balance Budget"; Cantú, "Private Water Industry Says Water Bills 'Have to Go Up.'"

16. Laura Bliss, "Guess Who's Paying the Price for America's Crumbling Water Infrastructure?," *CityLab*, July 13, 2015; Food and Water Watch, "American Water: A Corporate Profile" (Washington, DC, November 2013); Cantú, "Private Water Industry Says Water Bills 'Have to Go Up'"; In the Public Interest, "How Privatization Increases Inequality" (Washington, DC, September 2016); Gretchen Metz, "Pa. American Customers Face Another Rate Hike," *Daily Local*, June 1, 2011.

17. Dean Starkman, "Cities and Private Equity Firms Fight over Ownership of Water Systems," *Los Angeles Times*, October 15, 2015.

18. "Apple Valley Ranchos Water Company Wants a 30 Percent Rate Increase—April 30 Public Hearing," *Mojave River Valley News*, April 23, 2014; Martin Kidston, "Missoula, California Town to Collaborate on Water System Fights," *Missoulian*, July 18, 2014; Starkman, "Cities and Private Equity Firms Fight over Ownership of Water Systems"; Chris Glorioso, "Water Company Spends Thousands on Brunch, Booze, Golf Balls, Then Asks for Rate Increase," *NBC New York*, November 25, 2014; Mitch Jones, "United Water Living Large, Customers Stuck with the Bill," *Food & Water Watch*, December 1, 2014, Page discontinued.

5. The Stuff of Life: Reclaiming Public Water

1. Emanuele Lobina, Satoko Kishimoto, and Olivier Petitjean, "Here to Stay: Water Remunicipalisation as a Global Trend" (Transnational Institute, Multinationals Observatory, Public Services International Research Unit, University of Greenwich, 2014).

2. "After 14 Years, Donna Set to Take Over Water Services," *Monitor*, July 20, 2015; Danielle Battaglia, "Reidsville to Cut Ties with United Water," *News & Advance*, September 14, 2013.

3. Allie Robinson Gibson, "Town Takes Over Coeburn's Public Works Department," *Bristol Herald Courier*, April 24, 2014; Kristi O'Connor, "Coeburn Water Issue Said to Be Clearing Up Soon," WCYB, January 5, 2016.

4. Lobina, Kishimoto, and Petitjean, "Here to Stay"; Food and Water Watch, "United Water: A Corporate Profile" (Washington, DC, July 2013); Sarah Rubenstein, "Atlanta and United Water Dissolve 20-Year Contract," *Atlanta Business Chronicle*, January 24, 2003.

5. Food and Water Watch, "Veolia Water North America: A Corporate Profile" (Washington, DC, August 2013); Lobina, Kishimoto, and Petitjean, "Here to Stay"; Gary R. Welsh, "Surprise, You're Paying $29 Million to Veolia for a Poorly Done Job Just to Go Away," *Advance Indiana*, October 28, 2010; Public Citizen, "Veolia Environnement: A Corporate Profile" (Washington, DC, February 2005).

6. Satoko Kishimoto, Lavinia Steinfort, and Olivier Petitjean, "The Future Is Public: Towards Democratic Ownership of Public Services" (Amsterdam and Paris: Transnational Institute, May 2020); Yvonne Wenger, "Hearing Scheduled for Concerns on City Water System Privatization," *Baltimore Sun*, October 27, 2014; Edward Ericson Jr., "Amid Protests, DPW Selects Efficiency Consultant for Water-Treatment Facilities," *Baltimore Sun*, December 4, 2014; Ayana Byrd, "Baltimore Set to Ban Privatization of Water System," *Color Lines*, August 8, 2018; Rusty Simpson, "Letter to the Editor: Citizens Stopped Veolia Contract in Its Tracks," *Baltimore Sun*, December 11, 2014; Lauren DeRusha, "Victory! People Power Ends Veolia's Major Water Privatization Scheme," *Corporate Accountability*, April 11, 2018, https://www.corporateaccountability.org/water.

7. "Senior US Economist Arthur Laffer Praises Turkish Economy, Proposes to Trade Obama for Erdoğan," *Daily Sabah*, September 9, 2016.

8. Kate Whittle, "A Privatized River Runs Through It," *In These Times*, May 19, 2015; Keila Szpaller, "City's Lawyer Says Mountain Water Order Strong, Will Withstand Appeal," *Missoulian*, June 16, 2015.

9. City of Missoula v. Mountain Water Company and Carlyle Infrastructure Partners, No. DV-14-352 (Montana Fourth Judicial District Court, Missoula County June 15, 2015).

10. Dean Starkman, "Missoula, Mont., Moves to Wrest Control of Privately Held Water System," *Los Angeles Times*, October 15, 2015.

11. Ibid.; Danielle Ivory, Ben Protess, and Griff Palmer, "In American Towns, Private Profits from Public Works," *New York Times*, December 24, 2016.

12. Whittle, "A Privatized River Runs Through It"; Starkman, "Missoula, Mont., Moves to Wrest Control of Privately Held Water System."

13. *Missoula v. Mountain Water.*

14. Kidston, "Missoula, California Town to Collaborate on Water System Fights"; Whittle, "A Privatized River Runs Through It."

15. Szpaller, "City's Lawyer Says Mountain Water Order Strong"; Whittle, "A Privatized River Runs Through It"; Starkman, "Missoula, Mont., Moves to Wrest Control of Privately Held Water System"; Ivory, Protess, and Palmer, "In American Towns, Private Profits from Public Works."

16. *Missoula v. Mountain Water.*

17. Peter Friesen, "City of Missoula Takes Ownership of Mountain Water," *Missoulian*, June 22, 2017; Szpaller, "City's Lawyer Says Mountain Water Order Strong."

18. Kidston, "Missoula, California Town to Collaborate on Water System Fights"; Whittle, "A Privatized River Runs Through It."

Part III: The Public Gets Us There

1. Joe Biden, "Remarks by President Biden on the American Jobs Plan," Carpenters Pittsburgh Training Center, Pittsburgh, Pennsylvania, March 31, 2021.

6. Economic Destiny and the Pitfalls of the Public-Private Partnership

1. Zachary Callen, *Railroads and American Political Development: Infrastructure, Federalism, and State Building* (Lawrence: University Press of Kansas, 2016).

2. Zachary Callen, "Where Infrastructure Takes Us," *Process: A Blog for American History*, June 6, 2017, http://www.processhistory.org/callen-infrastructure.

3. Quoted in Callen, *Railroads and American Political Development*, 23.

4. H.W. Brands, *American Colossus: The Triumph of Capitalism, 1865–1900* (New York: Doubleday, 2010).

5. One solid summary of P3s is: National Conference of State Legislatures, "Public-Private Partnerships: A Toolkit for Legislators" (Washington, DC, October 2010).

6. Municipal Securities Rulemaking Board, "Municipal Securities: Financing the Nation's Infrastructure" (Washington, DC, 2019); Barnet Sherman, "Municipal Bonds:

Good for Your Portfolio's Health," *Forbes*, July 16, 2019; Barnet Sherman, "Municipal Bonds: Investing in Our Communities," *Forbes*, July 9, 2019.

7. Timothy Lee, "The Trump Administration Says It Has to Have Private Help to Fund Roads and Bridges. It's Wrong," *Vox*, January 11, 2017; Wilson Sayre, "HUD Secretary Ben Carson: Public-Private Partnerships Are 'the Answer' to Affordable Housing," WLRN, April 13, 2017.

8. Lee, "The Trump Administration Says It Has to Have Private Help"; Donald Cohen, "Why We Can't Let Trump and Congress Tax Public Infrastructure Investment," *Huffington Post*, May 8, 2017; Hunter Blair, "No Free Bridge: Why Public-Private Partnerships or Other 'Innovative' Financing of Infrastructure Will Not Save Taxpayers Money" (Economic Policy Institute, March 21, 2017).

9. Cohen, "Why We Can't Let Trump and Congress Tax Public Infrastructure Investment"; Robert W. Poole Jr. and Austill Stuart, "Federal Barriers to Private Capital Investment in U.S. Infrastructure" (Washington, DC: Reason Foundation, January 2017); Scott Greenberg, "Reexamining the Tax Exemption of Municipal Bond Interest," *Tax Foundation*, July 21, 2016; Rachel Greszler, Kevin Dayaratna, and Michael Sargent, "Why Tax Reform Should Eliminate State and Local Tax Deductions" (Washington, DC: Heritage Foundation, October 16, 2017).

10. Cohen, "Why We Can't Let Trump and Congress Tax Public Infrastructure Investment"; Matthew Goldstein and Patricia Cohen, "Public-Private Projects Where the Public Pays and Pays," *New York Times*, June 6, 2017.

11. Bill Panos quoted in Lynn Hume, "Senate Panel Told P3s Won't Work for Rural Areas, Tax-Exempts Are Key," *Bond Buyer*, February 8, 2017.

12. John Lauritz Larson, *Internal Improvement: National Public Works and the Promise of Popular Government in the Early United States* (Chapel Hill: University of North Carolina Press, 2001); Roy T. Sawyer, *America's Wetland: An Environmental and Cultural History of Tidewater Virginia and North Carolina* (Charlottesville: University of Virginia Press, 2010); Robert J. Kapsch, *The Potomac Canal: George Washington and the Waterway West* (Morgantown: West Virginia University Press, 2007).

13. Larson, *Internal Improvement*, 95–96.

14. Charles Royster, *The Fabulous History of the Dismal Swamp Company: A Story of George Washington's Times* (New York: Knopf, 1999).

15. Larson, *Internal Improvement*, 22, 74.

16. Daniel Walker Howe, *What Hath God Wrought: The Transformation of America, 1815–1848* (New York: Oxford University Press, 2007), 120.

17. Bart Elias, "Air Traffic Inc.: Considerations Regarding the Corporatization of Air Traffic Control" (Washington, DC: Congressional Research Service, May 16, 2017); Federal Aviation Administration, "Air Traffic by the Numbers," November 14, 2017.

18. Elias, "Air Traffic, Inc."; Linda Tsang and Jared Cole, "Legal Analysis of Title II of H.R. 2997, 21st Century Aviation, Innovation, Reform, and Reauthorization (AIRR) Act," Memorandum to Peter A. DeFazio (Congressional Research Service, July 18, 2017); Editorial Board, "Don't Privatize Air Traffic Control," *New York Times*, February 15, 2016; Curtis Tate and Alex Daugherty, "In the Battle over Who Controls U.S. Airspace, It's Big Lobbyists vs. Small Airports," *McClatchy*, March 6, 2017; Julie Hirschfeld Davis, "Trump Backs Air Traffic Control Privatization," *New York Times*, June 5, 2017.

19. Trump quoted in Davis, "Trump Backs Air Traffic Control Privatization."

20. Quoted in Tate and Daugherty, "In the Battle over Who Controls U.S. Airspace."

21. Ibid.

7. Toll Roads at America's Crossroads

1. Editorial Board, "A Continuing Toll," *Journal Gazette*, December 3, 2015; Lydia O'Neal and David Sirota, "Trump's $1 Trillion Infrastructure Plan Is Actually Pence's—and It's All About Privatization," *Newsweek*, September 4, 2017; Kyle Hannon, "Indiana Toll Road Deal Getting It Right," *South Bend Tribune*, September 1, 2017.

2. Quoted in Lydia O'Neal and David Sirota, "Companies Linked to Mike Pence Seek an Upper Hand in Infrastructure Policy," *International Business Times*, August 15, 2017.

3. Karen Francisco, "The Toll of Driving: Lawmakers Plan for a Future Where Gas Taxes Are Obsolete," *Journal Gazette*, November 12, 2017; John B. Gilmour, "The Indiana Toll Road Lease as an Intergenerational Cash Transfer," *Public Administration Review* 72, no. 6 (December 2012): 856–64.

4. O'Neal and Sirota, "Trump's $1 Trillion Infrastructure Plan"; Daniel Vock, "Indiana Governor Mitch Daniels' Toll Road Lease Will Have Major Impact on His Legacy and the State," *Stateline*, June 19, 2012, http://www.pewtrusts.org/en/research-and-analysis/blogs/stateline/2012/06/19/indiana-highway-building-ramps-up-as-daniels-term-winds-down; Phineas Baxandall, Kari Wohlschlegel, and Tony Dutzik, "Private Roads, Public Costs: The Facts About Toll Road Privatization and How to Protect the Public" (US PRIG Education Fund, Spring 2009).

5. Gilmour, "The Indiana Toll Road Lease as an Intergenerational Cash Transfer."

6. Baxandall, Wohlschlegel, and Dutzik, "Private Roads, Public Costs"; Angie Schmitt and Payton Chung, "The Indiana Toll Road and the Dark Side of Privately Financed Highways," *Streetsblog USA*, November 18, 2014; Angie Schmitt and Payton Chung, "How Macquarie Makes Money by Losing Money on Toll Roads," *Streetsblog USA*, November 19, 2014.

7. Gilmour, "The Indiana Toll Road Lease as an Intergenerational Cash Transfer."

8. Vock, "Indiana Governor Mitch Daniels' Toll Road Lease Will Have Major Impact on His Legacy and the State"; Andrew Steele, "Motorists to Pay Higher Indiana Toll Road Rates Beginning in June," *Northwest Indiana Times*, May 1, 2017.

9. Pelath quoted in Mark Peterson, "Drastic Indiana Toll Road Rate Hike Begins," WNDU, June 1, 2017; Indiana Department of Transportation quoted in O'Neal and Sirota, "Trump's $1 Trillion Infrastructure Plan."

10. Francisco, "The Toll of Driving."

11. Henry Petroski, *The Road Taken: The History and Future of America's Infrastructure* (New York: Bloomsbury, 2016), 266; O'Neal and Sirota, "Trump's $1 Trillion Infrastructure Plan"; Francisco, "The Toll of Driving"; Congressional Budget Office, "Using Public-Private Partnerships to Carry Out Highway Projects" (Washington, DC: United States Congress, January 2012).

12. Petroski, *The Road Taken*, 266; Francisco, "The Toll of Driving."

13. Baxandall, Wohlschlegel, and Dutzik, "Private Roads, Public Costs."

14. Vock, "Indiana Governor Mitch Daniels' Toll Road Lease Will Have Major Impact on His Legacy and the State"; Baxandall, Wohlschlegel, and Dutzik, "Private Roads, Public Costs"; Petroski, *The Road Taken*, 266; O'Neal and Sirota, "Trump's $1 Trillion Infrastructure Plan"; Stewart quoted in Bill Dolan, "State to Pay for Indiana Toll Road Free Time," *Northwest Indiana Times*, September 20, 2008.

15. Keith Benman, "Reports: Indiana Toll Road Again Facing Debt Problems," *Northwest Indiana Times*, March 31, 2014; Keith Benman, "Indiana Toll Road Operators Declare Bankruptcy," *Northwest Indiana Times*, September 22, 2014.

16. O'Neal and Sirota, "Trump's $1 Trillion Infrastructure Plan"; Editorial Board, "A Continuing Toll"; Luke H. Britt, "Letter to Shaw Friedman Re: Formal Complaint 15-FC-302; Alleged Violation of the Access to Public Records Act by the State of Indiana, Indiana Finance Authority," December 29, 2015, https://www.in.gov/pac/advisory/files/15 -FC-302.pdf.

17. Shaw Friedman quoted in O'Neal and Sirota, "Trump's $1 Trillion Infrastructure Plan."

18. Peterson, "Drastic Indiana Toll Road Rate Hike Begins."

19. Gilmour, "The Indiana Toll Road Lease as an Intergenerational Cash Transfer."

20. Ibid.; Vock, "Indiana Governor Mitch Daniels' Toll Road Lease Will Have Major Impact on His Legacy and the State."

8. Who Owns the Journey? Recentering the Public

1. Daniel B. Klein and John Majewski, "Economy, Community, and Law: The Turnpike Movement in New York, 1797–1845," *Law & Society Review* 26, no. 3 (1992): 469–512, https://doi.org/10.2307/3053736.

2. Ibid.; Howe, *What Hath God Wrought*; Gordon S. Wood, *Empire of Liberty: A History of the Early Republic, 1789–1815* (Oxford; New York: Oxford University Press, 2009).

3. Charles River Bridge v. Warren Bridge, 36 US 420 (1837).

4. Jeremy Mohler, "No One Asks How Are We Going to Pay for War. So, Why Should We for Public Transit?," In the Public Interest, January 16, 2020.

5. Trevor Bach, "Kansas City Bets on Free Bus Fares to Address Inequality," *US News & World Report*, December 17, 2019.

6. Ibid.; Yavor Tarinski, "Free Public Transport and the Right to the City," *Resilience*, July 25, 2018.

7. Nicole Daniels, "Should Public Transit Be Free?," *New York Times*, January 16, 2020; Mohler, "No One Asks How Are We Going to Pay for War"; Alissa Walker, "Kansas City Is First Major U.S. City to Make Public Transit Free," *Curbed*, December 6, 2019; Bach, "Kansas City Bets on Free Bus Fares to Address Inequality"; Lisa Rodriguez, "Kansas City Council Unanimously Votes to Get Rid of Bus Fares," KCUR, December 5, 2019.

8. Eric Jaffe, "How Free Transit Works in the United States," *CityLab*, March 6, 2013; Dave Colon, "MTA Will Spend $249M on New Cops to Save $200M on Fare Evasion," *Streetsblog New York City*, November 14, 2019; Alissa Walker, "Climate Mayors Ask Congress for Swifter Transportation Action," *Curbed*, July 17, 2019, https://www.curbed.com /2019/7/17/20698169/climate-mayors-transportation-senate-bill-peduto.

9. Hiroko Tabuchi, "How the Koch Brothers Are Killing Public Transit Projects Around the Country," *New York Times*, June 19, 2018; Julia Conley, "Public Transit Plans for Milwaukee and Cities Nationwide at Risk from Koch-Funded Activists," *Milwaukee Independent*, August 29, 2019.

10. Evan Wyloge, "Why Are Koch-Funded Activists Trying to Derail a US City's Public Transit?," *Guardian*, August 27, 2019; Bailey Vogt, "Phoenix Voters Dismiss Koch-Backed Proposal Killing Future Public Transportation Expansions," *Washington Times*, August 28, 2019; Steven Hsieh, "Koch-Funded Group Helped Develop Plan to Kill Future of Phoenix Light Rail," *Phoenix New Times*, August 6, 2019.

11. Tabuchi, "How the Koch Brothers Are Killing Public Transit Projects Around the Country."

12. . Mohler, "No One Asks How Are We Going to Pay for War"; Robin Young and Allison Hagan, "Public Transportation Ridership Is on the Rise," WBUR, October 16, 2019; E. Tammy Kim, "How Uber Hopes to Profit from Public Transit," *New York Times*, May 30, 2019; Alexander Sammon, "When Cities Turn to Uber, Instead of Buses and Trains," *American Prospect*, August 13, 2019.

13. Uber Technologies, Inc., "Form S-1 Registration Statement," February 15, 2019, https://www.sec.gov/Archives/edgar/data/1543151/000095012319002420/filename1.htm.

14. Allan Holmes, "How Big Telecom Smothers City-Run Broadband," Center for Public Integrity, August 29, 2014; Allan Holmes and Jared Bennett, "Behind the Municipal Broadband Battle," Center for Public Integrity, February 14, 2015.

15. Holmes, "How Big Telecom Smothers City-Run Broadband."

16. Holmes and Bennett, "Behind the Municipal Broadband Battle"; Holmes, "How Big Telecom Smothers City-Run Broadband."

17. Holmes and Bennett, "Behind the Municipal Broadband Battle"; Susan Crawford, "Koch Brothers Are Cities' New Obstacle to Building Broadband," *Wired*, December 16, 2017; Josh Harkinson, "City Wifi: Fast, Cheap, and No You Can't Have It.," *Mother Jones*, January 22, 2015; Holmes, "How Big Telecom Smothers City-Run Broadband"; Michael Hiltzik, "Cable and Telecom Firms Score a Huge Win in Their War to Kill Municipal Broadband," *Los Angeles Times*, August 12, 2016; Executive Office of the President, "Community-Based Broadband Solutions: The Benefits of Competition and Choice for Community Development and Highspeed Internet Access" (Washington, DC, January 2015).

18. Harkinson, "City Wifi"; Hiltzik, "Cable and Telecom Firms Score a Huge Win in Their War to Kill Municipal Broadband"; Leticia Miranda, "How States Are Fighting to Keep Towns from Offering Their Own Broadband," *ProPublica*, June 26, 2015; Holmes and Bennett, "Behind the Municipal Broadband Battle"; Katie Kienbaum, "Preemption Detente: Municipal Broadband Networks Face Barriers in 19 States," Community Networks, August 8, 2019.

19. Harkinson, "City Wifi"; Hiltzik, "Cable and Telecom Firms Score a Huge Win in Their War to Kill Municipal Broadband"; Jon Brodkin, "Republican Fight Against Municipal Broadband Heats Up in Michigan," *Ars Technica*, October 18, 2017.

20. Tamara Chuang, "19 More Colorado Cities and Counties Vote in Favor of City-Owned Internet, While Fort Collins Approves $150 Million to Move Forward," *Denver Post*, November 8, 2017; Brodkin, "Republican Fight Against Municipal Broadband Heats Up in Michigan."

21. Harkinson, "City Wifi"; Miranda, "How States Are Fighting to Keep Towns from Offering Their Own Broadband"; Holmes and Bennett, "Behind the Municipal Broadband Battle."

22. Lisa González, "Totals Are In: Comcast Spends $900K in Fort Collins Election," Community Networks, December 9, 2017, https://muninetworks.org/content/totals-are -comcast-spends-900k-fort-collins-election; Harkinson, "City Wifi"; Hiltzik, "Cable and Telecom Firms Score a Huge Win in Their War to Kill Municipal Broadband"; Chuang, "19 More Colorado Cities and Counties Vote in Favor of City-Owned Internet, While Fort Collins Approves $150 Million to Move Forward"; Jon Brodkin, "Sorry, Comcast: Voters Say 'Yes' to City-Run Broadband in Colorado," *Ars Technica*, November 8, 2017.

23. González, "Totals Are In"; Sean Gonsalves, "Chicago and Denver Voters Say Yes to Expanded Broadband Options," Community Networks, November 5, 2020.

Part IV. Privatization's Slow Coup:
The Undermining of Democracy and Justice

1. Charles River Bridge v. Warren Bridge, 36 US; Georgia et al. v. PublicResource.org, Inc., 590 US __ (2020).

2. Joe Mullin, "If You Publish Georgia's State Laws, You'll Get Sued for Copyright and Lose," *Ars Technica*, March 3, 2017; American Civil Liberties Union et al., "Brief of Amici Curiae, Georgia v. Public Resource.Org, Inc., Case 17-11589," May 24, 2017, https://www.acluga.org/sites/default/files/public_resource_11th_cir_amicus_brief.pdf.

3. Supreme Court quoted in American Civil Liberties Union et al., "Amici Curiae, Georgia v. Public Resource.Org"; Georgia v. Public.Resource.Org, Inc., No. 1:15-cv-02594-MHC (US District Court, Northern District of Georgia March 28, 2017).

4. See also David Kravets, "Georgia Sues Legal Rebel for Posting State's Copyrighted Law Online," *Ars Technica*, July 27, 2015; Vera Eidelman, "Georgia Is Fighting to Keep Its Laws Secret—Unless You Pay," *Speak Freely*, November 16, 2017, https://www.aclu.org/blog/free-speech/georgia-fighting-keep-its-laws-secret-unless-you-pay; Kate Brumback, "Judge: Annotations to Georgia Law Are Protected by Copyright," *US News & World Report*, March 28, 2017.

9. When the Contract Is King:
How Privatization Trumps Democracy

1. Hollie Russon Gilman, "Why Kansas City, Missouri, Plans to Privatize Sidewalks," *Vox*, January 29, 2018; Andrea Tudhope, "Kansas City Police Confirm Violent Crime in Westport Spikes on the Weekends," KCUR, December 13, 2017.

2. Lynn Horsley, "Privatize Westport Streets? Proposal Has Supporters, Detractors," *Kansas City Star*, June 2, 2017; Gilman, "Why Kansas City, Missouri, Plans to Privatize Sidewalks"; Thomas, "The Great Westport Giveaway: Turning Public Streets into Private Property," *Urban Angle*, May 24, 2017; Tudhope, "Kansas City Police Confirm Violent Crime in Westport Spikes on the Weekends."

3. See also Lisa Rodriguez, "Desperate to Stop Gun Violence, Westport Pushes for Private Sidewalks," KCUR, accessed March 7, 2018, http://kcur.org/post/desperate-stop-gun-violence-westport-pushes-private-sidewalks; Lynn Horsley, "Westport Street Privatization Proposal Postponed in an Effort to Find Consensus," *Kansas City Star*, June 6, 2017.

4. Colin Woodard, *American Character: A History of the Epic Struggle Between Individual Liberty and the Common Good* (New York: Viking Penguin, 2016), 291–95; Sven Beckert, *The Monied Metropolis: New York City and the Consolidation of the American Bourgeoisie, 1850–1896* (Cambridge, UK ; New York: Cambridge University Press, 2001), 293–95.

5. Gordon S. Wood, *Empire of Liberty: A History of the Early Republic, 1789–1815* (Oxford; New York: Oxford University Press, 2009).

6. Sumner quoted in Eric Foner, *The Story of American Freedom* (New York: W.W. Norton, 1998), 121; Woodard, *American Character*, 116.

7. Foner, *The Story of American Freedom*, 119, 123–24.

8. Quoted in Lizabeth Cohen, *Making a New Deal: Industrial Workers in Chicago, 1919–1939* (Cambridge, UK; New York: Cambridge University Press, 1990), 264.

9. Letters to FDR administration quoted in Foner, *The Story of American Freedom*, 204; Franklin D. Roosevelt, "Acceptance Speech for the Renomination for the Presidency, Philadelphia, PA, June 27, 1936," The American Presidency Project, accessed April 20, 2018, http://www.presidency.ucsb.edu/ws/?pid=15314; Cohen, *Making a New Deal*.

10. Foner, *The Story of American Freedom*; Nancy MacLean, *Democracy in Chains: The Deep History of the Radical Right's Stealth Plan for America* (New York: Viking, 2017), 144; Stuart M. Butler, "Changing the Political Dynamics of Government," *Proceedings of the Academy of Political Science* 36, no. 3 (1987): 4–13, https://doi.org/10.2307/1174092.

11. Jon D. Michaels, *Constitutional Coup: Privatization's Threat to the American Republic* (Cambridge, MA; London: Harvard University Press, 2017).

10. Democracy in Darkness:
Privatization's Shadow over Transparency

1. In the Public Interest, "Closing the Books: How Government Contractors Hide Public Records" (Washington, DC, March 2015).

2. Hope Academy Broadway Campus v. White Hat Mgt., LLC, No. 2013-Ohio-911 (Court of Appeals of Ohio, Tenth Appellate District March 12, 2013); Hope Academy Broadway Campus v. White Hat Mgt. LLC, No. 145 Ohio St.3d 29, 2015-Ohio-3716 (Supreme Court of Ohio September 15, 2015); AFL-CIO Food and Allied Service Trades Division and Ohio Federation of Teachers, "Education Empire: David Brennan's White Hat Management Inc.," March 2006; Doug Livingston, "Board Members at White Hat Charter Schools Say They Have Little Control over Public Funds," *Akron Beacon Journal*, March 30, 2014; Aaron Marshall, "10 Northeast Ohio Charter School Boards Sue White Hat Management Firm," *Cleveland Plain Dealer*, May 17, 2010; John C. Veauthierand and Karen S. Bell, "More Than 100 Publicly Funded Charter Schools Fail to Disclose Who Is in Charge," *Akron Beacon Journal*, March 29, 2014.

3. *New Flyer of America, Inc. vs. Los Angeles Metropolitan Transportation Authority*, Final Ruling on Petition for Writ of Mandate, No. BC621090 (Superior Court of the State of California for the County of Los Angeles, October 12, 2017); *New Flyer of America Inc. vs. Los Angeles County Metropolitan Transportation Authority* (Superior Court of California, County of Los Angeles, March 26, 2018).

4. Ohio is just one example. See Philip Mattera et al., "Public-Private Power Grab: The Risks in Privatizing State Economic Development Agencies" (Washington, DC: Good Jobs First, January 2011).

5. Nicholas Kusnetz, "State Pro-Business Organizations Are Publicly Funded, but Privately Controlled," Center for Public Integrity, October 23, 2013, https://www.publicintegrity.org/2013/10/23/13576/state-pro-business-organizations-are-publicly-funded-privately-controlled.

6. Greg LeRoy et al., "Creating Scandals Instead of Jobs: The Failures of Privatized State Economic Development Agencies" (Washington, DC: Good Jobs First, October 2013), http://www.goodjobsfirst.org/sites/default/files/docs/pdf/scandalsnotjobs.pdf.

7. Randy Ludlow, "Despite 34 Making Six Figures, True Amounts of JobsOhio Salaries Still Lowballed," *Columbus Dispatch*, March 22, 2018; Darrel Rowland and Joe Vardon, "Auditor to Examine Potential Conflicts of Interest at JobsOhio," *Columbus Dispatch*, September 26, 2013; LeRoy et al., "Creating Scandals Instead of Jobs"; Laura A. Bischoff, "Board Has Ties to Firms That Got Help," *Dayton Daily News*, July 31, 2013.

8. Mike DeWine, "Ohio Sunshine Laws 2018: An Open Government Resource Manual" (Attorney General of the State of Ohio, 2018); LeRoy et al., "Creating Scandals Instead of Jobs."

9. Robert Higgs, "How Effective Is JobsOhio? Experts Say Private Nature of Gov. John Kasich's Brainchild Makes Evaluation Tough," *Cleveland Plain Dealer*, August 24, 2013; Mya Frazier, "Amazon Is Getting a Good Deal in Ohio. Maybe Too Good," *Bloomberg*, October 26, 2017.

11. Skin in the Game: Environmental and Planning Policy in Privatization's Grip

1. Donald Cohen and Stephanie Farmer, "Why Chicago's Botched Parking Meter Privatization Is Also Bad for the Environment," *Next City*, June 4, 2014; Fran Spielman, "Parking Meter Deal Keeps Getting Worse for City as Meter Revenues Rise," *Chicago Sun-Times*, May 14, 2018; Chris Lentino, "Chicago to Pay $20 Million to Parking Meter Company in 2018," *Illinois Policy*, November 2, 2017.

2. Stephanie Farmer, "Cities as Risk Managers: The Impact of Chicago's Parking Meter P3 on Municipal Governance and Transportation Planning," *Environment and Planning* 46, no. 9 (September 2014): 2160–74, https://doi.org/10.1068/a130048p.

3. Ibid.

4. Martin E. Comas, "Less Garbage Could Cost Lake," *Orlando Sentinel*, February 15, 2009; Lori Lovely, "A Dirty MRF for Indy?," *MSW Management*, March 26, 2015, https://www.mswmanagement.com/collection/article/13015918/a-dirty-mrf-for-indy.

5. Comas, "Less Garbage Could Cost Lake"; Global Alliance for Incinerator Alternatives, "Waste Incinerators: Bad News for Recycling and Waste Reduction," October 2013.

6. Global Alliance for Incinerator Alternatives, "Waste Incinerators: Bad News for Recycling and Waste Reduction"; Laura Sullivan, "Prison Economics Helped Drive Immigration Law," *Morning Edition*, October 28, 2010; Trevor Aaronson and Mc Nelly Torres, "Florida Home to Seven Air Polluters on EPA Watch List," *Florida Center for Investigative Reporting*, November 7, 2011.

7. Michael Jackman, "Why the Detroit Incinerator Is Costly, Dirty, Smelly, Dangerous— and Unnecessary," *Detroit Metro Times*, April 11, 2018.

8. Violet Ikonomova, "Calling Trash-Burning an Impediment to Recycling, Detroit Environmentalists Urge Shutdown of Incinerator," *Detroit Metro Times*, November 15, 2017; Melissa Cooper Sargent and William Copeland, "Letter: Detroit Incinerator an Assault on Justice," *Detroit News*, July 20, 2017; Ryan Felton, "Detroit Incinerator Is Hotspot for Health Problems, Environmentalists Claim," *Guardian*, October 23, 2016; Larry Gabriel, "Toward a Sustainable Detroit," *Detroit Metro Times*, April 11, 2018; Sarah Cwiek, "Detroit's Incinerator Is in Trouble—but Not Enough, According to Some," Michigan Radio, March 10, 2017; Sarah Cwiek, "Detroit Incinerator Announces It Will Permanently Shut Down," Michigan Radio, March 28, 2019.

9. "City Sued over Recycling Center," *Indianapolis Star*, September 11, 2014; John Touhy, "City's New Recycling Plan Trashed by Critics," *Indianapolis Star*, June 10, 2014; "Covanta to Build Recycling Plant in Indianapolis," *Recycling Today*, June 18, 2014; Ed Wenck, "How Indy's New Recycling Deal Could Cost Taxpayers Millions," *NUVO*, November 8, 2015.

10. Wenck, "How Indy's New Recycling Deal Could Cost Taxpayers Millions"; Ed Wenck, "Covanta Defends Its Position," *NUVO*, October 6, 2015.

11. Wenck, "How Indy's New Recycling Deal Could Cost Taxpayers Millions"; Wenck, "Covanta Defends Its Position."

12. "Mixed Feelings on Mixed Waste, Still," *Earth911*, July 12, 2016, https://earth911 .com/business-policy/mixed-waste-mixed-feelings; Barry Shanoff, "Why a Deal Between Indianapolis and Covanta Hit a Legal Roadblock," *Waste360*, May 6, 2016, https://www .waste360.com/legal/why-deal-between-indianapolis-and-covanta-hit-legal-roadblock.

13. "Organize a March or Rally," *Crowds on Demand*, accessed January 27, 2020, https: //crowdsondemand.com/protests-rallies-and-advocacy; Michael Isaac Stein, "Actors Were Paid to Support Entergy's Power Plant at New Orleans City Council Meetings," *The Lens*, May 4, 2018.

14. Stein, "Actors Were Paid to Support Entergy's Power Plant at New Orleans City Council Meetings."

12. Freedom Has a Price: Privatization's Assault on the Justice System

1. Ann Imse, "Colorado Paying Millions for Unneeded Private Prisons," Colorado Public News, March 11, 2013.

2. In the Public Interest, "Criminal: How Lockup Quotas and 'Low-Crime Taxes' Guarantee Profits for Private Prison Corporations" (Washington, DC, September 2013).

3. Ann Imse, "State Pays Millions as Prison Populations Sink," *Colorado Springs Gazette*, March 9, 2013.

4. In the Public Interest, "Criminal."

5. Dean DeChiaro, "Private Prisons Boost Lobbying as Federal Detention Needs Grow," *Roll Call*, October 25, 2017.

6. Justice Policy Institute, "Gaming the System: How the Political Strategies of Private Prison Companies Promote Ineffective Incarceration Policies," June 2011, http:// www.justicepolicy.org/uploads/justicepolicy/documents/gaming_the_system.pdf; Minnesota Association of Professional Employees, "House Hearing Shut Down by Protesters Opposing Private Prison," March 23, 2016, https://www.mape.org/mape/news/house -hearing-shut-down-protesters-opposing-private-prison; General Accounting Office, "Private and Public Prisons: Studies Comparing Operational Costs and/or Quality of Service" (Washington, DC, August 1996); In the Public Interest, "The Cost of Private Prisons" (Washington, DC, April 2014); Southern Poverty Law Center, "Private Prisons: The Wrong Choice for Alabama" (Montgomery, AL, October 2017); Government Accountability Office, "Cost of Prisons: Bureau of Prisons Needs Better Data to Access Alternatives for Acquiring Low and Minimum Security Facilities" (Washington, DC, October 2007); Brad Lundahl et al., "Prison Privatization: A Meta-Analysis of Cost Effectiveness and Quality of Confinement Indicators" (Utah Criminal Justice Center, University of Utah, April 26, 2007); Associated Press, "Audit: Private Prisons Cost More Than State-Run Prisons," AP News, January 1, 2019; Megan Mumford, Diane Whitmore Schanzenbach, and Ryan Nunn, "The Economics of Private Prisons" (Washington, DC: Hamilton Project, 2016).

7. Douglas McDonald et al., "Private Prisons in the United States: An Assessment of Current Practice" (Boston, MA: Abt Associates, Inc., July 16, 1998); U.S. Department of Justice Office of the Inspector General, "Review of the Federal Bureau of Prisons' Monitoring of Contract Prisons" (Washington, DC: U.S. Department of Justice, August

2016); In the Public Interest, "How Private Prison Companies Increase Recidivism" (Washington, DC, June 2016); Bloomberg News, "Assaults Peak at Private Prison Where Gangs Best Guards," *Bloomberg.com*, accessed August 16, 2020, https://www.bloomberg .com/graphics/infographics/assaults-peak-at-private-prison-where-gangs-best-guards .html.

8. Justice Policy Institute, "Gaming the System"; Grant Duwe and Valerie Clark, "The Effects of Private Prison Confinement in Minnesota on Offender Recidivism" (St. Paul, MN: Minnesota Department of Corrections, March 2013), https://www.prisonlegalnews .org/news/publications/mn-doc-private-prison-recidivism-study-2013; In the Public Interest, "How Private Prison Companies Increase Recidivism"; Andrew Spivak and Susan Sharp, "Inmate Recidivism as a Measure of Private Prison Performance," *Crime and Delinquency* 54, no. 3 (July 2008): 482–508.

9. Scott D. Camp and Gerald G. Gaes, "Growth and Quality of U.S. Private Prisons: Evidence from a National Survey" (Federal Bureau of Prisons, Office of Research and Evaluation, September 21, 2001), https://www.bop.gov/resources/research_projects /published_reports/pub_vs_priv/oreprres_note.pdf.

10. Casey Tolan, "A Private-Prison CEO Is Actually Testifying About a Brutal Assault in His Facility," *Vice*, February 13, 2017; Rebecca Boone, "FBI Investigates Prison Company CCA in Idaho," *Idaho Press*, March 7, 2014; Harrison Berry, "Cost of Understaffing Idaho's Private Prison: $1 Million," *Boise Weekly*, February 5, 2014; Rebecca Boone, "Judge: CCA in Contempt for Prison Understaffing," *Idaho Press*, September 17, 2013; Kathy Griesmyer, "CCA Private Prison Transfer to State Hands Is Right for Idaho," *ACLU of Idaho* (blog), July 1, 2014, https://acluidaho.org/en/news/cca-private-prison-transfer-state -hands-right-idaho; Rebecca Boone and Cynthia Sewell, "Feds Will Not Charge Former Private Idaho Prison Operator over Falsified Timecards," *Idaho Statesman*, May 20, 2015; David Dayen, "The True Cost: Why the Private Prison Industry Is About So Much More Than Prisons," *Talking Points Memo*, June 23, 2016; Rebecca Boone, "CCA-Run Prison Remains Idaho's Most Violent Lockup," *San Diego Union-Tribune*, October 9, 2011.

11. American Civil Liberties Union, "Banking on Bondage" (New York, November 2011); Department of Justice Office of Public Affairs, "Department of Justice Releases Investigative Findings on the Walnut Grove Youth Correctional Facility in Mississippi," March 21, 2012, https://www.justice.gov/opa/pr/department-justice-releases-investigative -findings-walnut-grove-youth-correctional-facility; Thomas E. Perez to Phil Bryant, "Investigation of the Walnut Grove Youth Correctional Facility," March 20, 2012, https: //www.justice.gov/sites/default/files/crt/legacy/2012/04/09/walnutgrovefl.pdf; R.L. Nave, "MDOC, Private Prisons on Trial," *Jackson Free Press*, April 8, 2015.

12. Grassroots Leadership, "The Dirty Thirty: Nothing to Celebrate About 30 Years of Corrections Corporation of America," June 17, 2013, http://grassrootsleadership.org/cca -dirty-30; In the Public Interest, "Criminal."

13. Suzanne Kirchhoff, "Economic Impacts of Prison Growth" (Congressional Research Service, April 13, 2010), https://fas.org/sgp/crs/misc/R41177.pdf; American Civil Liberties Union, "Banking on Bondage"; Norval Morris and David J. Rothman, eds., *The Oxford History of the Prison: The Practice of Punishment in Western Society* (New York: Oxford University Press, 1997); Michelle Alexander, *The New Jim Crow: Mass Incarceration in the Age of Colorblindness* (New York: New Press, 2012).

14. DeChiaro, "Private Prisons Boost Lobbying as Federal Detention Needs Grow."

15. Grassroots Leadership, "The Dirty Thirty"; Johnson, "5 Ways Privatization Is Fleecing American Taxpayers"; In the Public Interest, "Criminal"; Beall, "Big Business, Legislators Pushed for Stiff Sentences"; Justice Policy Institute, "Gaming the System."

16. Grassroots Leadership, "The Dirty Thirty"; Justice Policy Institute, "Gaming the System"; Sullivan, "Prison Economics Helped Drive Immigration Law"; American Civil Liberties Union, "Banking on Bondage"; Madison Pauly, "A Brief History of America's Corporate-Run Prison Industry," *Mother Jones*, August 2016.

17. Center for Constitutional Rights Detention Watch Network, "Banking on Detention: Local Lockup Quotas and the Immigrant Dragnet," 2015, https://www .detentionwatchnetwork.org/sites/default/files/reports/DWN%20CCR%20Banking%20 on%20Detention%20Report.pdf; Sentencing Project, "Private Prisons in the United States" (Washington, DC, October 24, 2019), https://www.sentencingproject.org/publications /private-prisons-united-states.

18. David Dayen, "How Private Contractors Enable Trump's Cruelties at the Border," *Nation*, June 20, 2018; Alan Gomez, "Trump Plans Massive Increase in Federal Immigration Jails," *USA Today*, October 17, 2017; Manny Fernandez and Katie Benner, "The Billion-Dollar Business of Operating Shelters for Migrant Children," *New York Times*, June 21, 2018.

19. DeChiaro, "Private Prisons Boost Lobbying as Federal Detention Needs Grow"; Prison Industry Divestment Movement, "Lobbying," *Prisondivest.com* (blog), November 29, 2013, https://prisondivest.com/private-prison-industry-industria-de-prisiones-privadas /lobbying; Center for Responsive Politics, "For-Profit Prisons," *Open Secrets*, December 16, 2019, https://www.opensecrets.org/industries/indus.php?ind=G7000; Gomez, "Trump Plans Massive Increase in Federal Immigration Jails."

20. J. Weston Phippen, "The For-Profit Probation Maze," *Atlantic*, December 16, 2015.

21. Human Rights Watch, "'Set Up to Fail': The Impact of Offender-Funded Private Probation on the Poor," 2018; Phippen, "The For-Profit Probation Maze."

22. Shaila Dewan, "Private Probation Company Accused of Abuses in Tennessee," *New York Times*, December 21, 2017; Human Rights Watch, "Set Up to Fail"; Human Rights Watch, "Private Probation Harming the Poor," 2018.

23. Human Rights Watch, "Set Up to Fail"; Sarah Stillman, "Get Out of Jail, Inc.," *New Yorker*, June 16, 2014.

24. Human Rights Watch, "Set Up to Fail."

25. Jessica Silver-Greenberg and Robert Gebeloff, "Arbitration Everywhere, Stacking the Deck of Justice," *New York Times*, October 31, 2015; Jessica Silver-Greenberg and Michael Corkery, "In Arbitration, a 'Privatization of the Justice System,'" *New York Times*, November 1, 2015.

26. Economic Policy Institute, "The Growing Use of Mandatory Arbitration" (Washington, DC, April 6, 2018), http://epi.org/144131; Katherine V. W. Stone and Alexander J. S. Colvin, "The Arbitration Epidemic: Mandatory Arbitration Deprives Workers and Consumers of Their Rights" (Washington, DC: Economic Policy Institute, December 7, 2015); Haley Sweetland Edwards, "What Arbitration Agreements in Nursing Homes Really Mean," *Time*, November 16, 2017.

27. Michael Corkery and Jessica Silver-Greenberg, "In Religious Arbitration, Scripture Is the Rule of Law," *New York Times*, November 2, 2015; Martha McCluskey et al., "Regulating Forced Arbitration in Consumer Financial Services: Re-Opening the Courthouse Doors to Victimized Consumers" (Center for Progressive Reform, May 2016); Aaron Jordan, "Repeal of Mandatory Arbitration Ban Is a Wall Street Giveaway," *Regulatory Review*, November 1, 2017, https://www.theregreview.org/2017/11/01/jordan-arbitration -ban-wall-street; Silver-Greenberg and Corkery, "In Arbitration, a 'Privatization of the Justice System.'"

28. Haley Sweetland Edwards, "An 87-Year-Old Nun Said She Was Raped in Her Nursing Home. Here's Why She Couldn't Sue," *Time*, November 16, 2017.

29. Ibid.; Silver-Greenberg and Corkery, "In Arbitration, a 'Privatization of the Justice System.'"

30. Heidi Shierholz, "Correcting the Record: Consumers Fare Better Under Class Actions Than Arbitration" (Economic Policy Institute, August 1, 2017), https://www.epi.org/publication/correcting-the-record-consumers-fare-better-under-class-actions-than-arbitration; Nina Totenberg, "Supreme Court Decision Delivers Blow to Workers' Rights," *NPR*, May 21, 2018.

31. Silver-Greenberg and Gebeloff, "Arbitration Everywhere, Stacking the Deck of Justice."

32. AT&T Mobility LLC v. Concepcion, 563 US 333 (2011).

33. Epic Systems Corporation v. Jacob Lewis, 584 US __ (2018).

34. Ibid.

35. Leslie Newell Peacock, "Visionary Arkansans 2017," *Arkansas Times*, November 9, 2017; Justice Network Inc. v. Craighead County et al., No. 17–3770 (United States Court of Appeals for the Eighth Circuit 2019).

36. *Justice Network Inc. v. Craighead County.*

Part V. Every Last Dime: Shredding the Social Safety Net, Generating Inequality

1. Virginia Eubanks, "How Big Banks Are Cashing In on Food Stamps," *American Prospect*, February 14, 2014; In the Public Interest, "How Privatization Increases Inequality."

2. Janell Ross, "California's Welfare Families Paid Banks Millions in Fees for Public Assistance," *Huffington Post*, November 18, 2011; In the Public Interest, "How Privatization Increases Inequality" (Washington, DC, September 2016); Andrea Luquetta, "'We Don't Need to Be Charged for Being Poor': The Cost to Families of Paying Fees to Access Public Assistance" (California Reinvestment Coalition, May 2015).

13. Teaching Them a Lesson: Privatization Versus the Poor

1. Andrew Flowers, "Most Welfare Dollars Don't Go Directly to Poor People Anymore," *FiveThirtyEight*, August 25, 2016.

2. Wendy Bach, "Welfare Reform, Privatization, and Power: Reconfiguring Administrative Law Structures from the Ground Up," CUNY Academic Works (CUNY School of Law, 2009), h9p://academicworks.cuny.edu/cl_pubs/204; Flowers, "Most Welfare Dollars Don't Go Directly to Poor People Anymore"; Ali Safawi and Ife Floyd, "TANF Benefits Still Too Low to Help Families, Especially Black Families, Avoid Increased Hardship" (Washington, DC: Center on Budget and Policy Priorities, October 30, 2014), https://www.cbpp.org/research/family-income-support/tanf-benefits-still-too-low-to-help-families-especially-black; Martin Gilens, "'Race Coding' and White Opposition to Welfare," *American Political Science Review* 90, no. 3 (1996): 593–604, https://doi.org/10.2307/2082611.

3. Caitlin Dewey, "They're the Think Tank Pushing for Welfare Work Requirements,"

Washington Post, May 18, 2018; Terry O'Donnell et al., "Act to Restore Hope, Opportunity and Prosperity for Everyone (HOPE Act)," Pub. L. No. H.B. 1270 (2018), http://webserver1.lsb.state.ok.us/cf_pdf/2017-18%20ENR/hB/HB1270%20ENR.PDF; Foundation for Government Accountability, "An Act to Restore Hope, Opportunity, and Prosperity for Everyone (HOPE)" (Naples, FL, 2017), https://thefga.org/wp-content/uploads/2017/01/Welfare-Reform-Bill-2017.pdf.

4. Michael Hiltzik, "He Was Convicted in a Historic Healthcare Fraud. Trump Is Letting Him Walk Free," *Los Angeles Times*, December 29, 2020; Greg Kaufmann, "A Cruel New Bill Is About to Become Law in Mississippi," *Nation*, March 31, 2017; O'Donnell et al., "Act to Restore Hope, Opportunity and Prosperity for Everyone (HOPE Act)"; Joel Ebert, "Tennessee Bill Would Restrict Where Welfare Money Is Spent," *Tennessean*, February 8, 2016.

5. Dale Denwalt, "Oklahoma Bill Aims at Reducing Medicaid Fraud," *Oklahoman*, September 29, 2017; Kaufmann, "A Cruel New Bill Is About to Become Law in Mississippi"; Ebert, "Tennessee Bill Would Restrict Where Welfare Money Is Spent"; Dewey, "They're the Think Tank Pushing for Welfare Work Requirements"; Jimmie E. Gates, "New Law Could Be a Waste of Taxpayers' Money," *Clarion Ledger*, April 8, 2017.

6. Michael B. Katz, *In the Shadow of the Poorhouse: A Social History of Welfare in America*, 10th anniversary ed. (New York: BasicBooks, 1996), 33.

7. Ibid., 50–52.

8. Ibid., 26–27.

9. Mike Konczal, "The Conservative Myth of a Social Safety Net Built on Charity," *Atlantic*, March 24, 2014.

10. Monica Potts, "The American Social Safety Net Does Not Exist," *Nation*, October 13, 2016.

11. Hoover quoted in Konczal, "The Conservative Myth of a Social Safety Net Built on Charity"; Hoover quoted in Jill Lepore, *These Truths: A History of the United States* (New York; London: W.W. Norton, 2018); Red Cross leadership quoted in Elisabeth Stephanie Clemens and Doug Guthrie, eds., *Politics and Partnerships: The Role of Voluntary Associations in America's Political Past and Present* (Chicago; London: University of Chicago Press, 2010), 85.

12. Clemens and Guthrie, *Politics and Partnerships*, 87, 89, 97, 91.

13. Ibid., 89, 94.

14. Elisabeth S. Clemens, "In the Shadow of the New Deal: Reconfiguring the Roles of Government and Charity, 1928–1940," in *Politics and Partnerships: The Role of Voluntary Associations in America's Political Past and Present*, ed. Elisabeth S. Clemens and Doug Guthrie, Kindle (Chicago; London: University of Chicago Press, 2010); Katz, *In the Shadow of the Poorhouse*, 18, 60.

15. Konczal, "The Conservative Myth of a Social Safety Net Built on Charity."

14. Privatized Medicaid and the Business of Denying Care

1. Kaiser Family Foundation, "Status of State Medicaid Expansion Decisions: Interactive Map," KFF, November 2, 2020; Jeff Stein, "Ryan Says Republicans to Target Welfare, Medicare, Medicaid Spending in 2018," *Washington Post*, December 6, 2017.

2. Jacob S. Hacker, "GOP Voters Want Medicaid Expansion. GOP Elites Don't. Something Has to Give," *Washington Post*, accessed January 26, 2021.

3. Brian Rosenthal, "Report: Privatized Medicaid Program Serves Fewer People, Costs More," *Houston Chronicle*, February 13, 2017.

4. Jason Clayworth, "Iowa Ends Public Bid Secrecy," *Des Moines Register*, August 9, 2016; Jason Clayworth, "Iowa Government Bids Shrouded in Secrecy," *Des Moines Register*, July 21, 2015.

5. Andy Marso, "Caregivers of Disabled Left in Dark Under Kansas' Private Healthcare System," *Kansas City Star*, November 12, 2017; Jason Clayworth, "Care Denied: How Iowa's Medicaid Maze Is Trapping Sick and Elderly Patients in Endless Appeals," *Des Moines Register*, 2018; Editorial Board, "Privatizing Iowa Medicaid Has Privatized Previously Public Information," *Des Moines Register*, January 16, 2018; Tricia Brooks, "Protecting and Promoting Medicaid's Guaranteed Benefits for Children: EPSDT and Managed Care Iowa Case Study" (Georgetown University Health Policy Institute Center for Children and Families, April 30, 2018), https://ccf.georgetown.edu/2018/04/30/protecting-and-promoting-medicaids-guaranteed-benefits-for-children-iowa-epsdt-and-managed-care.

6. Chelsea Keenan, "Iowa's Private Medicaid Insurers to Lose $450 Million in First Year," *Gazette*, February 22, 2017; Tony Leys, "Medicaid Firms Spending Less on Care for Iowa's Poor, Disabled," *Des Moines Register*, March 15, 2017; In the Public Interest, "Privatizing the VA: Lessons from Privatized Medicaid in Kansas and Iowa" (Washington, DC, March 2018).

7. Tony Leys, "Iowa Medicaid Payment Shortages Are 'Catastrophic,' Private Managers Tell State," *Des Moines Register*, December 21, 2016; Brooks, "Protecting and Promoting Medicaid's Guaranteed Benefits for Children: EPSDT and Managed Care Iowa Case Study"; Keenan, "Iowa's Private Medicaid Insurers to Lose $450 Million in First Year"; Anthem, Inc., "Form 10-K for the Fiscal Year Ended December 31, 2017" (Indianapolis, IN, 2017), https://www.sec.gov/Archives/edgar/data/1156039/000115603918000003/antm-2017123110kq42017.htm#sA671F2759A855DA38F0B2543AC27DACE; Anthem, Inc., "2018 Proxy Statement" (Indianapolis, IN, May 16, 2018), https://www.sec.gov/Archives/edgar/data/1156039/000155837018002704/antm-20180516xdef14a.htm#ExecutiveCompensation; UnitedHealth Group Incorporated, "Form 10-K for the Fiscal Year Ended December 31, 2017," 2017, https://www.unitedhealthgroup.com/viewer.html?file=/content/dam/UHG/PDF/investors/2017/UNH-Q4-2017-Form-10-K.pdf; UnitedHealth Group Incorporated, "Proxy Statement" (Minnetonka, MN, April 20, 2018), https://www.unitedhealthgroup.com/viewer.html?file=/content/dam/UHG/PDF/investors/2017/UNH-2018-Proxy.pdf.

8. Clayworth, "Care Denied."

9. Jason Clayworth, "How Privatized Medicaid Is Systematically Denying Hundreds of Disabled Iowans the Medical Equipment Their Doctors Say They Need," *Des Moines Register*, April 8, 2018; Clayworth, "Care Denied"; Jason Clayworth, "'Stubborn and Absurd.' Iowa's Ombudsman Slams Private Medicaid Managers for Denying Medical Care to Disabled," *Des Moines Register*, April 2, 2018.

10. Editorial Board, "Reynolds' Medicaid Director Is Dedicated to Privatization, Secrecy," *Des Moines Register*, February 28, 2018; Editorial Board, "Iowa Needs Answers on Medicaid Savings, Not a Kansas-Style Shell Game," *Des Moines Register*, June 21, 2018; Tony Leys and Barbara Rodriguez, "Audit: Privatized Medicaid Is Saving Iowa Millions of Dollars. Democrats Aren't Convinced," *Iowa City Press-Citizen*, November 26, 2018; Paul Brennan, "Gov. Reynolds Supports Bill That Cuts Reporting Requirements on State's Privatized Medicaid Program," *Little Village*, February 12, 2018; Tony Leys, "Iowa's Estimated Savings from Medicaid Privatization Keeps Changing, Without Explanation," *Des Moines Register*, May 19, 2018; Editorial Board, "Iowa Needs Answers on Medicaid Sav-

ings, Not a Kansas-Style Shell Game"; Tony Leys, "Iowa Medicaid Director: Privatization Is Saving Money but It's Hard to Say How Much," *Des Moines Register*, June 13, 2018.

11. Jason Clayworth, "A Private Medicaid Company That Pulled Out of Iowa Has Yet to Pay Thousands of Medical Bills," *Des Moines Register*, August 31, 2018.

12. David Hall and Tue Anh Nguyen, "Economic Benefits of Public Services," *Real-World Economics Review* no. 84 (2018): 135, http://www.paecon.net/PAEReview/issue84 /HallNguyen84.pdf; The Advisory Board, "How Much of Americans' Paychecks Go to Health Care, Charted," May 2, 2019, https://www.advisory.com/en/daily-briefing/2019/05 /02/health-care-costs.

15. What's in It for Wall Street:
Public Assistance in the Hands of Big Finance

1. Tom Jones and Bob Hasen, "Ambulance Bills Sent Straight to Collections," *NBC News 7 San Diego* (San Diego, CA: NBC, August 18, 2016); Danielle Ivory, Ben Protess, and Kitty Bennett, "When You Dial 911 and Wall Street Answers," *New York Times*, June 25, 2016.

2. In the Public Interest, "Evaluating Pay for Success Programs and Social Impact Bonds" (Washington, DC, July 2015); Vibeka Mair, "Pay-for-Success: The Latest Thinking on Social Impact Bonds," *Responsible Investor*, May 9, 2018; Rick Cohen, "Social Impact Bonds: Phantom of the Nonprofit Sector," *Nonprofit Quarterly*, July 25, 2014; Rick Cohen, "Does 'Pay for Success' Actually Pay Off? The ROI of Social Impact Bonds," *Nonprofit Quarterly*, October 17, 2014; National Conference of State Legislatures, "Social Impact Bonds," nscl.org, September 22, 2016, https://www.ncsl.org/research/labor-and -employment/social-impact-bonds.aspx.

3. Liz Farmer, "First 'Pay for Success' Project for Veterans Underway," *Governing*, November 4, 2018; Tristan Horrom, "Individual Placement and Support More Effective Than Transitional Work for Veterans with PTSD," *VA Research Currents*, February 28, 2018.

4. Hunter quoted in Cohen, "Social Impact Bonds: Phantom of the Nonprofit Sector"; "Pay for Success," U.S. Department of Education, October 24, 2017, https://www2.ed.gov /about/inits/ed/pay-for-success/index.html.

5. Hunter quoted in Kenneth Saltman, "Wall Street's Latest Public Sector Rip-Off: Five Myths About Pay for Success," *Counterpunch*, August 23, 2016; Cohen, "Does 'Pay for Success' Actually Pay Off?"

6. Cohen, "Does 'Pay for Success' Actually Pay Off?"; Saltman, "Wall Street's Latest Public Sector Rip-Off"; Rick Cohen, "Casting a Skeptical Eye on Goldman Sachs' Pre-school SIB Program in Chicago," *Nonprofit Quarterly*, November 6, 2014; Melissa Sanchez, "For the Record: Paying for Preschool with Social Impact Bonds," *Chicago Reporter*, November 3, 2014.

7. Saltman, "Wall Street's Latest Public Sector Rip-Off"; Michael J. Roy, Neil McHugh, and Stephen Sinclair, "A Critical Reflection on Social Impact Bonds," *Stanford Social Innovation Review*, May 1, 2018; Valerie Strauss, "Wall Street's New Way of Making Money from Public Education—and Why It's a Problem," *Washington Post*, September 14, 2016.

8. McKinsey quoted in In the Public Interest, "Evaluating Pay for Success Programs and Social Impact Bonds"; Roy, McHugh, and Sinclair, "A Critical Reflection on Social Impact Bonds"; Donald Cohen and Jeniffer Zelnick, "What We Learned from the Failure of the Rikers Island Social Impact Bond," *Nonprofit Quarterly*, August 7, 2015.

9. In the Public Interest, "Evaluating Pay for Success Programs and Social Impact Bonds"; Daniel Edmiston and Alex Nicholls, "Social Impact Bonds: The Role of Private Capital in Outcome-Based Commissioning," *Journal of Social Policy* 47, no. 1 (January 2018): 57–76, https://doi.org/10.1017/S0047279417000125; Roy, McHugh, and Sinclair, "A Critical Reflection on Social Impact Bonds"; Saltman, "Wall Street's Latest Public Sector Rip-Off"; Martin Carnoy and Roxana Marachi, "Investing for 'Impact' or Investing for Profit? Social Impact Bonds, Pay for Success, and the Next Wave of Privatization of Social Services and Education" (Boulder, CO: National Education Policy Center, February 2020), https://nepc.colorado.edu/sites/default/files/publications/PB%20Carnoy-Marachi_1.pdf.

10. Goldberg quoted in Mair, "Pay-for-Success: The Latest Thinking on Social Impact Bonds"; Farmer, "First 'Pay for Success' Project for Veterans Underway."

11. Saltman, "Wall Street's Latest Public Sector Rip-Off"; Richard Johnson, "The Work Programme's Only Success Is at 'Creaming and Parking,'" *Guardian*, February 20, 2013.

12. Clive Belfield and Ellen S. Peisner-Feinberg quoted in Nathaniel Popper, "Success Metrics Questioned in School Program Funded by Goldman," *New York Times*, January 19, 2018; Carnoy and Marachi, "Investing for 'Impact' or Investing for Profit? Social Impact Bonds, Pay for Success, and the Next Wave of Privatization of Social Services and Education."

13. Lenny Bernstein, "'Government Only Pays for the Positive Outcomes.' A Strikingly New Approach to Social Problems," *Washington Post*, February 16, 2016; Roy, McHugh, and Sinclair, "A Critical Reflection on Social Impact Bonds"; Cohen, "Does 'Pay for Success' Actually Pay Off?"

14. Devin Fergus, *Land of the Fee: Hidden Costs and the Decline of the American Middle Class* (New York: Oxford University Press, 2018), 53; James B. Steele and Lance Williams, "Who Got Rich off the Student Debt Crisis," *Reveal*, June 28, 2016; Zack Friedman, "Student Loan Debt Statistics in 2020: A Record $1.6 Trillion," *Forbes*, February 3, 2020.

15. Steele and Williams, "Who Got Rich off the Student Debt Crisis"; Fergus, *Land of the Fee.*

16. Susan M. Dynarski, "The RNC Wants to Make Student Loans Competitive Again. They Never Were" (Washington, DC: Brookings Institution, July 21, 2016); New America Foundation, "Student Loan History," accessed January 25, 2019, https://www.newamerica.org/education-policy/topics/higher-education-funding-and-financial-aid/federal-student-aid/federal-student-loans/federal-student-loan-history; Steele and Williams, "Who Got Rich off the Student Debt Crisis"; Enyu Zhou and Pilar Mendoza, "Financing Higher Education in the United States: A Historical Overview of Loans in Federal Financial Aid Policy," in *The Neoliberal Agenda and the Student Debt Crisis in U.S. Higher Education*, ed. Nicholas Daniel Hartlep, 13 (New York: Routledge, 2017), 3–18.

17. Steele and Williams, "Who Got Rich off the Student Debt Crisis"; Dynarski, "The RNC Wants to Make Student Loans Competitive Again. They Never Were."

18. New America Foundation, "Student Loan History"; Steele and Williams, "Who Got Rich off the Student Debt Crisis."

19. Steele and Williams, "Who Got Rich off the Student Debt Crisis."

20. Ibid.; New America Foundation, "Student Loan History"; Dynarski, "The RNC Wants to Make Student Loans Competitive Again. They Never Were."

21. Steele and Williams, "Who Got Rich off the Student Debt Crisis"; Tim Chen, "Student Loans Have Become Our Modern-Day Debtors Prisons," *USA Today*, June 5, 2018; Deanne Loonin and Persis Yu, "Pounding Student Loan Borrowers: The Heavy Costs of the Government's Partnership with Debt Collection Agencies" (National Consumer Law Center, September 2014); G. Michael Bedinger VI, "Time for a Fresh Look at the

'Undue Hardship' Bankruptcy Standard for Student Debtors," *Iowa Law Review* 99 (2014): 1817–39.

22. Jonathan D. Glater, "Millions to Be Repaid After College Loan Inquiry," *New York Times*, April 3, 2007; Stacy Cowley and Jessica Silver-Greenberg, "Loans 'Designed to Fail': States Say Navient Preyed on Students," *New York Times*, January 20, 2018; Steele and Williams, "Who Got Rich off the Student Debt Crisis"; New America Foundation, "Student Loan History"; Beckie Supiano, "Campuses Turn to Remote Call Centers to Handle Flood of Calls," *Chronicle of Higher Education*, September 3, 2012; Kelly Field, "The Selling of Student Loans," *Chronicle of Higher Education*, June 1, 2007, https://www.chronicle.com/article/the-selling-of-student-loans; Nancy Solomon, "Probe Targets College Financial Aid Kickbacks," *All Things Considered* (NPR, April 5, 2007).

23. Cowley and Silver-Greenberg, "Loans 'Designed to Fail.'"

24. Ibid.

25. Dynarski, "The RNC Wants to Make Student Loans Competitive Again. They Never Were"; New America Foundation, "Student Loan History"; Molly Hensley-Clancy, "Betsy DeVos Picked a Student Loan CEO to Run the Student Loan System," *BuzzFeed News*, June 20, 2017.

26. Michael Stratford, "Student-Loan Behemoth Tightens Its Ties to Trump and DeVos," *Politico*, September 9, 2019.

27. Fergus, *Land of the Fee*; Rachel M. Cohen, "College, the Skills Gap, and the Student Loan Crisis," *American Prospect*, February 25, 2016.

16. Privatizing Pays Us Less

1. In the Public Interest, "Race to the Bottom: How Outsourcing Public Services Rewards Corporations and Punishes the Middle Class" (Washington, DC, June 2014).

2. Ibid.

3. Ibid.

4. Amy Traub and Robert Hiltonsmith, "Underwriting Bad Jobs: How Our Tax Dollars Are Funding Low-Wage Work and Fueling Inequality" (New York: Demos, May 2013); Good Jobs Nation, "Promises Broken #1: Trump Is America's Top Low Wage Job Creator" (Washington, DC, August 2018).

5. Mike Elk, "US Government Failing Millions by Paying Below $15 an Hour, Study Finds," *Guardian*, August 10, 2018.

6. Randi Weingarten, "Support Chavez Prep Staff & Students!," Press Release (American Federation of Teachers, February 14, 2019) (quote).

7. "D.C. Charters Have Some of the Highest Salaries for Administrators. So Why Are Their Teachers Making So Little?," *Kojo Nnamdi Show*, February 5, 2019; Perry Stein, "Cesar Chavez Public Charter Schools Announces It Will Close Two Campuses in D.C.," *Washington Post*, January 23, 2019; Weingarten, "Support Chavez Prep Staff & Students!"; Perry Stein, "D.C.'s Only Unionized Charter School Filed Another Federal Labor Complaint—This Time as Its Campus Is Shutting Down," *Washington Post*, March 6, 2019; Valerie Jablow, "Another School Year, More High Teacher Attrition," *Educationdc* (blog), February 26, 2018, https://educationdc.net/2018/02/26/another-school-year-more-high-teacher-attrition.

8. "D.C. Charters Have Some of the Highest Salaries for Administrators. So Why Are Their Teachers Making So Little?"; Administrator salaries from Rachel M. Cohen, "D.C.

Charter Administrators Have Some of the Highest School Salaries in Town; Their Teachers, Some of the Lowest," *Washington City Paper*, January 30, 2019. Pupil totals from DCPS data.

Part VI. Things in Common:
Privatization and the Erosion of Community

1. Christopher Solomon, "Our Pampered Wilderness," *New York Times*, May 23, 2015.

2. Bonnie Honig, *Public Things: Democracy in Disrepair* (New York: Fordham University Press, 2017).

17. Public Places: Parks, Presidents, and Privatization

1. Frederick Law Olmsted, *Writings on Landscape, Culture, and Society*, ed. Charles E. Beveridge (New York: Library Of America, 2015).

2. Ibid.

3. Ibid.; Illinois Central Railroad Co. v. Illinois, 146 US 387 (1892).

4. Lolly Bowean, "Obama Foundation Responds to Group's Lawsuit over Use of Jackson Park," *Chicago Tribune*, September 18, 2018; Richard Epstein, "Chicago's New Obama Burden," *Defining Ideas*, December 17, 2018; "The Trouble with Obama's Presidential Center," *New York Times*, February 28, 2019; Kriston Capps, "The Legal Struggle over Obama's Presidential Center Will Go On," *CityLab*, February 21, 2019.

5. Anthony Clark, "Barack Obama's Presidential Library Is Making a Mockery of Transparency," *Daily Beast*, March 3, 2019; Anthony Clark, "Presidential Libraries Are a Scam. Could Obama Change That?," *Politico Magazine*, May 7, 2019; Bob Clark, "In Defense of Presidential Libraries: Why the Failure to Build an Obama Library Is Bad for Democracy," *Public Historian* 40, no. 2 (May 1, 2018): 96–103, https://doi.org/10.1525/tph.2018.40.2.96.

6. Naftali quoted in Bob Garfield, "The Obama Presidential Center Will Curate Its Own Story," *On the Media*, March 8, 2019.

7. Ibid.

8. Naftali quoted in ibid.

9. Robert McClure, "Public Parks for Sale," *InvestigateWest*, June 11, 2012; Brianna Bailey, "Lake Texoma Area Residents, State Officials Grow Frustrated with Stalled Pointe Vista Development," *Oklahoman*, June 23, 2013.

10. Joe Wertz, "The Death of OK's Lake Texoma State Park and the Promises of Privatization," *StateImpact Oklahoma*, June 11, 2012.

11. Robert McClure, "Oklahoma Park Bought and Paid For," *InvestigateWest*, June 11, 2012; Brianna Bailey, "Chickasaw Nation Plans Resort Hotel, Casino on Lake Texoma," *Oklahoman*, October 27, 2016.

12. Bailey, "Lake Texoma Area Residents, State Officials Grow Frustrated with Stalled Pointe Vista Development"; Logan Layden, "From State Park to Hotel-Casino: Texoma Residents Eager for Progress but Question Public Process," KGOU, December 8, 2016.

13. McClure, "Public Parks for Sale"; Bailey, "Lake Texoma Area Residents, State Officials Grow Frustrated with Stalled Pointe Vista Development."

14. Logan Layden, "Settlement Over Texoma Park Privatization Worries Locals, Costs State," *StateImpact Oklahoma*, July 14, 2016; Davis quoted in Bailey, "Lake Texoma Area Residents, State Officials Grow Frustrated with Stalled Pointe Vista Development."

15. Bailey, "Chickasaw Nation Plans Resort Hotel, Casino on Lake Texoma."

16. Bailey, "Lake Texoma Area Residents, State Officials Grow Frustrated with Stalled Pointe Vista Development"; Layden, "From State Park to Hotel-Casino."

17. Bailey, "Lake Texoma Area Residents, State Officials Grow Frustrated with Stalled Pointe Vista Development."

18. School Choice and Resegregation

1. Chris Ford, Stephenie Johnson, and Lisette Partelow, "The Racist Origins of Private School Vouchers" (Washington, DC: Center for American Progress, July 12, 2017); Leo Casey, "When Privatization Means Segregation: Setting the Record Straight on School Vouchers," *Dissent*, August 9, 2017.

2. Nikole Hannah-Jones, "It Was Never About Busing," *New York Times*, July 12, 2019; Clint Smith, "The Desegregation and Resegregation of Charlotte's Schools," *New Yorker*, October 3, 2016.

3. Wesley Whistle, "Trump: School Choice Is the Civil Rights Statement of the Year," *Forbes*, June 16, 2020.

4. Quoted in Frank Adamson, Channa Cook-Harvey, and Linda Darling-Hammond, "Whose Choice? Student Experiences and Outcomes in the New Orleans School Marketplace" (Stanford, CA: Stanford Center for Opportunity Policy in Education, 2015).

5. Erica Frankenberg et al., "Choice Without Equity: Charter School Segregation and the Need for Civil Rights Standards" (Los Angeles, CA: The Civil Rights Project/Proyecto Derechos Civiles at UCLA, June 26, 2012), https://escholarship.org/uc/item/4r07q8kg.

6. Ibid.

7. Emmanuel Felton, "'It's like a Black and White Thing': How Some Elite Charter Schools Exclude Minorities," NBC News, June 17, 2018.

8. Kris Nordstrom, "With HB 514, Legislature Unambiguously Embraces School Segregation," *Progressive Pulse*, May 31, 2018, http://pulse.ncpolicywatch.org/2018/05/31/with -hb-514-legislature-unambiguously-embraces-school-segregation.

9. Denise Forte, "Segregation's History Repeats Itself in North Carolina's HB 514," The Century Foundation, June 26, 2018, https://tcf.org/content/commentary/segregations -history-repeats-north-carolinas-hb-514. Author's demographic data has been updated with latest Census data.

10. Nordstrom, "With HB 514, Legislature Unambiguously Embraces School Segregation"; Jim Morrill, "Controversial NC Charter Bill Approved. Now, These Four Towns Could Open Schools.," *Charlotte Observer*, June 6, 2018.

11. Morrill, "Controversial NC Charter Bill Approved"; Nordstrom, "With HB 514, Legislature Unambiguously Embraces School Segregation"; Kimberly Quick, "Segregation's History Repeats Itself in North Carolina's HB 514," The Century Foundation, June 26, 2018, https://tcf.org/content/commentary/segregations-history-repeats-north-carolinas-hb -514; James E. Ford, "Matthews vs. CMS: Yes, the Fight About Charter Schools Is About Race," *Charlotte Observer*, April 27, 2018; Ann Doss Helms, "Governor Cites 'Taxpayer-Funded Resegregation' of Meck Schools in Veto of NC Bill," *Charlotte Observer*, December 21, 2018.

12. Ford, "Matthews vs CMS"; Quick, "Segregation's History Repeats Itself in North Carolina's HB 514"; Clara Leonard, "I Went to Matthews Schools, and I See the Value of Diversity," *Charlotte Observer*, June 9, 2018.

13. Victor Leung, Roxanne H. Alejandre, and Angelica Jongco, "Unequal Access: How Some California Charter Schools Illegally Restrict Enrollment" (Los Angeles: ACLU Foundation of Southern California and Public Advocates, April 25, 2017).

14. Dana Goldstein, "'Threatening the Future': The High Stakes of Deepening School Segregation," *New York Times*, May 10, 2019.

15. Ricard D. Kahlenberg, Halley Potter, and Kimberly Quick, "A Bold Agenda for School Integration," The Century Foundation, April 8, 2019, https://tcf.org/content/report /bold-agenda-school-integration; Richard D. Kahlenberg and Halley Potter, "Diverse Charter Schools: Can Racial and Socioeconomic Integration Promote Better Outcomes for Students?" (Poverty & Race Research Action Council; The Century Foundation, May 2012); Emma García, "Schools Are Still Segregated, and Black Children Are Paying a Price" (Washington, DC: Economic Policy Institute, February 12, 2020), https://files.epi .org/pdf/185814.pdf.

16. Richard N. Pitt and Josh Packard, "Activating Diversity: The Impact of Student Race on Contributions to Course Discussions," *Sociological Quarterly* 53, no. 2 (2012): 295–320, https://doi.org/10.1111/j.1533-8525.2012.01235.x; Amy Stuart Wells, Lauren Fox, and Diana Cordova-Cobo, "How Racially Diverse Schools and Classrooms Can Benefit All Students" (The Century Foundation, February 9, 2016), https://tcf.org/content/report /how-racially-diverse-schools-and-classrooms-can-benefit-all-students.

17. Wells, Fox, and Cordova-Cobo, "How Racially Diverse Schools and Classrooms Can Benefit All Students"; Jennifer A. Richeson, Sophie Trawalter, and J. Nicole Shelton, "African Americans' Implicit Racial Attitudes and the Depletion of Executive Function After Interracial Interactions," *Social Cognition* 23, no. 4 (2005): 336–52, https://doi.org /10.1521/soco.2005.23.4.336; Jennifer A. Richeson and Sophie Trawalter, "Why Do Interracial Interactions Impair Executive Function? A Resource Depletion Account," *Journal of Personality and Social Psychology* 88, no. 6 (June 2005): 934–47, https://doi.org/10.1037 /0022-3514.88.6.934.

18. Eliza Shapiro, "How White Progressives Undermine School Integration," *New York Times*, August 21, 2020.

19. Public Libraries and Apple Pie

1. Sue Halpern, "In Praise of Public Libraries," *New York Review of Books*, April 18, 2019.

2. Deborah Fallows, "When Libraries Are 'Second Responders,'" *Atlantic*, May 23, 2019.

3. David Streitfeld, "As L.S.S.I. Takes Over Libraries, Patrons Can't Keep Quiet," *New York Times*, September 26, 2010; Wayne Hanson, "Outsourcing the Local Library Can Lead to a Loud Backlash," *Government Technology*, June 1, 2011.

4. CEO Brad King quoted in Hanson, "Outsourcing the Local Library Can Lead to a Loud Backlash"; James Nash, "Privately-Run Libraries Expand Throughout U.S.," *Government Technology*, November 3, 2015; Jane Jerrard, Nancy Bolt, and Karen Strege, *Privatizing Libraries* (Chicago: American Library Association, 2012).

5. CLA president quoted in Jeremy Mohler, "There's an Amazon-like Corporation Trying to Take over Public Libraries," In the Public Interest, July 26, 2018; Ruth Metz Associ-

ates, "Jackson County Library Services Performance Review and Quality Assessment," November 17, 2016.

6. Ruth Metz Associates, "Jackson County Library Services Performance Review and Quality Assessment"; Librarian quoted in Doug Porter, "Saving Escondido's Only Public Library," *Escondido Grapevine*, July 29, 2017, https://escondidograpevine.com/2017/07/29/saving-escondidos-only-public-library.

7. Pezzanite quoted in Streitfeld, "As L.S.S.I. Takes Over Libraries, Patrons Can't Keep Quiet."

8. Ruth Metz Associates, "Jackson County Library Services Performance Review and Quality Assessment"; "Abed, Masson, Gallo: 'Screw You, Library,'" *Escondido Grapevine*, August 31, 2017, https://escondidograpevine.com/2017/08/31/abed-masson-gallo-screw-you-library.

9. Streitfeld, "As L.S.S.I. Takes Over Libraries, Patrons Can't Keep Quiet"; "As Escondido Mayor Dismisses Community Sentiment, Council Moves to Privatize Library," *San Diego Free Press*, August 25, 2017; Eric Klinenberg, "To Restore Civil Society, Start with the Library," *New York Times*, September 8, 2018.

10. Harry J. Jones, "Opposition to Escondido Library Outsourcing Grows," *San Diego Union-Tribune*, August 9, 2017; Sharon Chen, "Escondido Privatizes Public Library," Fox 5 San Diego, August 24, 2017.

11. "Abed, Masson, Gallo: 'Screw You, Library'"; Porter, "Saving Escondido's Only Public Library"; Jones, "Opposition to Escondido Library Outsourcing Grows."

12. Michael Hiltzik, "A Handy Sign That a Local Government Is Shirking Its Public Duty: Privatizing the Library," *Los Angeles Times*, November 18, 2013.

20. Communities Take Care: How Social Security Defines Us

1. Winnie Pineo, "Social Security 70th Anniversary" (News Conference, Washington, DC, August 12, 2005), https://www.c-span.org/video/?188456-1/social-security-70th-anniversary.

2. Cynthia Crossen, "Before Social Security, Most Americans Faced Very Bleak Retirement," *Wall Street Journal*, September 25, 2004; Robin Toner, "'A Great Calamity Has Come Upon Us,'" *New York Times*, January 23, 2005; Harriet Edleson, "More Americans Working or Looking for Work After 65," AARP, April 22, 2019, https://www.aarp.org/work/employers/info-2019/americans-working-past-65.html.

3. Quoted in Nancy J. Altman, *The Battle for Social Security: From FDR's Vision to Bush's Gamble* (Hoboken, NJ: Wiley, 2005).

4. Ibid.

5. Ibid.; Judie Svihula and Carroll Estes, "Social Security Privatization: An Ideologically Structured Movement," *Journal of Sociology & Social Welfare* 35, no. 1 (March 1, 2008), https://scholarworks.wmich.edu/jssw/vol35/iss1/5.

6. Altman, *The Battle for Social Security*; investigation quoted in Svihula and Estes, "Social Security Privatization."

7. David R. Francis, "One Man's Retirement Math: Social Security Wins," *Christian Science Monitor*, December 27, 2004.

8. Jason Furman, "Would Private Accounts Provide a Higher Rate of Return Than Social Security?" (Center on Budget and Policy Priorities, June 2, 2005), https://www.cbpp.org/research/would-private-accounts-provide-a-higher-rate-of-return-than-social-security.

9. Bush's strategist quoted in Altman, *The Battle for Social Security*; Peter J. Ferrara, "The New Progressivism: Personal Social Security Accounts for Working People (Testimony before the President's Commission to Strengthen and Preserve Social Security, San Diego Marriot Hotel and Marina San Diego, California, September 6, 2001)" (Washington, DC: Americans for Tax Reform, September 6, 2001).

10. Altman, *The Battle for Social Security*; *Congressional Record* 159, no. 132 (September 30, 2013): S7018–29.

11. Nancy J. Altman, "Securing Healthcare," *Los Angeles Times*, August 14, 2009; Jeff Shesol, "Shutdown: The Hysterical Style in American Politics," *New Yorker*, September 30, 2013.

12. Elizabeth Bauer, "Just What Is Social Insurance, Anyway? (and Why Isn't It Earned?)," *Forbes*, September 24, 2018; Ross Douthat, "Government and Its Rivals," *New York Times*, January 28, 2012.

Part VII. Privatization Doesn't Want You to Know: The Corruption of Public Education

1. Gerry Canavan, "Replying to @KRGilbertson," Twitter, February 25, 2015, https://twitter.com/gerrycanavan/status/570668164683587585?s=20.

21. School Choice and Competition: When Creative Destruction Is Just Destruction

1. DeVos quoted in Jason Blakely, "How School Choice Turns Education into a Commodity," *Atlantic*, April 17, 2017.

2. Matthew S. Schwartz, "How One D.C. Elementary's 5th Grade Enrollment Highlights Concerns About Middle School," *American University Radio* (Washington, DC: WAMU, March 2, 2016), https://wamu.org/story/16/03/02/5th_grade_dropoff.

3. Julie P. Combs et al., "Academic Achievement for Fifth-Grade Students in Elementary and Intermediate School Settings: Grade Span Configurations," *Current Issues in Education* 14, no. 1 (April 18, 2011), https://cie.asu.edu/ojs/index.php/cieatasu/article/view/677; Gahan Bailey, Rebecca Giles, and Sylvia Rogers, "An Investigation of the Concerns of Fifth Graders Transitioning to Middle School," *Research in Middle Level Education* 38, no. 5 (2015), https://files.eric.ed.gov/fulltext/EJ1059740.pdf; Jennifer Palmer, "Are 5th Graders Ready for Middle School? Oklahoma City Schools Says Yes, but Parents Worry," *Oklahoma Watch* (KGOU, January 28, 2019); Philip J Cook et al., "Should Sixth Grade Be in Elementary or Middle School? An Analysis of Grade Configuration and Student Behavior," Working Paper (National Bureau of Economic Research, August 2006), https://doi.org/10.3386/w12471; Duke Today Staff, "Sixth Graders in Middle Schools Fare Worse Than Peers in Elementary Schools, Study Finds," *Duke Today*, February 26, 2007, https://today.duke.edu/2007/02/sixth_grade.html; Elissa Gootman, "Taking Middle Schoolers Out of the Middle," *New York Times*, January 22, 2007.

4. Patrick Lester, "Laboratories of Innovation: Building and Using Evidence in Charter Schools" (Washington, DC: IBM Center for the Business of Government, 2018).

5. Obama quoted in Jack Schneider, "Charters Were Supposed to Save Public Education. Why Did People Turn on Them?," *Washington Post*, May 30, 2019; Greg Richmond, "Collaborating, Not Competing: Charters as 'Laboratories of Innovation,'" *Educa-*

tion Post, September 17, 2014; Rachel Cohen, "The Untold History of Charter Schools," *Democracy: A Journal of Ideas*, April 27, 2017; Richard D. Kahlenberg and Halley Potter, "The Original Charter School Vision," *New York Times*, August 30, 2014.

6. Albert Shanker, "National Press Club Speech" (Washington, DC, March 31, 1988), https://reuther.wayne.edu/files/64.43.pdf.

7. Jubilee Academic Center, Inc., "Employee Handbook," August 2014, in author's possession.

8. Chavez Schools, "Employee Handbook," August 2016, in author's possession; Bright Star Schools, "Employee Handbook," April 2012, in author's possession.

9. Morgan Smith, "When Private Firms Run Schools, Financial Secrecy Is Allowed," *New York Times*, December 14, 2013; David Safier, "BASIS Charters' Educational Trade Secrets," *Blog for Arizona*, September 18, 2013, https://arizona.typepad.com/blog/2013/09 /basis-charters-educational-trade-secrets.html; Yoohyun Jung, "Public School Inc.: When Public Education Turns into Big Business," *Reveal/Center for Investigative Reporting*, September 29, 2017.

10. Rachel M. Cohen, "Fining Teachers for Switching Schools," *American Prospect*, November 3, 2016; Cynthia Howell, "State Pulls Charter of Troubled Little Rock School," *Arkansas Democrat Gazette*, February 16, 2019; Cynthia Howell, "Little Rock School Closing When Charter Lapses in June," *Arkansas Democrat Gazette*, January 16, 2019.

11. Cohen, "Fining Teachers for Switching Schools."

12. Shanker, "National Press Club Speech."

22. Higher Education: Who Fills the Void?

1. American Academy of Arts and Sciences, "Public Research Universities: Serving the Public Good" (Cambridge, MA, 2016).

2. Ibid.

3. David Adam, "Situation Improves Slightly for U Alaska, Major Changes Ahead," *Scientist Magazine*, September 24, 2019; Chancy Croft, "University of Alaska Should Be Free for Alaskans," *Anchorage Daily News*, September 9, 2019; Adam Harris, "Higher Education Has Become a Partisan Issue," *Atlantic*, July 5, 2019; Joanne Boyer, "'The Boundaries of the University Shall Be the Boundaries of the State': A Lesson Wisconsin and Scott Walker Forgot," *OpEdNews*, January 30, 2015; American Academy of Arts and Sciences, "Public Research Universities: Recommitting to Lincoln's Vision—An Educational Compact for the 21st Century" (Cambridge, MA, 2016); State Higher Education Executive Officers Association, "State Higher Education Finance: FY 2018" (Boulder, CO, 2019); Century Foundation, "Recommendations for Providing Community Colleges with the Resources They Need," April 25, 2019.

4. James Hohmann, "Koch Network Laying Groundwork to Fundamentally Transform America's Education System," *Washington Post*, January 30, 2018.

5. Dave Levinthal, "Spreading the Free-Market Gospel," *Atlantic*, October 30, 2015; Richard Fink, "From Ideas to Action: The Role of Universities, Think Tanks, and Activist Groups," *Philanthropy*, Winter 1996, https://archive.org/stream /TheStructureOfSocialChangeLibertyGuideRichardFinkKoch.

6. Dave Levinthal, "Koch Foundation Proposal to College: Teach Our Curriculum, Get Millions" (Center for Public Integrity, September 12, 2014), https://publicintegrity.org

NOTES

/federal-politics/koch-foundation-proposal-to-college-teach-our-curriculum-get-millions; Levinthal, "Spreading the Free-Market Gospel"; Travis Waldron, "FSU Accepts Funds from Charles Koch in Return for Control over Its Academic Freedom," *ThinkProgress*, May 10, 2011.

7. Erica L. Green and Stephanie Saul, "What Charles Koch and Other Donors to George Mason University Got for Their Money," *New York Times*, May 5, 2018; Anemona Harto-collis, "Revelations over Koch Gifts Prompt Inquiry at George Mason University," *New York Times*, May 1, 2018.

8. Green and Saul, "What Charles Koch and Other Donors to George Mason University Got for Their Money."

9. Levinthal, "Spreading the Free-Market Gospel."

10. Joel Rosenblatt, "Trump's Education Chief in Hot Seat over Student-Debt Collection," *Bloomberg*, October 7, 2019; Tareq Haddad, "Betsy DeVos Could Face Jail After Judge Rules She Violated 2018 Order on Student Loans," *Newsweek*, October 8, 2019.

11. Helaine Olen, "A Judge Calls Betsy DeVos to Account," *Washington Post*, October 10, 2019; Andrew Kreighbaum, "DeVos: Borrower-Defense Rule Offered 'Free Money,'" *Inside Higher Ed*, September 26, 2017.

12. Robert Shireman quoted in Annie Waldman, "How a For-Profit College Targeted the Homeless and Kids with Low Self-Esteem," *ProPublica*, March 18, 2016.

13. Hannah Appel and Astra Taylor, "Education with a Debt Sentence: For-Profit Colleges as American Dream Crushers and Factories of Debt," *New Labor Forum* 24, no. 1 (2015): 31–36, https://doi.org/10.1177/1095796014562860; Danielle Douglas-Gabriel, "How Dozens of Failing For-Profit Schools Found an Unlikely Savior: A Debt Collector," *Washington Post*, November 28, 2014; Jillian Berman, "Trump Administration Wants to Overhaul the Way You Repay Student Loans," *MarketWatch*, May 21, 2017.

14. Ray Fisman, "Sweden's School Choice Disaster," *Slate*, July 16, 2014; Sam Dillon, "Online Colleges Receive a Boost from Congress," *New York Times*, March 1, 2006.

15. David Halperin, "Abuses at Corinthian Are Mirrored at Other Big For-Profit Colleges," *Republic Report*, April 22, 2015, https://www.republicreport.org/2015/abuses-at -corinthian-are-mirrored-at-other-big-for-profit-colleges; Appel and Taylor, "Education with a Debt Sentence"; David Halperin, "EDMC Professors and Students Speak: How Lobbyists and Goldman Sachs Ruined For-Profit Education," *Huffington Post*, September 24, 2012.

16. Waldman, "How a For-Profit College Targeted the Homeless and Kids with Low Self-Esteem"; Halperin, "EDMC Professors and Students Speak"; Douglas-Gabriel, "How Dozens of Failing For-Profit Schools Found an Unlikely Savior: A Debt Collector"; Molly Hensley-Clancy, "Whistleblower Suit Alleges For-Profit College Tricked Veterans into Debt," *BuzzFeed News*, December 16, 2014.

17. Halperin, "EDMC Professors and Students Speak."

18. Halperin, "Abuses at Corinthian Are Mirrored at Other Big For-Profit Colleges"; Appel and Taylor, "Education with a Debt Sentence"; Halperin, "EDMC Professors and Students Speak"; Annie Waldman, "Who's Regulating For-Profit Schools? Execs from For-Profit Colleges," *ProPublica*, February 26, 2016.

19. Waldman, "Who's Regulating For-Profit Schools?"; Roger Yu, "DeVry to Pay $49M to Students for Misleading Ads," *USA Today*, July 5, 2017; Stephanie Saul, "For-Profit College Operator EDMC Will Forgive Student Loans," *New York Times*, November 16, 2015.

20. Annie Waldman, "For-Profit Colleges Gain Beachhead in Trump Administration," *ProPublica*, March 14, 2017.

21. Michael Stratford, "Trump Administration Selects Former DeVry Official to Lead College Enforcement Unit," *Politico*, August 30, 2017; Gail Collins, "No Profit in Betsy DeVos," *New York Times*, October 27, 2017.

22. Pauline Abernathy, executive vice president of the Institute for College Access and Success, quoted in Michael Stratford, "Trump and DeVos Fuel a For-Profit College Comeback," *Politico*, August 31, 2017; Danielle Douglas-Gabriel, "Trump Administration Let Nearly $11 Million in Student Aid Go to Unaccredited For-Profit Colleges," *Washington Post*, October 22, 2019; Robert C. Scott to Betsy DeVos, October 22, 2019, https://edlabor .house.gov/imo/media/doc/Chairman%20Scott%20Threatens%20to%20Subpoena%20 Secretary%20DeVos.pdf.

23. Ray Fisman and Michael Luca, "Betsy DeVos Wants to Bring a Business Mindset to Education. It's Backfired Before and Will Again," *Slate*, February 7, 2017.

24. Appel and Taylor, "Education with a Debt Sentence."

Part VIII. "The Cash Just Pours Out": The Privatization of Public Science and Research

1. Deborah Levine, "The Case for a Free or Inexpensive Coronavirus Vaccine," *Washington Post*, March 2, 2020.

2. Michael Hiltzik, "What Should Pfizer and Moderna Earn from Vaccines?," *Los Angeles Times*, January 4, 2021.

3. Achal Prabhala, Arjun Jayadev, and Dean Baker, "Want Vaccines Fast? Suspend Intellectual Property Rights," *New York Times*, December 7, 2020; Michael Hiltzik, "Private Firms Keep Stranglehold on COVID Vaccines, Though You Paid for the Research," *Los Angeles Times*, November 16, 2020.

23. Academic Publishing: How to Pay for Knowledge Three Times Over

1. Vinken quoted in Stephen Buranyi, "Is the Staggeringly Profitable Business of Scientific Publishing Bad for Science?," *Guardian*, June 27, 2017.

2. Robert M. Kaplan, "Op-Ed: Why You Should Care About the Raging Battle for Free Access to Research Findings," *Los Angeles Times*, April 9, 2019; Buranyi, "Is the Staggeringly Profitable Business of Scientific Publishing Bad for Science?"; Peter Suber, *Open Access*, 2019, https://openaccesseks.mitpress.mit.edu/pub/ktf344br.

3. Brian Resnick and Julia Belluz, "The War to Free Science," *Vox*, June 3, 2019; Kaplan, "Why You Should Care."

4. Buranyi, "Is the Staggeringly Profitable Business of Scientific Publishing Bad for Science?"; Resnick and Belluz, "The War to Free Science."

5. Buranyi, "Is the Staggeringly Profitable Business of Scientific Publishing Bad for Science?"

6. Resnick and Belluz, "The War to Free Science."

7. Suber, *Open Access*.

8. Resnick and Belluz, "The War to Free Science"; Kaplan, "Why You Should Care";

Michael Hiltzik, "UC Achieves Another Big Win in Its Long Battle with Major Scientific Publishers," *Los Angeles Times*, March 16, 2021.

9. Suber, *Open Access.*

10. Ibid.

24. They Even Want to Own the Weather

1. Andrew Blum, *The Weather Machine: A Journey Inside the Forecast* (Ecco, 2019); John F. Kennedy, "State of the Union" (Speech, Washington, DC, January 30, 1961), https://millercenter.org/the-presidency/presidential-speeches/january-30-1961-state-union; Nate Silver, *The Signal and the Noise: Why So Many Predictions Fail—but Some Don't* (New York: Penguin Press, 2012); Devin Leonard and Brian K. Sullivan, "Trump's Pick to Lead Weather Agency Spent 30 Years Fighting It," *Bloomberg*, June 14, 2018.

2. Michael Lewis, *The Fifth Risk* (New York: W.W. Norton, 2018); Lulu Garcia-Navarro, "How the Advance Weather Forecast Got Good," *NPR*, June 30, 2019.

3. Blum, *The Weather Machine.*

4. Lewis, *The Fifth Risk.*

5. Leonard and Sullivan, "Trump's Pick to Lead Weather Agency Spent 30 Years Fighting It."

6. Ibid.; Jane Lubchenco, "The Senate Should Reject Trump's NOAA Nominee," *New York Times*, May 1, 2019.

7. Leonard and Sullivan, "Trump's Pick to Lead Weather Agency Spent 30 Years Fighting It"; Rick Santorum, "S. 786, National Weather Services Duties Act of 2005" (109th Congress 1st Session, 2005), https://www.govinfo.gov/content/pkg/BILLS-109s786is/pdf/BILLS-109s786is.pdf.

8. Lewis, *The Fifth Risk*; Leonard and Sullivan, "Trump's Pick to Lead Weather Agency Spent 30 Years Fighting It"; Andrew Freedman, "National Weather Service Hold on Mobile Apps Stirs Controversy," *Washington Post*, January 9, 2012; Cliff Mass, "Cliff Mass Weather and Climate Blog: Do We Need Local National Weather Service Offices If We Have Weather Apps, Accuweather, and the Weather Channel?," *Cliff Mass Weather and Climate Blog*, June 11, 2016.

9. Pam Wright, "Trump Administration Proposes Slashing National Weather Service Budget by 8 Percent, Eliminating Hundreds of Jobs," *Weather Channel*, February 13, 2018; Eric Katz, "Lawmakers Accuse Trump Administration of Circumventing Congress on Weather Service Staffing," *Government Executive*, August 7, 2019; Dennis Mersereau, "The President's Proposed Budget Would Fire Hundreds of Meteorologists and Slash Tornado Research," *Forbes*, March 31, 2019.

10. Silver, *The Signal and the Noise.*

11. Fuqing Zhang et al., "What Is the Predictability Limit of Midlatitude Weather?," *Journal of the Atmospheric Sciences* 76, no. 4 (January 15, 2019): 1077–91, https://doi.org/10.1175/JAS-D-18-0269.1; Matthew Cappucci, "How Far into the Future Can Meteorologists Forecast the Weather?," *Washington Post*, July 11, 2019; Maddie Stone, "AccuWeather's 90-Day Forecast Tool Is Misleading as Hell," *Gizmodo*, April 19, 2016; Eric Berger, "AccuWeather Issues 90-Day Forecasts and Meteorologists Are Not Amused," *Ars Technica*, April 17, 2016; Silver, *The Signal and the Noise.*

12. Silver, *The Signal and the Noise.*

13. Barry Myers interviewed by CNBC, rebroadcast on John Oliver, "Weather," *Last Week Tonight* (HBO, October 13, 2019), https://www.youtube.com/watch?v=qMGn9T37eR8.

14. For more on AccuWeather and tornado forecasting, see Lewis, *The Fifth Risk*; Jason Samenow, "AccuWeather Rips Weather Service for Dismissing Tornado Threat in Oklahoma Wednesday and Delayed Warning," *Washington Post*, March 27, 2015; Angela Fritz and Sarah Larimer, "U-Md. Used a Private Company for a Tornado Warning. That Can Be Problematic," *Washington Post*, September 18, 2018; AccuWeather also erroneously warned about a tsunami; Leonard and Sullivan, "Trump's Pick to Lead Weather Agency Spent 30 Years Fighting It."

15. Silver, *The Signal and the Noise*.

25. Drug Prices and the Pirates of the Patent System

1. Mariana Mazzucato, *The Value of Everything: Making and Taking in the Global Economy* (New York: Public Affairs, 2018).

2. Alfred B. Engelberg, "Hatch Amendment Would Delay Generic Competition and Increase Drug Costs," *Health Affairs Blog*, November 9, 2018, https://www.healthaffairs .org/do/10.1377/hblog20181106.747590/full.

3. Abbey Meller and Hauwa Ahmed, "How Big Pharma Reaps Profits While Hurting Everyday Americans," Center for American Progress, August 30, 2019, https://www .americanprogress.org/issues/democracy/reports/2019/08/30/473911/big-pharma-reaps -profits-hurting-everyday-americans; Katherine Ellen Foley, "Big Pharma Is Taking Advantage of Patent Law to Keep OxyContin from Ever Dying," *Quartz*, November 18, 2017, https://qz.com/1125690/big-pharma-is-taking-advantage-of-patent-law-to-keep -oxycontin-from-ever-dying; Arti Rai and Barak Richman, "A Preferable Path for Thwarting Pharmaceutical Product Hopping," *Health Affairs Blog*, May 22, 2018, https://www .healthaffairs.org/do/10.1377/hblog20180522.408497/full; Erin Fox, "How Pharma Companies Game the System to Keep Drugs Expensive," *Harvard Business Review*, April 6, 2017; Katie Thomas, "Patents for Restasis Are Invalidated, Opening Door to Generics," *New York Times*, October 16, 2017.

4. Engelberg, "Hatch Amendment Would Delay Generic Competition and Increase Drug Costs"; I-MAK, "Overpatented, Overpriced: How Excessive Pharmaceutical Patenting Is Extending Monopolies and Driving Up Drug Prices," 2018, http://www.i-mak.org /wp-content/uploads/2018/08/I-MAK-Overpatented-Overpriced-Report.pdf.

5. Fox, "How Pharma Companies Game the System to Keep Drugs Expensive"; Meller and Ahmed, "How Big Pharma Reaps Profits While Hurting Everyday Americans"; Mazzucato, *The Value of Everything*.

6. Meller and Ahmed, "How Big Pharma Reaps Profits While Hurting Everyday Americans."

7. Mazzucato, *The Value of Everything*.

8. NIH stats in Mariana Mazzucato, "How Taxpayers Prop up Big Pharma, and How to Cap That," *Los Angeles Times*, October 27, 2015; Amin Tahir, "High Drug Prices Caused by US Patent System, Not 'Foreign Freeloaders,'" CNBC, June 27, 2018.

9. Mazzucato, "How Taxpayers Prop Up Big Pharma"; Rai and Richman, "A Preferable Path for Thwarting Pharmaceutical Product Hopping."

10. Amy Kapczynski and Aaron S. Kesselheim, "'Government Patent Use': A Legal Approach to Reducing Drug Spending," *Health Affairs* 35, no. 5 (May 2016): 791–97, https:

//doi.org/10.1377/hlthaff.2015.1120.

11. Ibid.

12. Meller and Ahmed, "How Big Pharma Reaps Profits While Hurting Everyday Americans"; Ricardo Alonso-Zaldivar and Hope Yen, "AP Fact Check: Trump Cites Drug-Price Drop That Isn't," *Associated Press*, May 14, 2019; Shefali Luthra and Amy Sherman, "Fact-Checking Donald Trump's Claim That Drug Prices Are Going Down," *Politifact*, May 22, 2019.

Part IX. Becoming Pro-Public

1. Corey Robin, "Reclaiming the Politics of Freedom" *Nation*, April 6, 2011.

2. Robert W. Poole, "Does U.S. Airport Privatization Have a Future?," *Public Works Financing*, May 2020.

3. Gwen Ifill, "Federal Cutbacks Proposed by Gore in 5-Year Program," *New York Times*, September 8, 1993; Lizabeth Cohen, *A Consumers' Republic: The Politics of Mass Consumption in Postwar America* (New York: Vintage Books, 2004), 397.

4. Melissa Denchak, "Flint Water Crisis: Everything You Need to Know," National Resources Defense Council, November 8, 2018.

5. Ethan Porter, *The Consumer Citizen* (New York: Oxford University Press, 2021).

6. Michael Tomasky, "The Greatest Story Never Told," *Democracy: A Journal of Ideas*, December 7, 2011; William J. Burns, "America Needs a Rebirth of Public Service," *Atlantic*, May 4, 2020.

7. David Leonhardt, "F.D.R. Got It. Most Democrats Don't," *New York Times*, January 12, 2020.

8. Suzanne Mettler, *The Submerged State: How Invisible Government Policies Undermine American Democracy* (Chicago: University of Chicago Press, 2011), 113, 122.

9. Christopher Newfield, "University Research and the Great Mistake," *University Research and the Great Mistake*, April 13, 2017; Fred L. Block and Matthew R. Keller, *State of Innovation: The U.S. Government's Role in Technology Development* (New York: Routledge, 2016).

Index

About the Authors

Donald Cohen is the founder and executive director of In the Public Interest, an Oakland, California–based national research and policy center that studies public goods and services. His opinion pieces and articles have appeared in the *New York Times*, Reuters, *Los Angeles Times*, and the *New Republic*, among others. He lives in Los Angeles.

Allen Mikaelian is a *New York Times* bestselling author and editor. He lives in Washington, DC.

Publishing in the Public Interest

Thank you for reading this book published by The New Press. The New Press is a nonprofit, public interest publisher. New Press books and authors play a crucial role in sparking conversations about the key political and social issues of our day.

We hope you enjoyed this book and that you will stay in touch with The New Press. Here are a few ways to stay up to date with our books, events, and the issues we cover:

- Sign up at www.thenewpress.com/subscribe to receive updates on New Press authors and issues and to be notified about local events
- Like us on Facebook: www.facebook.com/newpressbooks
- Follow us on Twitter: www.twitter.com/thenewpress
- Follow us on Instagram: www.instagram.com/thenewpress

Please consider buying New Press books for yourself; for friends and family; or to donate to schools, libraries, community centers, prison libraries, and other organizations involved with the issues our authors write about.

The New Press is a 501(c)(3) nonprofit organization. You can also support our work with a tax-deductible gift by visiting www .thenewpress.com/donate.